WILLS & PROBATE RECORDS

A Guide for Family Historians

WILLS & PROBATE RECORDS

A Guide for Family Historians

Karen Grannum
& Nigel Taylor

The National Archives

This second edition published in 2009 by
The National Archives
Kew, Richmond
Surrey TW9 4DU
United Kingdom

www.nationalarchives.gov.uk

The National Archives brings together the Public Record Office, Historical Manuscripts Commission, Office of Public Sector Information and Her Majesty's Stationery Office.

A catalogue card for this book is available from the British Library.

ISBN 978 1 905615 41 4

Jacket, typographic design and typesetting by
Ken Wilson | point 918

Printed in the UK by
TJ International Ltd, Padstow, Cornwall

Cover images: (centre) Thomas Braithwaite of Ambleside (*d.* 1607) making his will (Bridgeman); (above) holograph will of Jane Austen (PROB 1/78).

Picture credits: the images featured inside this book are to be found in the files of the National Archives and are © Crown copyright.

ACKNOWLEDGEMENTS

We are indebted to the following colleagues at the National Archives for their assistance with this publication: Adrian Ailes, Hugh Alexander, Catherine Bradley, Brian Carter, Sean Cunningham, Carol Dickson for her assistance in extracting statistical data from DocumentsOnline, Paul Johnson, Sheila Knight, Malcolm Mercer for his help on Latin translations, Stephen O'Connor and Tom Wharton.

Special thanks go to Amanda Bevan, who gave invaluable help and assistance.

Karen would particularly like to thank Guy, Lauren and James.

KAREN GRANNUM AND NIGEL TAYLOR

CONTENTS

USING THE NATIONAL ARCHIVES

The National Archives is the national repository for government records in the UK. Its main site at Kew holds the surviving records of government back to the Domesday Book (1086) and beyond.

Most of the records described in this guide can be consulted at the National Archives, Kew, Richmond, Surrey, TW9 4DU. The archives are open 09:00–17:00 on Mondays and Fridays, 09:00–19:00 on Tuesdays and Thursdays, 10:00–17:00 on Wednesdays and 09:30–17:00 on Saturdays. They are closed on Sundays, public holidays and for annual stocktaking. The website address is:

www.nationalarchives.gov.uk

The archives are about 10 minutes' walk from Kew Gardens Underground Station, which is on London Transport's District Line, as well as the London Overground Service. For motorists, it is just off the South Circular Road (A205). There is adequate parking.

The National Archives can be a confusing place to use. If you are new to researching there, it is a good idea to allow plenty of time to find your feet. The staff are both knowledgeable and friendly, and are happy to help if you get lost. There is a public restaurant and a well-stocked bookshop on site. Self-service lockers are available to store your belongings.

Accessing the records is simple. First you need to obtain a reader's ticket, which is free, when you arrive. Please bring two forms of identity, such as a passport or driving licence, and something with an address, such as a utility bill or bank statement. If you are not a British citizen, you will need your passport. For further information see:

www.nationalarchives.gov.uk/visit/whattobring.htm

It is possible to get photocopies and/or digital copies of most documents you find: please ask the staff for details. It is also possible for you to use your own digital camera to copy documents.

In order to protect the documents, each one of which is unique, security in the reading rooms is tight. You are only permitted to take a camera, laptop, notebook and notes into the reading rooms and can only use a pencil. Eating and drinking are not permitted in the reading rooms.

The records held by the National Archives are described and ordered using a three-part reference. The first element is known as the 'department' and takes the form of letters. The 'department' denotes which government department created the records. The second element is known as the 'series' and collects together records of a similar type. The second element is in the form of numbers. The third and final element of a document reference is known as the 'piece' and this is usually just a number, but occasionally may include letters.

Over time, terminology used to describe the document references at the National Archives has changed and you may hear terms such as 'letter codes' and 'class' still being used. Letter codes are, of course, the 'department' and 'class' is the 'series'. Whilst such terminology is interchangeable, many of the 'department' identities, irrespective of whether they are being called 'department' or 'letter code', are obvious, with PROB being the Prerogative Court of Canterbury, TS being the Treasury Solicitor and IR being the Inland Revenue. Other 'department' identities are not so obvious; the records of MI5, for example, are identified by the letters KV (it is an anagram of significance for you to work out) and the Welsh Office uses BD.

Brief descriptions of every document ('piece' is the term used by the National Archives) are in the series lists. Several sets of lists are available in the Open Reading Room and other locations. The series list gives you the exact reference of the document you want. This is what you order on the computer terminal. Occasionally in this guide we use the full reference, written thus: PROB 2/356, which is the inventory (dated 1559) of John Abyn, a merchant from Salisbury.

An increasing number of probate records are available on microfilm, microfiche or in digitized format. Where this is the case, the fact is noted in the text. You do not need to order microfilms on the computer as you can help yourself to them in the Open Reading Room.

In addition, there are various other finding aids for genealogists. The best general overview is provided by Amanda Bevan's revised *Tracing Your Ancestors in The National Archives* (7th edition, TNA, 2006).

The National Archives Online

As well as giving information on where the National Archives is, opening times and how to gain access, the National Archives website gives details about popular records, including research guides and lists of independent researchers. Most importantly, the website allows readers to access the National Archives Catalogue (series lists).

The Catalogue can be searched by using keywords, dates and, if you know them, the department (letter code) and series (class) where records are known to exist.

Follow these simple steps to identify the documents you require:

1 Locate the Catalogue
2 Click on Search the Catalogue
3 Type keyword(s) into the top box, the year range (as appropriate) into the two boxes below the keyword box and, if known, the departmental code and series (optional) into the last (bottom) box
4 It is possible to use more than one keyword, either by just putting the words in or by doing a combined word search linking the words together with AND
5 Click on Search.

The computer will then search for documents of interest that include the search term(s) you used and that are included in a document description. Document descriptions and the references under which they will need to be ordered will be listed as either individual items or, in the case of multiple results, under the department code (the letters) and then with the number of results in blue at the right-hand side. Click on the blue number to obtain more detailed descriptions of these results.

Many records have been or are in the process of being digitized and placed on the DocumentsOnline section of the National Archives website. Among these records are the Prerogative Court of Canterbury copy wills (PROB 11), famous original wills (PROB 1), Death Duty registers of the Country Courts (IR 26) and Royal Naval wills (ADM 48). In each case it is possible to search these records by name and, where appropriate, to download them (for a fee).

Records Held Elsewhere

Many records of value for family and local history are held in other record offices and libraries. The National Register of Archives—maintained by TNA and available on the National Archives website—contains information about the whereabouts of records in local record offices and local studies libraries and in other repositories in England and Wales. Probate records held by the British Library and the Bank of England are described in chapter 9. For the whereabouts of probate records relating to Scotland, Northern Ireland, the Republic of Ireland, the Channel Islands and the Isle of Man, see chapter 10.

Useful addresses and websites are given in full on pages 152–4.

INTRODUCTION

In the five years since the first edition of this book, the growth of the internet has significantly changed the way we access wills and other probate records. Wills make really good indexing projects, not just for family historians, but also financial and economic historians, and many record offices and commercial websites are capitalizing on this. Speculative searches through series previously available only on microfilm are replaced with numerous hits at the touch of a button. Other online tools are now available to assist your research; for example, palaeography tutorials to help you read the documents and newspapers and discover further information, particularly with regard to disputes. In this revised second edition, we describe how you can use the internet to make searching easier, and all addresses and websites are updated, along with the further reading.

We were interested in wills and probate records from the start of our National Archives careers, when we worked in the old Public Record Office in Chancery Lane, in the heart of legal London. In a room called the Rolls Room, and later the Rolls Chapel, we helped readers find wills, inventories, and documents relating to disputes.

Wills and other associated probate records are also a key source for local, social, financial and economic historians and for biographers and historians generally. Associated records such as inventories and accounts often provide an intriguing glimpse of how our ancestors lived and may give the value of their personal property in minute detail.

Although wills can be dry and formulaic, they are also one of the few 'official' records that can convey personal feelings and thoughts. From what other source could you learn that David Davis despised his wife to such an extent that in 1788 he left her 'the sum of five shillings', which he thought 'sufficient to enable her to get drunk for the last time at my expense'? Some wills are even written in the hand of the deceased themselves—for example, that of Jane Austen, held at the National Archives and featured opposite and on the front cover.

Our experience helping people with their enquiries highlighted the need for a practical guide that reveals how to find probate records, including less well-known records such as administration bonds and probate accounts. This guide explains the content of these records and places them in context with the relevant legislation. It also covers the primary sources for wills and related records from the earliest to the most modern—from wills found among ancient documents to those of the recently deceased.

In addition to the holdings of the National Archives and the Borthwick Institute of Historical Research, at the University of York, we have covered those of the various county archives throughout the country. The book's coverage also extends to the records held at institutions such as the Bank of England and the British Library, and looks beyond England to holdings in other parts of the British Isles and in the Republic of Ireland.

Also included are chapters on death duty records—a key source for measuring wealth—and on litigation over wills, which can reveal unexpected aspects of an ancestor's life and character. As well as covering disputes brought before the church courts, this guide also refers to those dealt with by the secular courts, such as the Court of Chancery and Court of King's Bench. It clearly explains some of the complexities of what was heard where, in language that can be understood by readers not familiar with ecclesiastical and legal history.

KAREN GRANNUM AND NIGEL TAYLOR

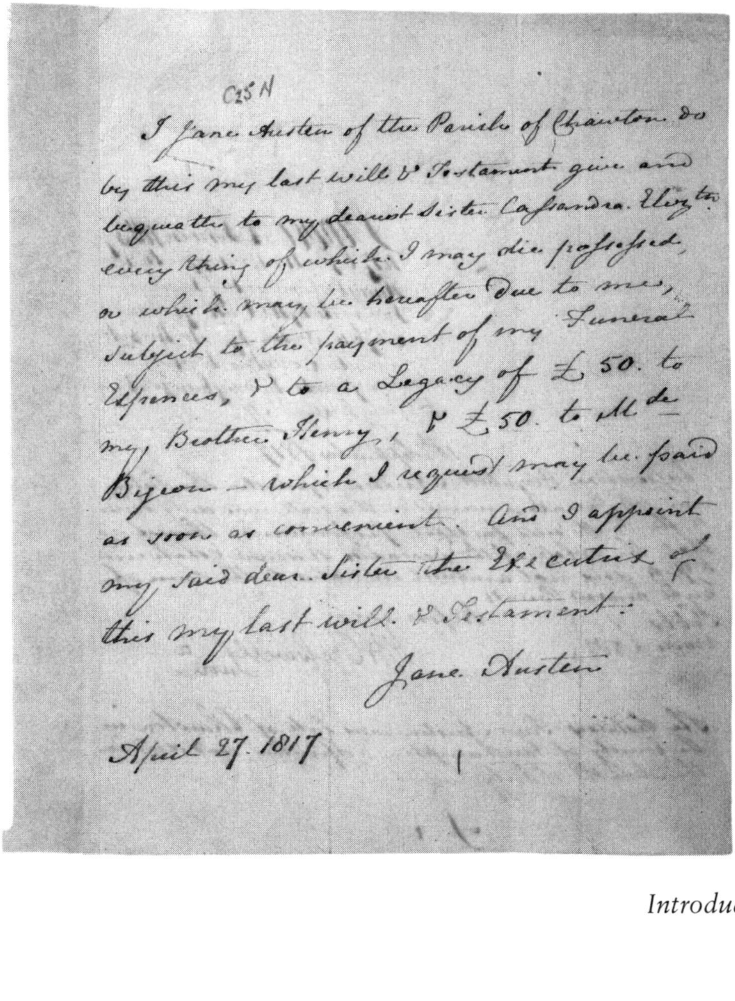
C25N
I Jane Austen of the Parish of Chawton do
by this my last Will & Testament give and
bequeath to my dearest Sister Cassandra Elizth
every thing of which I may die possessed,
or which may be hereafter due to me,
subject to the payment of my Funeral
Expences, & to a Legacy of £50. to
my Brother Henry, & £50. to Mde
Bijeon — which I request may be paid
as soon as convenient. And I appoint
my said dear Sister the Executrix of
this my last will & Testament.
Jane Austen
April 27. 1817

Fig. 1 *The will of Jane Austen, written in her own hand (holograph) and dated 27 April 1817.* PROB 1/78

1 UNDERSTANDING WILLS

1.1 Why Wills Matter

1.1.1 *Wills for family history*

Wills are an important resource for family historians. They can give the names of numerous people associated with the deceased—though wills vary from the very short, naming maybe just one beneficiary, to extensive documents, running to as many as a hundred pages, with many individuals mentioned.

Wills can give an insight into the lifestyle and status of a family. For example, a series of bequests of scholarly books would indicate an interest in learning. They may display deeply felt emotions: love, hate, exasperation, or protectiveness. References to non-family members—trusted servants, business associates, local worthies—can help to reveal aspects of family life and may provide clues to a wider story. Also, if one member of a family left a written will, it is likely that other members of the family, from earlier and later generations, may have left wills too.

Wills can also give clues to occupations, which in turn can reveal other potential sources for research. For example, a will of a serviceman in the Royal Navy could lead to additional information in Ships' Logs, service records, muster rolls and medal entitlements.

1.1.2 *Wills for local, social and economic history*

Until recently wills were not generally regarded as a prime source for local, social or economic history. This is possibly because of the difficulties in locating wills according to trade or place. But now many more wills are searchable online by place or occupation, and so the types of research for which they can be used are greatly extended. Wills can, for example, be a helpful source in plotting the growth of a village or a trade, or the influence of landed families in an area or the spread of business contacts.

Identifying farmers, yeomen, butchers, wheelwrights, clergymen or lawyers and examining their wills in conjunction with linked evidence, such as inventories and accounts, can allow the identification of social trends, or patterns of activity such as booms and slumps, across places and time. A number of important studies (some on a national basis and others on a regional basis) of the various social classes have drawn extensively on such records. (For some of the academic publications that have used these sources, see Further Reading, p.155.)

Charitable bequests—including those that actually create a charity—can offer an insight into the religious and philanthropic nature of society. In addition, a particularly generous bequest may prompt further research, to try to ascertain the motive for the testator's generosity.

1.2 What is a Will?

Wills are documents in which people try to exert control over their property—and their heirs—after their death. Over the centuries, what would happen to property in the absence of a will was governed by a variety of laws and customs. These generally allowed a proportion to support the deceased's widow and other dependants, a proportion to the next heir, and so on. A will gives greater scope, allowing the testator to support a wider range of people and to leave property exactly as he or she wishes—for example, to a best friend, a trusted servant, the poor of the local parish, or even to a favourite pet. For example, Elizabeth Orby Hunter in 1813 left, 'to my beloved parrot the faithful companion of twenty five years an annuity for its life of two hundred guineas a year to be paid half yearly as long as this beloved parrot lives' (PROB 11/1545).

Centuries or decades after the creation of a will, we are able to use it as a prime source for finding out more about the testator's life, family and times. As with all documents that serve as sources for family history, this is not the purpose the writer had in mind. We therefore need to learn what can be taken at face value and what is merely traditional wording; what is meaningful and what is not necessarily significant; whether all close relatives or property that might be of interest are mentioned; and if not, where else to look. It can be very easy to jump to conclusions—and not necessarily the right ones.

Every so often, over the centuries, the state displayed an interest in wills, whether to inhibit avoidance of taxes or dues payable to the Crown or to try to eliminate fraud. But making a will has never been obligatory. In some instances where no will was made, the transfer of property took place

and direct that all the residue and remainder of my property
real and personal of every denomination shall be security
for the payment of the following annuities and that the
yearly interest arising from the aforesaid property may be
applied half yearly to the payment of the following annuities
first I give and bequeath to my beloved parrot the faithful
companion of twenty five years an Annuity for its life
of two hundred guineas a year to be paid half yearly
as long as this beloved parrot lives to whoever may have the
care of it and prove its identity but the above annuity to
cease on the death of my parrot and if the person who shall
or may have the care of it should substitute any other parrot

Fig. 2 *The will of Elizabeth Orby Hunter, which includes an unusual bequest to her parrot (proved 1813).* PROB 11/1545

according to local knowledge or custom, perhaps through manorial courts or informally. In other cases, the next of kin or creditors were able to go to court to obtain authority to administer and dispose of the deceased's property—again, according to set rules.

1.3 The Origin of Wills

The early history of wills is not clear and has generated much discussion among historians. We do not know to what extent wills were made orally, even after the Norman Conquest. These oral wills were probably just a few sentences spoken in the presence of witnesses, and not always committed to writing. It is likely that this kind of will (or rather testament—see 1.4.1) persisted among the poor and those unable to make wills (such as married women—see 5.5.1) for centuries, with relatives and husbands disposing of small possessions and keepsakes quite informally. For more about early wills, see Michael M. Sheehan's *The Will in Medieval England* (Pontifical Institute of Mediaeval Studies, Toronto, Studies and Texts No. 6, 1963) and Dorothy Whitelock's *Anglo-Saxon Wills* (Cambridge University Press, 1930).

The church developed a virtual monopoly on the probate of wills until 1858 when it became the responsibility of the state. This may seem strange, but at the time, the church was in an excellent position to take this responsibility. Priests made it clear that the dying man was duty-bound to make atonement for the wrongs he had committed—particularly the non-payment of tithes (church taxes)—and to use part of his wealth for the relief of the poor. When a written will was made, it was likely that an educated priest drafted it; and it was the clergy who received the will or heard the testator's final wishes during his or her last hours. Following the testator's death, it was the clergy who, if necessary, clarified points within the will. And when someone died without leaving a will, it was the clergy who advised on the wishes of the deceased regarding his or her estate. Charitable bequests were a notable feature of pre-Reformation testaments, often tied in with requests for prayers for the testator's soul. Unfortunately, this meant that the charitable bequests were appropriated by the Crown when prayers for the dead were forbidden by Henry VIII and Edward VI. Later charitable bequests were framed so as not to fall foul of laws against 'superstitious uses'.

It is not known whether there was a conscious decision to grant the clergy this responsibility or whether this simply evolved. The role of the secular courts in the probate process should not, however, be overlooked. Although the ecclesiastical courts were responsible for the proving of wills and the granting of administrations, they had jurisdiction over personal goods only—such as furniture, livestock, leaseholds, crops, jewellery and fabrics. Secular courts claimed jurisdiction over real estate. Certainly secular courts were unable to grant probate without the help of the church. See

3.3 for more information on the ecclesiastical court structure and history.

1.3.1 *Why did people leave wills?*

People drafted a will in order to settle their affairs, to ensure that their family or dependants were provided for, to make charitable bequests, and to remember friends. Generally, people did this later in life and often on their deathbed or when seriously ill. There was much superstition among the medieval and early modern populace, and it was thought that making a will too early in life might tempt fate and accelerate death.

Some people sorted out their estate and any marriage settlements years before they died, thus making the necessity for a will redundant. However, a husband with a young wife probably considered a will a prudent precaution, as her possessions would become the property of her new husband (see 5.3.7). Also, a will may well have been judged necessary if a dispute seemed possible.

1.3.2 *How many people left wills?*

Before 1858, it is not easy to say what proportion of the population left wills. The most straightforward method of determining this is to compare the number of wills with the number of adults buried, given in records such as parish registers. Unfortunately this is not as straightforward as it sounds. Many burial records give only the name and date of death of the deceased, so it is impossible to tell whether the death was of a child or an adult. Also, certain members of society, such as married women, were barred from making wills.

In 1861 the Registrar General produced an analysis of the number of wills that went to probate during 1858 and the number of administrations granted. The number of persons who died during the year was 210,972. Out of these, some 21,653 left wills (since the new Court of Probate was not operative for the first 10 days of 1858, this figure had been adjusted to compensate for the missing days). Therefore only one person in 10 left a will. The average value of property disposed of was £2,998 by will and £759 by administration.

During 1858, out of the 102,049 men aged 21 or over who died in England and Wales, 15,558 (15.2 per cent) left personal property by will and 5,896 (5.8 per cent) by administration. So 21 per cent of adult males left personal property and 79 per cent made no bequests.

Out of the 108,923 women who died aged 21 or over, 6,095 (5.6 per cent) left personal property by will and 3,274 (3 per cent) by administration. So, for women, the average amount left by will was £1,793 and the average amount left by administration was £587. However, it should be borne in mind that this was before the Married Women's Property Act of 1882, and so a large percentage of adult women were still excluded from making wills.

1.4 Some Key Terms

1.4.1 *Is a will and a testament the same thing?*

Basically, a will is a declaration of the testator's wishes and instructions regarding his or her property that are to be put into effect after death. Strictly, the terms 'will' and 'testament'—which are often used together in the preamble to a will—relate to different categories of property:

> Originally, under common law, the *will* was solely concerned with land held on a freehold basis (see 5.3.6), also referred to as *real estate*. This was *devised*, not bequeathed. However, by the sixteenth century the expressions 'will' and 'testament' had become interchangeable.
>
> Originally, the term *testament* dealt with the testator's *personal estate* (or *personalty*)—including cash, credits, leases, goods and chattels (moveable possessions)—which are *bequeathed* as *bequests*.

1.4.2 *What is the difference between a testator and an intestate?*

A *testator* is a person who leaves a will. A female testator is sometimes referred to as a *testatrix*. An *intestate* is someone who dies without making a will, or who leaves a will that is invalid. The legal term for such a situation is *intestacy*. In these cases, an individual with a claim on the estate can apply to the court for permission to pay outstanding debts and distribute the estate in accordance with the law. The court issues the *administrator* with *letters of administration* authorizing the distribution of the estate. See 4.1.

1.4.3 *What is an estate?*

The possessions of the deceased—whether a humble cottage or a stately home, a single cooking pot or a porcelain dinner service and an array of valuable paintings—are collectively known as his or her estate.

1.4.4 *What is an executor?*

An *executor* is someone nominated by the testator to put the provisions of the will into effect, by *executing* (carrying out) the wishes of the testator. The testator may nominate one or more executors. A female executor is sometimes referred to as an *executrix*.

1.4.5 *What is probate?*

Probate is the official recognition by a relevant court of law that a will has been *proved*—accepted as legally valid, in that it has been properly witnessed, has not been tampered with, and conforms to all other requirements of the law. Probate does not concern itself with the detailed contents of the will. The granting of probate allows the executor or executors to *administer* the will—the legal term for putting the provisions of a will into effect.

Generally, the court would give an executor a copy of the will with the text of the grant of probate added to it to work from as he or she administered the testator's estate. Such a copy of the will is sometimes referred to as a *probate*. Following the grant of probate, a probate clause was attached to the will by seal by the ecclesiastical court. In later years, the confirmation of probate was annotated (formally noted), usually on the last page of the will. Probate clauses are formulaic and merely confirm that probate was granted on a particular day. As a result, they provide little in the way of personal information about the testator and his or her family. Before 1733 —except during the Interregnum (1651–1660)—probate clauses were written in Latin. For an example of a Latin probate clause and English translation, see 5.3.15.

1.5 The Probate Process

An act of 1529 ('concerning fines and sums of money to be taken by ministers of bishops and other ordinaries of Holy Church for the probate of Testaments') specified that probate should be granted with 'convenient speed without any frustratory delay'. Although the exact procedure and practices differed between the various courts, the act did serve as a general template. It set out the court fees that were to be paid and stipulated that the certification of the oath, sometimes called a *jurat*, had to be written on the back of the will, declaring when, where and before whom it was sworn.

This was done before the executor presented him/herself to be sworn by the surrogate (deputy judge) on behalf of the archbishop, bishop or archdeacon (depending on the type of church court) as to the due execution of the will. The executor's oath states that he/she would faithfully execute the same, paying debts and legacies, and bring in a 'true and perfect inventory'. After the swearing of the oath, a transcript or copy of the will was copied on parchment and delivered to the register scribe or other officer of the bishop, etc.

By the second half of the nineteenth century, simple instructions on how to gain probate were given in such publications as *Whitaker's Almanack*. The 1896 edition advised that when applying for probate executors should bring a registrar's certificate of death or an official certificate of burial, together with the will and full details of the property and debts of the deceased. It added that if there was no will, or no executor appointed, then two sureties would have to attend and enter into a bond for the faithful administration of the estate.

1.6 Which Probate Court?

This depended on the date. Until 1858, church courts mainly proved wills, and there were more than 200 of them, in all. Most people lived within reach of a church court of some kind. Unfortunately for family historians and other researchers, all these courts kept separate registers of wills and there was no central index. However, archives are increasingly making either wills, or indexes to them, available on the internet, which makes searching much easier.

1.7 Case Study

1.7.1 *The will of Lady Hamilton*

Emma, Lady Hamilton, mistress of Lord Horatio Nelson, left a will of 1811 in her own handwriting called a holograph will, written on multiple sheets of paper. Both the original and probate register copy are held in the National Archives. Fig. 3 shows the last page of the original, with the signature and seal of Emma Hamilton. The probate copy is also shown. This was written in a court hand by a clerk in the Registry of the Prerogative Court of Canterbury and covers just one page, with the probate clause at the end extending into the second page.

In her will, Lady Hamilton left all her possessions to her daughter Horatia, otherwise known as Nelson Thompson, 'the daughter of the great and glorious Nelson'. She states her alleged claims to public bounty, which Lord Nelson had included in the last codicil to his will but which had been rejected by the Treasury. Lady Hamilton, however, had large debts, despite bequests from Lord Nelson and her late husband, and she was committed to the Kings' Bench Debtors Prison in 1813. She was to die in poverty in Calais in 1815.

Fig. 3 *The original will and registered copy will of Emma Hamilton (proved 6 March 1816).* PROB 11/1578 PROB 1/25 (*inset*)

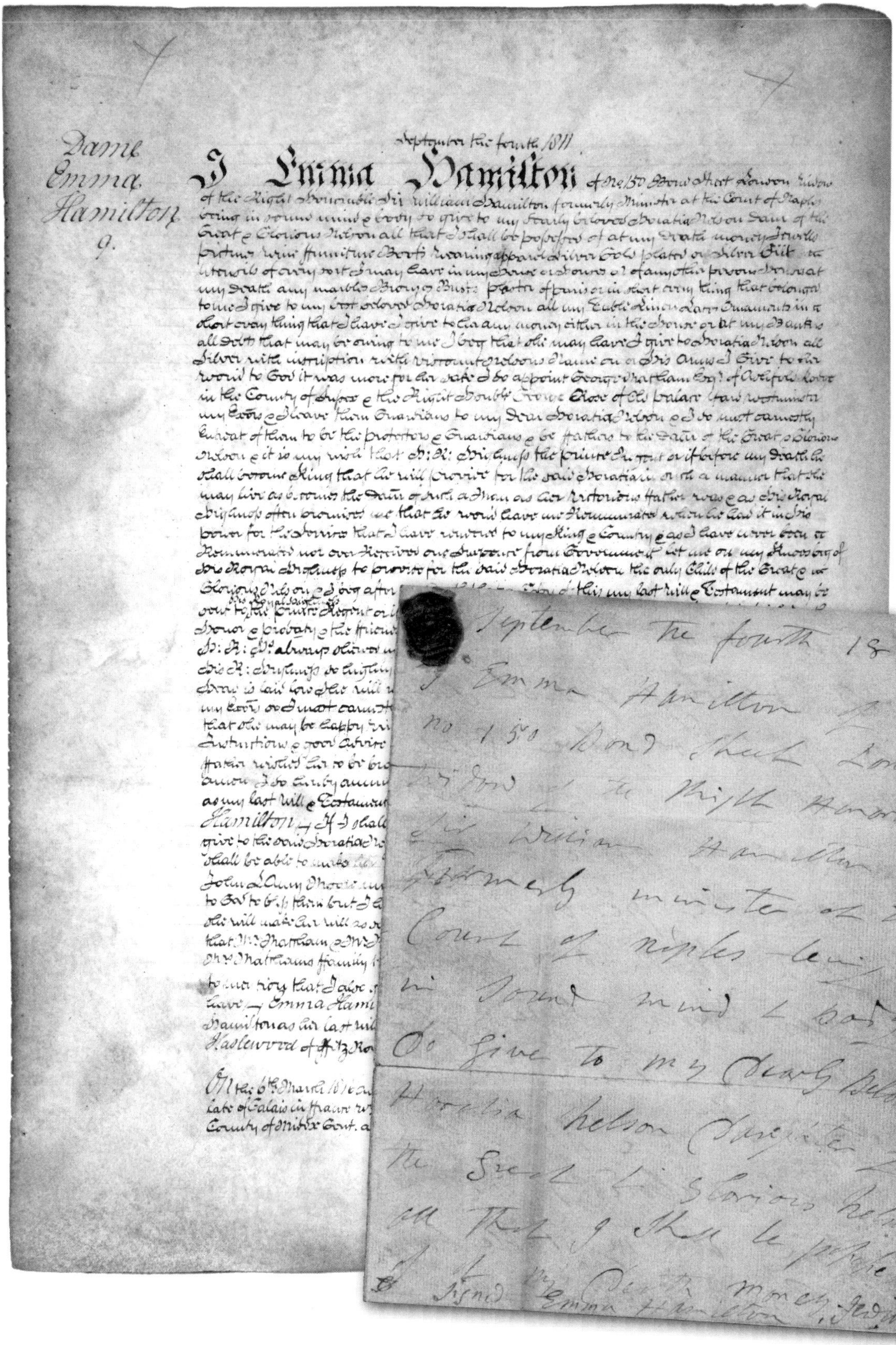
Dame Emma Hamilton 9.

September the fourth 1811

I Emma Hamilton of No 150 Bond Street London Widow of the Right Honourable Sir William Hamilton formerly Minister at the Court of Naples being in sound mind & body do give to my dearly beloved Horatia Nelson daughter of the Great & Glorious Nelson all that I shall be possessed of at my death money jewells pictures wine furniture books wearing apparel silver gold plated or silver gilt …

September the fourth 1811

I Emma Hamilton of
No 150 Bond Street London
Widow of the Right Honorable
Sir William Hamilton
formerly minister at the
Court of Naples being
in sound mind & body
do give to my dearly beloved
Horatia Nelson daughter of
the Great & Glorious Nelson
all that I shall be possessed
of at my death money, jewells
Signed Emma Hamilton

2 WILLS AND ADMINISTRATIONS FROM 1858

2.1 The Probate Act 1857

A new Act of Parliament came into force in 1857 which removed probate jurisdiction from the church courts and set up a secular national Court of Probate for England and Wales. There was no change to the law of probate, and the new court followed the rules, orders and practice of the church courts.

Although often described as a centralized court, the new Court of Probate was also a very local institution, with a network of 40 district registries to cover wills of lower value. Indeed, by 1879, three-fifths of all grants of probate and administration were issued by the district registries.

One of the advantages of the post-1858 Court of Probate, compared with the church courts, was that it was much easier for executors to appear in person. Previously, specialized ecclesiastical lawyers called proctors appeared on behalf of executors.

2.2 Wills Proved in England and Wales

The general impression of a single universal court was created by the production of a union index of all wills and administrations. This was compiled annually by the Principal Probate Registry from information sent in by the local registries. The new court made its first grants of probate and administration on 12 January 1858. As a result, finding wills proved since 12 January 1858 is much easier than finding wills proved before then.

2.2.1 *The National Probate Calendar*

There are National Probate Calendars for each year from 1858 to the current year. From 1871, wills and administrations are indexed in a single sequence; before then they were given in separate indexes. All are arranged in strictly alphabetical order.

From 1858 to 1968, the following information appears:

The full name and address of the deceased (and sometimes occupation)
The full name of executors or administrators (and addresses up to 1892)
The relationship, if any, of the executors or administrators to the deceased (up to 1892)
The date and place of death
The date and place of grant of probate or administration
In the case of women, marital status was noted, with name of husband if still alive at time of probate or administration (husband's name not given from 1958).

From 1968 onwards, the only information given is:

The name and address of the deceased
The date and place of death
The date and place of grant of probate or administration
The value of estate.

The only complete run of the annual National Probate Calendars is at:

London Probate Department,
Principal Registry of the Family Division,
First Avenue House,
42–49 High Holborn,
London
WC1V 6NP
Telephone: 020 7947 7191
Website: *www.hmcourts-service.gov.uk*

They are in the following formats:

1858–1992	In books
1993–5	On microfiche
1996 onwards	On computer (also available at Manchester District Probate Registry)

However, the National Archives and a number of county archives/record offices and local studies centres hold microfiche copies of the National Probate Calendars for 1858–1943. The Society of Genealogists in London and some record offices have microfilm or microfiche copies for the slightly shorter period of 1858–1930. Additionally, hard copies that were held at district registries are now deposited at a number of local record offices.

The National Probate Calendars are also available at district probate registries, although these registries are only required to hold the indexes to wills and administrations for the last 50 years and most do not hold any for earlier years. The addresses of the district registries and the network of sub-registries are listed on the Her Majesty's Court Service website (*www.courtservice.gov.uk*).

Although the National Probate Calendars are not at present accessible via the internet, there is currently a proposal to digitize the indexes to wills and administrations and to provide online ordering and payment for copies of wills and grants. Check Her Majesty's Court Service website for the latest developments.

2.3 Obtaining a Copy of a Will

Note down the following if you have found an entry in the National Probate Calendar for a will or administration that is of interest:

The name of the deceased
The date
The type of grant (i.e. will or administration).

For the years 1940–46, you may find Llandudno mentioned when you were expecting London as the place of probate or administration. The reason for this is that the Principal Registry moved from London to Llandudno, in North Wales, as part of the evacuation of certain government records during the war years.

2.3.1 *In person*

You can go to the Probate Searchroom at the Principal Registry of the Family Division in London or any of the district registries to request a copy of a will, grant of probate or grant of administration.

If you are using the calendars for 1858–1930 at the Probate Searchroom in London, make a note of the handwritten folio number that appears in the margin of the index, as you will need it to access the will itself. These numbers do not appear on the microfiche or microfilm copies. Also, there are handwritten additions to show further grants of probate, or where the original value of an estate was re-sworn because it had been recalculated.

2.3.2 *By post*

The Probate Registry offers a postal search service. For applications for searches and copies of wills and administrations contact:

Postal Searches and Copies Department
York Probate Sub-Registry
1st Floor, Castle Chambers
Clifford Street
York
YO1 9RG
Telephone: 01904 6667777
Website: *www.hmcourts-service.gov.uk*

For more detailed information about the postal search service (including a downloadable application form), see Her Majesty's Court Service website.

2.4 The Court of Probate

In addition to the Principal Registry, which served London and the surrounding counties, the Court of Probate had 40 district registries.

Within a county, poorer people did not even have to travel to the district registry. An executor of a will of low value could apply for probate at the local Inland Revenue Office, if that was more convenient. Taking one year at random, 1899, we find that 'low value' was then defined as where the gross real and personal estate did not exceed £500. So, in Middlesex, for example, many people had the option of going to Inland Revenue offices at Acton, Enfield, Kilburn, Staines, Sudbury, Tottenham and Uxbridge; and in Devon low-value wills were proved at Barnstaple, Bideford, Honiton, Ilfracombe, North Tawton, Okehampton, Parracombe, Plymouth, South Molton, Tiverton and Totnes, as well as Exeter. Although local church courts had gone, there was still local provision for getting wills proved as cheaply as possible. This was of great importance for the success of the court, and also for the extension of death duties. There was even a provision allowing applications for administrations to be made to the registrar of a county court, if the value of the estate was small (for example, £100 in 1896) and the applicant lived more than 3 miles from a district registry.

Today, there are 30 district and sub-district registries. Contact details for these registries are given on Her Majesty's Court Service website.

2.4.1 *Do all wills go to probate?*

Probate is unnecessary if the sum involved is small (currently the threshold for England and Wales is £5,000 for money held in accounts). However, many wills involving smaller amounts go to probate, as this is often the easiest way to fulfil the instructions contained in the will.

2.5 Location of Records

When probate was taken out at a district registry, the registry retained the original will and made a registered copy, which was bound into a volume. A further copy was forwarded to the Principal Registry in London. The original wills and associated records—apart from those lodged during the last two years, which are still held by the district registries—are now held in a central repository in Birmingham. The centre receives requests for copies from the registries, scans a copy and sends it back electronically. It does not deal directly with members of the public.

Registered copies originally held by the relevant district registry that are more than 50 years old are now mainly held at local county archives. The central repository in Birmingham also holds associated records for the Principal Registry, including oath bonds and, in some cases, correspondence from solicitors and internal registry notes. These have been kept for the last 50 years (earlier records have been destroyed).

In addition, the repository in Birmingham holds surviving records for the last 50 years of wills and grants issued by courts in former British colonies and resealed (probate confirmed or grants of administration authorized) in the Court of Probate in London. These are for people who lived and worked abroad but held property in England or Wales. Again, earlier records have been destroyed.

2.5.1 *England*

County	Registered copy wills
Bedfordshire	Up to 1930 at Northamptonshire Record Office
Cambridgeshire	Up to 1926 at Northamptonshire Record Office
Cheshire	Up to 1940 at Cheshire and Chester Archives
Cornwall	Up to 1941 at Cornwall Record Office
Cumberland	Up to 1941 at Cumbria Record Office, Carlisle
Derbyshire	Up to 1928 at Derbyshire Record Office, Matlock
Dorset	Up to 1941 at Dorset Archive Service
Durham	Up to 1940 at Durham University Library Archives and Special Collections
Essex	Up to 1941 at Suffolk Record Office, Ipswich
Gloucestershire	Up to 1941 for Gloucester at Gloucestershire Record Office Up to 1941 for Bristol at Bristol Record Office
Hampshire and Isle of Wight	Up to 1941 at Hampshire Record Office
Herefordshire	Up to 1928 at the National Library of Wales
Huntingdonshire	Up to 1941 at Northamptonshire Record Office
Lancashire	Up to 1941 at Lancashire Record Office
Leicestershire	Up to 1940 at Leicestershire Record Office
Lincolnshire	Up to 1941 at Lincolnshire Record Office
Norfolk	Up to 1941 at Norwich Record Office
Northamptonshire	Up to 1930 at Northamptonshire Record Office
Northumberland	Up to 1941 at Northumberland Record Office
Nottinghamshire	Up to 1939 at Nottinghamshire Record Office
Rutland	Up to 1941 at Leicestershire Record Office
Shropshire	Up to 1940 at Shropshire Records and Research Centre
Staffordshire	Up to 1928 at Lichfield Record Office
Suffolk	Up to 1928 for Bury St Edmunds at Suffolk Record Office, Bury St Edmunds Up to 1941 for Ipswich at Suffolk Record Office, Ipswich
Sussex	Up to 1928 (West Sussex) for Chichester at West Sussex Record Office
Warwickshire	Up to 1941 at Birmingham Reference Library, Local Studies Department
Westmorland	Up to 1941 at Cumbria Record Office, Carlisle
Wiltshire	Up to 1928 at Wiltshire and Swindon Record Office
Worcestershire	Up to 1928 at Worcestershire Record Office
Yorkshire	Up to 1939 for Wakefield at West Yorkshire County Record Office

2.5.2 *Wales*

County	Registered copy wills	County	Registered copy wills
Anglesey	Up to 1941 at NLW	Glamorganshire	Up to 1940 at NLW
Brecknockshire	Up to 1928 at NLW	Merionethshire	Up to 1928 at NLW
Cardiganshire	Up to 1941 at NLW	Monmouthshire	Up to 1940 at NLW
Caernarvonshire	Up to 1941 at NLW	Montgomeryshire	Up to 1940 at Shropshire Records and Research Centre
Carmarthenshire	Up to 1941 at NLW		
Denbighshire	Up to 1928 at NLW		
Flintshire	Up to 1928 at NLW	Pembrokeshire	Up to 1941 at NLW
		Radnorshire	Up to 1928 at NLW

NLW = National Library of Wales

2.6 Estates Without Next of Kin

If someone dies intestate and is not survived by a lawful heir, or dies leaving a will but fails to dispose of the residue of his or her estate, the estate (or residue) reverts to the Crown. Such estates are known as *bona vacantia* (ownerless goods).

The Bona Vacantia Division of the Treasury Solicitor's Department (*http://www.bonavacantia.gov.uk/*) administers the estates of people who die intestate in most of England and Wales, and collects the assets of dissolved companies and failed trusts. You can search their website to see whether you are entitled to the estate of a deceased relative. Estates of people dying within the Duchy of Lancaster and the Duchy of Cornwall are administered differently. See the website for more information.

The National Archives holds selected case papers relating to estates of this kind administered by the Treasury Solicitor (the government lawyer) and HM Procurator General. Among them you will find papers relating to property in England and Wales belonging to dissolved companies and to trusts that failed or were wound up.

The main series is TS 17 (*Bona Vacantia*, Administration of Estate Papers, 1698–1981), which contains selected case papers (TS 17/1–301 and TS 17/1245–1390) and letters of administration (TS 17/302–1244) extracted by HM Procurator General in favour of the Treasury Solicitor. The files are arranged by the name of the person or organization whose estate is under administration, but later files within the series relate to the wider policy questions concerning *bona vacantia*.

Other records of the Treasury Solicitor and HM Procurator General concerning *bona vacantia* business include:

TS 8	Letter Books, 1804–15
TS 9	Letter Books, 1815–44
TS 30	Royal Warrants and Treasury Authorities, 1804–1936
TS 33	Pedigrees, 1794–1944

For details of *bona vacantia* estates in Scotland and Ireland, see 10.1.5 and 10.2.1.

2.7 Resealing in London of Scottish and Irish Wills

Wills of Scots and Irish persons with property in England and Wales were resealed (that is, the grant of probate was confirmed) in London and are therefore listed in the general indexes. From 1858 to 1876, these resealed wills are indexed after the letter Z in each year. However, only the grants of probate were lodged in London and these do not usually contain more information than included in the probate calendars. The wills themselves were lodged in the respective countries. For more information about Scottish and Irish wills, see chapter 10.

2.8 Wills of the Royal Family

When an application for probate involving a member of the royal family is submitted, the will is sealed pursuant to an order by the President of the Family Division of the High Court. No one may inspect the original will and no copies may be made, though the grant of probate is usually made available (an exception was made in 1998, when both a will and a grant of probate were made available in respect of the estate of Diana, Princess of Wales).

A list of royal wills is kept by the Principal Registry of the Family Division, but this is not available to the public and approval from a senior district judge would be needed to release it. However, the now out-of-print *Wills, inventories and death duties: The records of the Prerogative Court of Canterbury and the Estate Duty Office, a provisional guide* by Jane Cox (Public Record Office, 1988)—copies of which are available at the National Archives—lists royal wills from the medieval period to the twentieth century. Also see 9.4 for a list of royal wills at the National Archives.

2.9 Case Study

2.9.1 *The will of a rich man*

Edward Cecil Guinness, the brewer and philanthropist, was born in Dublin in 1847. He joined the family's brewery business aged 15 and became a very rich young man on the death of his father, Sir Benjamin Lee Guinness, in 1868. The family fortune was mainly split between Edward and his elder brother Arthur. They also shared the profits of the business and valuable land and property, Arthur inheriting the family estates in County Galway, Ireland and Edward the building at 80 St Stephen's Green, Dublin that is now the headquarters of the Irish Department of Foreign Affairs. Probate had to be gained for the part of the estate of Benjamin Guinness that was in England and the will was resealed in the Principal Registry of the Family Division in London. The 1868 death duty register entry for Sir Benjamin Guinness can be found at the National Archives under reference IR 26/2555. His entry in the Scottish and Irish section of the 1868 National Probate

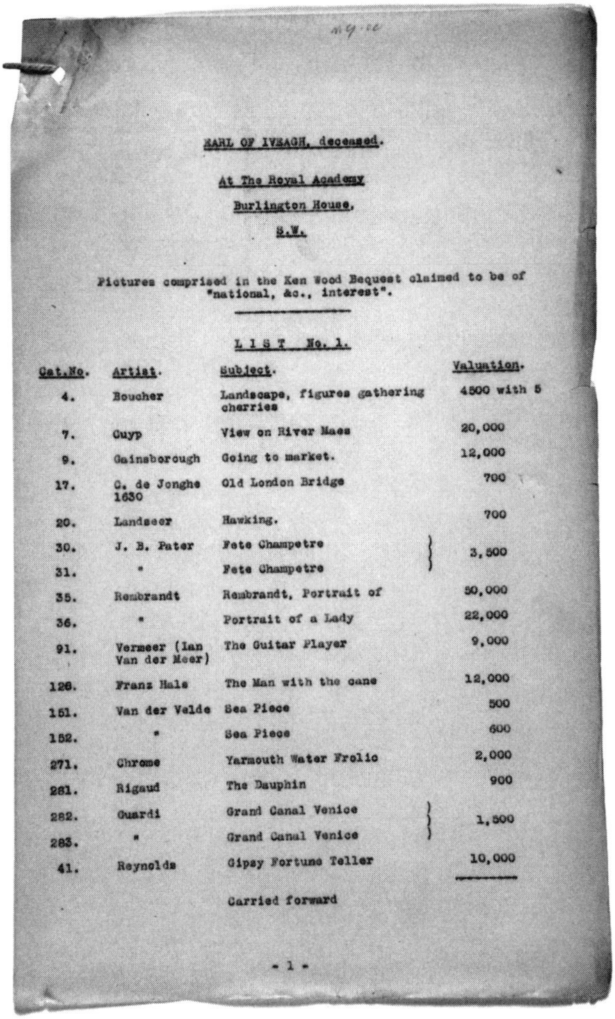

EARL OF IVEAGH, deceased.

At The Royal Academy

Burlington House,

S.W.

Pictures comprised in the Ken Wood Bequest claimed to be of "national, &c., interest".

L I S T No. 1.

Cat.No.	Artist.	Subject.	Valuation.
4.	Boucher	Landscape, figures gathering cherries	4500 with 5
7.	Cuyp	View on River Maes	20,000
9.	Gainsborough	Going to market.	12,000
17.	C. de Jonghe 1630	Old London Bridge	700
20.	Landseer	Hawking.	700
30.	J. B. Pater	Fete Champetre	3,500
31.	"	Fete Champetre	
35.	Rembrandt	Rembrandt, Portrait of	50,000
36.	"	Portrait of a Lady	22,000
91.	Vermeer (Ian Van der Meer)	The Guitar Player	9,000
126.	Franz Hals	The Man with the cane	12,000
151.	Van der Velde	Sea Piece	500
152.	"	Sea Piece	600
271.	Chrome	Yarmouth Water Frolic	2,000
281.	Rigaud	The Dauphin	900
282.	Guardi	Grand Canal Venice	1,500
283.	"	Grand Canal Venice	
41.	Reynolds	Gipsy Fortune Teller	10,000
		Carried forward	

- 1 -

Fig. 4 *The death duty account of Edward Guinness, dated 1926–9.* IR 59/1201

Calendar gives a valuation of the estate in England as well as providing the date of probate in Dublin, Ireland.

The Guinness business became increasingly profitable and in 1886 it became a public company. During this period of growth the company gained a reputation in terms of social welfare, including a system of social security for its workforce introduced in 1900. Edward Guinness showed wider generosity towards the end of his life, when he bought Kenwood House in Hampstead, London, setting up a trust to maintain the house and its collection as an art gallery open to the public.

Made a viscount in 1905 and an earl in 1919, Edward Lord Iveagh died on 7 October 1927 at Grosvenor Place, London. The National Probate Calendar entry for his probate will shows that his estate was valued at £11 million, which was then the highest-ever valuation. His various properties were divided between his three sons and the residue of the estate, after all the bequests had been paid, went again to his three sons and their children, who received the income for their lives only. He also left large sums to the King Edward VII Hospital Fund for London and to St Patrick's Cathedral, Dublin. The will also confirmed the status of Kenwood House and the surrounding estate, with the intention that it should pass to the nation in 1935.

The estate was somewhat reduced by the requirement to pay over £4 million in death duties, the scourge of the rich. In the National Archives there are no fewer than eight death duty files in the series IR 59, concerning his estate, all but one of which are still closed. The one file that is open to be seen (IR 59/1201) includes lists and valuations of the many paintings in various houses, including those painted by Reynolds, Gainsborough, Stubbs and Rubens. Those in Kenwood House are shown as exempted from death duty because of their donation to the nation.

3 FINDING A WILL BEFORE 1858

Before 1858 the task of proving wills and granting administrations was the responsibility of the church. Many different church courts were able to prove wills and grant administrations, so it is not always straightforward to find the documents you are looking for, although the increasing number of online sources helps. To find a will before 1858, you need to have some idea of the family name and the area where they lived—but families do not always stay put, and records of individuals may appear in unexpected areas because of church court rules. Below, you will find a practical guide to finding wills and administrations before 1858. See 3.3 for an overview of the church court structure and their records.

3.1 Online Search Strategies

Because of their popularity among family and social historians and their relevance for one-name searches, wills make good indexing projects and there are several major collections on the internet. The location of church court records can be confusing, so it is worth eliminating any relevant online sources first. As the location and availability of online sources changes rapidly, it is best to regularly check websites that list current online will databases. Unfortunately there is not a comprehensive list, but Genuki (*www.genuki.org.uk/big/eng/Probate.html*) and Cyndi's List (*www.cyndislist.com/wills.htm*) are worth consulting along with the sites listed below.

When using online sources, you should bear in mind that only the testator is indexed and therefore other key people such as executors, witnesses and beneficiaries are not easily found.

3.1.1 *Your Archives (http://yourarchives.nationalarchives.gov.uk/)*

This is the National Archives' Wiki. It allows contributors to add and amend information that complements the Catalogue. Users have also posted transcribed Prerogative Court of Canterbury wills. To access the index to other online wills, type 'online probate indexes' into the search box.

3.1.2 *DocumentsOnline (www.nationalarchives.gov.uk/documentsonline)*

Searching the Prerogative Court of Canterbury (PCC) registered wills on DocumentsOnline can be very rewarding as the site contains more than 1,016,000 wills from 1384 to 1858 (also see 3.3). The index is free to search and, as the Prerogative Court of Canterbury was the busiest of all the church courts, it is worth eliminating. There is a small charge to download a will, but they can be viewed free of charge at the National Archives (see 3.4 for the jurisdiction of the PCC).

You should remember that these wills are reproductions of the registered copies and not the original wills (see 3.7). As the executor had to pay to have the will copied into the register, there may be some gaps in the series.

DocumentsOnline does not include administrations. Remember to try variants of spelling for surnames if your initial search is unsuccessful. Up to 200 characters can be entered in the Quick Search box, which can accommodate between 20 and 30 search terms, depending on the length of the words you enter. You can significantly narrow down your search by entering even four keywords—for example, 'james taylor innkeeper middlesex'. Simply separate the words with spaces; there is no need to use capital letters.

3.1.3 *Access to Archives* (A2A)

The A2A database contains catalogues describing archives held locally in England and Wales and dating from the eighth century to the present day. The catalogues range from detailed individual files to summary information. It is possible to find, for example, catalogues of the family archives of named families and catalogues of archives relating to the study of genealogy as a subject. Via the A2A site (*www.nationalarchives.gov.uk/a2a*) you can search for records from particular ecclesiastical courts. The database is updated regularly, so is worth revisiting from time to time for newly included catalogues.

3.2 Records Held Locally

Where there is no online source available, you need to establish which church court proved the will. However, some ecclesiastical jurisdictions covered more than one county. For example, someone who died in Berkshire could have had his or her will proved by the Archdeaconry Court of Berkshire, the Consistory Court of Salisbury or the Prerogative Court of Canterbury, depending upon the value and the location of his or her goods; and the records of these three courts are in different locations.

The table below offers a basic guide to finding wills and administrations before 1858. Detailed guidance is in *Probate Jurisdictions: Where To Look For Wills* by Jeremy Gibson and Else Churchill (FFHS, 5th edn, 2002).

You can find contact details for all of the record offices listed below online in the ARCHON directory (*www.nationalarchives.gov.uk/archon*) on the National Archives website.

3.2.1 *England*

Deceased's place of residence	**Local church court records at:**
Bedfordshire[1]	Bedfordshire and Luton Archives and Records Service
Berkshire[1]	Berkshire Record Office
	Oxfordshire Record Office
	Wiltshire and Swindon Record Office
Buckinghamshire[1]	Buckinghamshire Record Office
	Oxfordshire Record Office
	Hertfordshire Archives and Local Studies
Cambridgeshire[1]	Cambridgeshire Archives
	Cambridge University Library
	Huntingdonshire Archives
	Suffolk Record Office
Cheshire[2]	Cheshire and Chester Archives and Local Studies Service
Cornwall[1]	Cornwall Record Office
Cumbria[2]	Cumbria Archive Service
	Lancashire Record Office
Derbyshire[2]	Lichfield Record office
Devon[1]	Devon Record Office
	Cornwall Record Office
	Dorset History Centre
	Wiltshire and Swindon Record Office
Dorset[1]	Dorset Archive Service
Durham[2]	Durham University Library Archives and Special Collections
Essex[1]	Essex Record Office
	London Metropolitan Archives
	Guildhall Library
Gloucestershire[1]	Gloucestershire Archives
	Bristol Record Office
Hampshire[1]	Hampshire Record Office
Herefordshire[1]	Herefordshire Archive Service
	National Library of Wales
Hertfordshire[1]	Hertfordshire Archives and Local Studies
	Huntingdon Archives
	Essex Record Office
	London Metropolitan Archives
	Guildhall Library
Kent[1]	Centre for Kentish Studies
	London Metropolitan Archives
Lancashire[2]	Lancashire Record Office
Leicestershire[1]	The Record Office for Leicestershire, Leicester and Rutland
Lincolnshire[1]	Lincolnshire Archives
Middlesex and London[1]	London Metropolitan Archives
	Guildhall Library
	City of London Records Office
	Lambeth Palace Library
	City of Westminster Archives Centre

Norfolk[1]	Norfolk Record Office
Northamptonshire[1]	Northamptonshire Record Office Lincolnshire Archives Service
Northumberland[2]	Northumberland Record Office
Nottinghamshire[2]	Nottinghamshire Archives Some may also be found among PCC records at TNA
Oxfordshire[1]	Oxfordshire Record Office Bodleian Library
Shropshire[1]	Lichfield Record Office Herefordshire Record Office National Library of Wales
Somerset[1]	Somerset Archives and Record Service Bristol Record Office
Staffordshire[1]	Lichfield Record Office
Suffolk[1]	Suffolk Record Office, Ipswich Suffolk Record Office, Bury St Edmunds Norfolk Record Office, Lowestoft
Surrey[1]	London Metropolitan Archives Lambeth Palace Library Hampshire Record Office
Sussex[1]	West Sussex Record Office East Sussex Record Office
Warwickshire[1]	Lichfield Record Office Worcestershire Record Office Shakespeare Birthplace Trust Warwickshire Record Office
Westmorland[2]	Cumbria Archive Service Lancashire Record Office
Wiltshire[1]	Wiltshire and Swindon Record Office Hampshire Record Office Gloucestershire Record Office
Worcestershire[1]	Worcestershire County Record Office Hertfordshire Archives and Local Studies
Yorkshire[2]	Cheshire and Chester Archives and Local Studies Cumbria Archive Service Durham University Library Archives and Special Collections Nottinghamshire Archives National Library of Wales Lancashire Record Office West Riding Registry of Deeds West Yorkshire Archive Service

1. Prerogative Court of Canterbury (PCC) records at the National Archives and online at *www.nationalarchives.gov.uk/documentsonline*
2. Prerogative Court of York (PCY) records at the Borthwick Institute and indexes partially available online at *www.britishorigins.com*

- Remember to check for online sources (see 3.1)

3.2.2 *Wales*

Deceased's place of residence	Where to look?
NORTH WALES[1] Anglesey, Caernarvonshire, Denbighshire, Flintshire, Merionethshire, Montgomeryshire	National Library of Wales
SOUTH WALES[1] Brecknockshire, Cardiganshire, Carmarthenshire, Glamorganshire, Monmouthshire, Pembrokeshire	National Library of Wales Herefordshire Archive Service

3.3 Ecclesiastical Courts

Ecclesiastical courts were established as a separate entity from the secular courts from at least the reign of William the Conqueror. The church courts operated under canon law and as well as dealing with testamentary affairs they were responsible for:

The discipline of the clergy
The fabric of church buildings
Suppressing recusancy (refusal to attend the parish church)
Non-payment of tithes
Matrimonial disputes
Defamation
Heresy.

The main punishments administered by the church were excommunication and public penance. Secular courts would hear more serious offences, such as rape, as they had the power to execute or imprison.

Before 1858, there were more than 200 church courts scattered across the country and there was no single, united pattern of church administration.

Like the secular courts, the church courts operated in a hierarchy. England and Wales were divided into two provinces: York and Canterbury. Each province consisted of a number of dioceses and was presided over by an archbishop. Each of the dioceses consisted of several archdeaconries and was presided over by two or more bishops. Each archdeaconry was presided over by an archdeacon and consisted of a number of rural deaneries.

3.3.1 *Canon law*

The rules for the proving of wills and the granting of administrations were a combination of statute and ecclesiastical canon law, which existed side by side. Canon law consisted of proclamations issued by convocations (assemblies of the clergy gathered by their representatives to discuss ecclesiastical affairs). Ecclesiastical canons are certain rules and regulations, mostly concerning conduct or belief, defined by the church.

1. Prerogative Court of Canterbury (PCC) records at the National Archives and online at *www.nationalarchives.gov.uk/documentsonline*

3.3.2 *Bona notabilia*

Before 1604 archbishops claimed exclusive rights to administer estates where a person had goods (*bona*) in more than one diocese. Attempts by bishops and archdeacons to curb the power of the archbishops, and so increase their own revenues, resulted in the influential canons of 1604. These specified that:

All witnesses, administrators and executors were to take an oath declaring whether or not there were any goods or debts in any other diocese within the province and their value. If there were goods in more than one diocese, then the case was referred to the archbishop's court within 40 days. No oath was required from executors or administrators by the archbishop's court unless there were objections.

The estates of people dying with *bona notabilia* ('noteworthy goods') totalling £5 or more (the practice in London was £10) in more than one diocese should be dealt with by the archbishop's court. The estate of any person without goods in more than one diocese to the value of £5 or more was dealt with by a lower ecclesiastical court (such as a bishop's or an archdeacon's court).

It is important to keep in mind the rule of *bona notabilia*, as it forms a crucial part of the probate and administration process. It was this rule that determined in which court a will was proved, and consequently where the documents are now located.

See *A Brief Treatise of Bona Notabilia Within the Province of York* by George Lawton (1825).

3.4 Which Ecclesiastical Court?

As explained earlier, before 1858 the amount of goods and property left by the deceased and where those goods were (in terms of ecclesiastical jurisdictions) determined in which court a will was proved.

To complicate matters further, testamentary court records are arranged by the date on which the probate or administration was granted, rather than by the date of death or the date on which the will was written—and, although wills were often written when the testator was on his or her deathbed, there is sometimes a large discrepancy between these dates. Straightforward wills might take a couple of months to prove, whereas complicated or disputed estates could take many years. It is therefore important to try to establish not only the name of the testator or intestate and the place where they were living, but also the approximate date on which the testator or intestate died.

The practicalities of how to find a will are explained in 3.1 and 3.2, but as a broad rule of thumb:

The will or administration would be granted by the Prerogative Court of York if the testator or intestate lived in the north of England

(Cheshire, Cumberland, Durham, Lancashire, Northumberland, Nottinghamshire, Westmorland and Yorkshire) and was reasonably wealthy (having goods totalling £5 or more in more than one diocese). See 3.5.

The will or administration would be granted by the Prerogative Court of Canterbury if the testator or intestate lived in the south of England or in Wales (Berkshire, Buckinghamshire, Cambridgeshire, Cornwall, Derbyshire, Devon, Dorset, Essex, Gloucestershire, Hampshire, Herefordshire, Hertfordshire, Huntingdonshire, Kent, Leicestershire, Lincolnshire, London, Middlesex, Norfolk, Northamptonshire, Oxfordshire, Rutland, Shropshire, Somerset, Staffordshire, Surrey, Sussex, Suffolk, Wales, Warwickshire, Wiltshire and Worcestershire) and was reasonably wealthy (having goods totalling £5 or more in more than one diocese). See 3.6).

The will or administration would be granted by the bishop's court (known as a consistory court or commissary court) if the testator or intestate had goods in more than one archdeaconry but all in the same diocese.

The will or administration would be granted by the archdeacon's court if the goods were in just one archdeaconry.

The records of archdeacons' and bishops' courts are generally in the local county or diocesan record office for the county of the deceased's residence, but changing boundaries and jurisdictions complicate this and it is worth consulting a guide to probate jurisdictions. See the table in 3.2.1 for the location of locally proved wills.

In the event of someone dying with *bona notabilia* in both the northern and the southern province, separate grants of probate or administration were issued to cover the effects in each. This was because the jurisdiction of each archbishop was confined to his own province.

Location of property	**Relevant court**	**Location of records**
In more than one diocese (with *bona notabilia*—goods amounting to £5 or more)	Archbishop's Prerogative Court	YORK: Borthwick Institute and partially on British Origins CANTERBURY: The National Archives and on DocumentsOnline
In more than one archdeaconry, but all in the same diocese	Bishop's court (known as a consistory or commissary court)	Local record office see 3.2.1
Within one archdeaconry	Archdeacon's court—or possibly a 'peculiar court'with local jurisdiction	Local record office see 3.2.1

3.5 Prerogative Court of York

The testamentary records of the Archbishop of York are held at the Borthwick Institute of Historical Research. Records survive from the fourteenth century to 1858, when the court was abolished. The Borthwick Institute also holds the records of minor church courts within the province of York. British Origins (*www.britishorigins.com*) is currently digitizing the indexes of the Prerogative and Exchequer Court of York wills. It is worth checking the website regularly for updates. Copies of probate records are available from the Postal Reprographic Service, Borthwick Institute.

Bishops dealt with the majority of probate business, and their court in northern England was known as the Exchequer Court of York. However, the Prerogative Court of York (PCY) claimed jurisdiction over estates in the northern province where the rule of *bona notabilia* applied.

Both the large number of peculiar courts (see 3.10.1) and changing boundaries complicate the jurisdiction of the Archbishop of York. More detailed information about the structure of the ecclesiastical courts in the north of England is on the Borthwick Institute's website (*www.york.ac.uk/inst/bihr/*) and in *Probate Jurisdictions: Where To Look For Wills* by Jeremy Gibson and Else Churchill (FFHS, 5th edn, 2002).

Published indexes to wills proved in the Exchequer and Prerogative courts are published by the Yorkshire Archaeological Record Series in the following volumes: 1389–1514 Vol. 6; 1514–53 Vol. 11; 1554–68 Vol. 14; 1568–85 Vol. 19; 1585–94 Vol. 22; 1594–1602 Vol. 24; 1603–11 Vol. 26; 1612–19 Vol. 28; 1620–7 Vol. 32; 1627–36 Vol. 35 (includes administrations 1627–52); 1636–52 Vol. 49; 1660–5 Vol. 49; 1666–72 Vol. 60; 1673–80 Vol. 68; 1681–8 Vol. 89. Many of the volumes contain appendices (mostly indexes to administrations). They are available at the National Archives, the Borthwick Institute and large reference libraries.

3.6 Prerogative Court of Canterbury

The testamentary records of the Prerogative Court of Canterbury are held by the National Archives. Wills from 1384–1858 are searchable on Documents Online.

The Prerogative Court of the Archbishop of Canterbury began to claim its right to grant wills and administrations as early as the reign of Henry III, although it was not until the fifteenth century that it emerged as an administrative organization in its own right. The court was based at Doctors' Commons in London. Up to 1858, when the court was abolished, it exercised jurisdiction where the deceased had *bona notabilia* within the southern province amounting to £5 or more.

During the first half of the fifteenth century, the Archbishop of Canterbury could also prove wills on his own account. These wills date from 1312 to 1637, although there are few after 1500. They are now held in Lambeth

Palace Library, but are published in the following:

Index of Wills Recorded in the Archiepiscopal Registers at Lambeth Palace, edited by J. C. Smith (reprinted from *The Genealogist*, vols 34–5, 1919)

Calendar of Lambeth Palace Administrations Recorded in the Archbishops' Registers (reprinted from *The Genealogist*, vols 7–8 (1883–4)

Micropublication of the Archbishops' Registers 1272–1640 (available from World Microfilms Publications).

For further information, see the Lambeth Palace Library website (*www.lambethpalacelibrary.org*).

Initially, wills proved by the PCC would have attracted only the wealthier sections of society, as the £5 limit was a barrier. The Prerogative Court of Canterbury also attracted business that should strictly perhaps have gone to lower ecclesiastical courts, but because of the PCC's prestige were directed to it. Eventually, due to inflation, the £5 threshold became less of a restriction, as the stipulated sum was not increased. From 1810 until the abolition of the court in 1858, the Bank of England would only accept probate from the PCC (see 9.6.2).

The PCC claimed jurisdiction over people dying overseas with property in England and Wales, and for soldiers and sailors who died abroad. However, in the case of soldiers and sailors, from 1817 the value of the estate had to exceed £20 before the PCC could act.

Many of the indexes to these wills and administrations are published by the British Record Society. A list of these publications is available on their website at *www.britishrecordsociety.org/volumespublished.htm*. Some of them are searchable (for a fee) on Ancestry (*www.ancestry.co.uk/search/rectype/vital/epr/main.aspx*). The publications are available at the National Archives and other reference libraries.

Fifty of the earliest PCC wills are transcribed in full and are free to search on the Corpus of Middle English Prose and Verse website (*http://quod.lib.umich.edu/cgi/t/text/text-idx?c=cme;idno=EEWills*).

See Appendix 1 for a complete list of PCC record series, with references.

3.6.1 *Statistical analysis*

Online access to more than a million wills via DocumentsOnline has made it possible to undertake some valuable statistical analysis. Where a county is identified within the will (for example, James Taylor of Bow Lane, Middlesex), it was included in the database. Consequently, from 1383 to 1858 the most common counties of residence for testators were:

1.	Middlesex	202,502
2.	London	87,750
3.	Surrey	70,610
4.	Kent	53,275

5.	Somerset	31,204
6.	Gloucestershire	30,943
7.	Essex	27,680
8.	Devon	27,045
9.	Hampshire	23,919
10.	Wiltshire	19,797

Although it is not possible to search DocumentsOnline by gender, most women were identified by their occupation or status. Adding together the most common female identifiers—for example, (by status), single lady, lady, dowager, widow, spouse, gentlewoman, mistress, spinster, wife, and (by occupation), dressmaker, nurse, housekeeper, school mistress, laundress—it is possible to estimate that at least 21 per cent of all PCC testators were female.

3.7 Types of Records

Although there were lots of different types of records generated during the course of testamentary business, the main records are:

3.7.1 *Original wills*

In order to obtain probate, the executor submitted the original will to the court. Generally it was retained by the court once the process was complete, though some courts made a copy of the will and returned the original to the executor (this was certainly the case with some wills in the Prerogative Court of Canterbury before 1600). Original wills are usually signed by the testator, but are generally not written in the testator's own hand. They are usually written on paper, or sometimes on parchment. As they are loose documents, their survival rate is not as great as that of registered copies. They tend not to survive in large numbers before 1600, although this varies from court to court.

• PCY: ORIGINAL WILLS 1427–1858. Although the original wills series begins in 1427, there are only one or two surviving items before 1591. From 1591 there are some original wills surviving for most years, and the series is generally complete from 1660 onwards. These records also include administration bonds, inventories, tuition bonds, renunciations and other testamentary paperwork. The records are in chronological bundles arranged according to month of probate by either the Prerogative Court or the Exchequer Court of York.

• PCC: ORIGINAL WILLS 1484–1858 (PROB 10). These survive sporadically before about 1600. Up to 1600 many of the so-called 'original wills' are in fact copies, since the original was returned to the executor.

• PCC: ORIGINAL WILLS OF FAMOUS PEOPLE 1552–1854 (PROB 1). The wills in this series were removed from PROB 10 due to the celebrity of the testators. They include the wills of Jane Austen, William Shakespeare and Samuel Pepys. They are accessible via DocumentsOnline as either the original will or the registered copy.

3.7.2 *Registered copies*

Once the probate process was complete, the executor could pay to have a copy of the will entered into the probate register. The registers are large bound ledgers, with wills copied into them page after page. It is these that many archives have microfilmed, and not the original wills. Check with the archive whether the records you are consulting are the original wills or the clerk's copies in the register. The survival rate of the registered copies is quite good, often extending back further than the original wills.

Ordinarily there is little difference between looking at the clerk's copy and the original. You should, however, bear the following points in mind:

The clerk's copy never includes the signature or seal of the testator. The testator's signature or seal is only on the original will—though it should be pointed out that a seal at the end of a will is not always the testator's but sometimes that of the scribe or his office.

Some executors did not pay to have the will copied. In such a case there will be either no entry in the registered copy will indexes or an entry with no corresponding will. In such circumstances the only full record is the original will, if it survives. If the original will has not survived, then the only available source is the probate act book (see below).

The handwriting on the original will and the registered copy will be different because different people wrote them. If the handwriting on either document is difficult to read, consult the other. Occasionally the clerk making the copy missed lines or names from the original document. If the registered copy does not seem to make sense, or something appears to be missing from it, compare the registered copy with the original will.

• PCY: PROBATE REGISTERS 1389–1858. There are gaps in the probate registers series during the fifteenth and seventeenth centuries. Inventories and grants of administration were never registered after the medieval period.

• PCC: REGISTERED COPY WILLS 1383–1858 (PROB 11). These are clerks' copies of original wills and only exist if the executor paid for the will to be registered. Before 1803 they include the 'sentence' (the final judgment in a cause) if the victorious party paid for it to be registered. The PCC registered copy wills are digitized in their entirety and are available on DocumentsOnline.

• PCC: INDEXES TO WILLS AND ADMINISTRATIONS 1383–1858 (PROB 12). The indexes (known as 'calendars') to PCC wills and administrations list the names of testators and intestates for whose estates grants were made during each year. They are arranged by year of probate and then by the initial letter of the surname. Many of the published name indexes available at the National Archives and elsewhere provide a reference based on the old register name. For example, the name John Small in the published index for 1649 gives the reference 64 Fairfax. This comprises the quire number and the name of the register which can be converted to a modern National Archives reference using the PROB 11 catalogue.

A quire is a traditional numbering system. It comprises eight folios (or 16 pages). The number is written at the top right-hand corner of the first page of the quire in roman numerals (early registers) or Arabic numbers. The index entry is to quire, and so the will should be in the following 16 pages. Access to wills via DocumentsOnline has largely made this series redundant. However, exceptions to the normal probate process such as double or limited probate are recorded here.

3.7.3 *Probate act books*

These books contain the ecclesiastical courts' own records of the initial grant of probate and of later letters of administration with will annexed and administration with will annexed of goods not administered (see 4.7).

When the grant of probate was issued, it was recorded on the original will, which was usually retained by the court. A record of the grant of probate was then copied into the probate act book. The probate act book may contain a valuation in the margin of the entry, alongside the date when the inventory was to be exhibited. This valuation can be useful if the inventory does not survive, although it will only relate to the personal estate of the deceased.

If the original will has not survived and the executor failed to pay the required fee to have the will copied into the probate register, then the probate act may be the only surviving item of testamentary documentation.

• PCY: PROBATE ACT BOOKS 1502–1858. From 1502, grants of probate and administration were entered in the act books of the various rural deanery courts. The earliest surviving act book of the Prerogative Court is dated 1587; before that date, prerogative business will be found in the act books of York City Deanery, held at the Borthwick Institute. There are gaps in the probate act books series during the sixteenth and seventeenth centuries.

• PCC: PROBATE ACT BOOKS 1526–1858 (PROB 8). These record the day-to-day business of the probate court and provide confirmation that probate was granted. If the original will has not survived and was not copied into the probate register, then this is likely to be one of the few documentary sources available. This series is arranged by 'seat' (see 4.3.2).

3.8 Other Prerogative Court of Canterbury Sources

Initial applications for a grant of probate are in PROB 14 (1657–1858). These records provide the executor's signature and an approximate date of the deceased's death.

If the executor was sworn by commission—and many executors were, as they could not afford the expense of travelling to London—the name and address of the local clergyman who administered the oath are in the commissions to swear executors in PROB 52 (1796–1858) and PROB 56 (before 1796), although this series is currently uncatalogued. These series can be used as a guide to the executor's place of residence. PROB 52 is arranged by 'seat' (see 4.3.2). If the court took over the distribution of the estate, details of this are in the Muniment Books in PROB 16 (1610–1858).

3.9 Interregnum

In the early stages of the English Civil War (May 1643 to November 1644) wills were not proved in London but in Oxford, where the judge of the Prerogative Court of Canterbury was based, along with Charles I. In November 1644 the Parliamentarians declared all grants of probate made in Oxford invalid, but allowed people to have the wills proved (or administrations granted) for a second time by a parliamentary court based in London.

In 1646 the records of these two courts (Oxford and London) were amalgamated, following the fall of Oxford to the Parliamentarians. The Oxford court did not keep registered copies of wills (see 3.7.2)—so unless the will proved in Oxford was proved and registered again in London, you will need to look for the original will (at the National Archives, in PROB 10/639–642).

When Parliament abolished the episcopacy in 1646, most ecclesiastical testamentary business went into abeyance. Then, following an act of 8 April 1653, all testamentary matters were transferred to a single court for England and Wales called the Court for the Probate of Wills and the Granting of Administrations, based in London. Records created by this court were written in English, instead of Latin (at that time the normal language of court records). The court ceased to function in 1659, and after the monarchy was restored in 1660 the records were incorporated into those of the Prerogative Court of Canterbury.

This effectively means that all probate records for England and Wales are in English for the brief period 1651 to 1660 and held centrally by the National Archives from 1653 to 1660. However, some executors and administrators in the north of England avoided the new court because of the expense and inconvenience of travelling to London. In such cases the wills—now held at the Borthwick Institute in York—either seem to have been implemented without formal probate or were proved retrospectively following the restoration of the ecclesiastical courts in 1660.

The document E 315/483 (1648–1659) at the National Archives contains copies of a number of wills and letters of administration extracted from the registers of the Prerogative Court of Canterbury during the Interregnum. These mainly relate to people in the service of the Commonwealth, either in the army or otherwise, the copies having been obtained by the government for the purposes of settling arrears of pay. The series is searchable by name on the Catalogue.

3.10 Other Testamentary Jurisdictions

3.10.1 *Peculiar jurisdictions*

Some clergy had the right to hold their own courts—for example, holders of monastic and abbey lands following Henry VIII's dissolution of the monasteries. Lords of the manor, universities and cathedrals also sometimes inherited such rights. These 'peculiar courts', as they were called, were exempt from the authority of their local archdeacon and sometimes even from the authority of the bishop. Examples of peculiar jurisdictions in the county of Dorset include Wimborne Minster, Sturminster Marshall, Great Canford and Poole, and Corfe Castle. Records of peculiar courts are deposited at the local or diocesan record office for the county.

3.10.2 *Manorial courts*

Under the feudal system, in theory, all land was held by the Crown and therefore the disposal of land, either through sale or inheritance, was a matter for the royal or manorial courts. Manorial courts recorded the passing on of title of copyhold land (literally 'held by copy of court roll') and the acquisition of copyhold land. Copyhold land could not be transferred to another person (whether by sale, mortgage or inheritance) without the permission of the manor court. See 5.3 for more on the devising of property.

In some parishes the manorial courts were virtually defunct by the eighteenth century; in others they continued until 1926, when copyhold tenure was abolished by the Law of Property Act 1922.

You can find the location of manorial court rolls and other documents by consulting the Manorial Documents Register located at the National Archives. You can search the Register (*www.nationalarchives.gov.uk/mdr*) for the following counties: Berkshire, Buckinghamshire, Cumberland, Hampshire, the Isle of Wight, Lancashire, Middlesex, North of the Sands (the Furness area, part of Cumbria since 1974), Norfolk, Surrey, Wales, Westmorland and the three Ridings of Yorkshire.

Court rolls for some manors are located at the National Archives. A will could be proved by a church court and enrolled on a manorial court roll. However, from 1815 there was no legal necessity to surrender (transfer) the copyhold and subsequently there may be no enrolment. For more information consult M. Ellis, *Using Manorial Records* (PRO revised edn, 1997).

3.11 Non-Anglican Wills

There was no special probate court for non-Anglicans and their wills were proved in the usual way.

3.11.1 *Jewish wills*

Wills of first-generation Jews can be particularly rewarding, as they often leave legacies to relatives living in their country of origin. A very useful source is *Anglo–Jewish Notabilities, Their Arms and Testamentary Dispositions*, compiled by A. P. Arnold (Jewish Historical Society of England, 1949). It includes a section giving details of wills and letters of administration of prominent members of Anglo–Jewry. A high percentage of Jewish wills were registered with the Prerogative Court of Canterbury (reflecting the concentration of Jews in London) and are accessible through DocumentsOnline.

3.11.2 *Quaker wills*

The wills of Quakers, like those of Jews, were proved or registered in the normal way. However, before the Affirmation Act 1696 Quaker executors were prevented by their beliefs from swearing an affidavit, because this entailed swearing an oath of allegiance to the monarch. However, some Quakers were not happy with the affirmation specified in the 1696 Act and had to wait until the Affirmation Act 1722 for satisfactory wording. Sometimes affirmation is mentioned in the probate clause of the will, but there are also instances of clerks using the word *jurat* to indicate that an oath was sworn by Quaker executors, who would probably not have sworn an oath.

3.11.3 *Roman Catholic wills*

Following an Act of Parliament in 1716, deeds and wills of papists were also enrolled in the Court of Chancery on the Close Rolls to create a permanent and authoritative record. They were known as 'letters closed' as they conveyed orders and instructions to royal officers and others and were therefore of a confidential nature. Before being dispatched, they were folded and then closed by the Great Seal. The records are in the series C 54 (1204–1903).

Lists of wills enrolled on the Close Rolls (from 13 William III to 5 George IV) are published in *The Genealogist*, Vol. 1, p. 267 (1877) and Vol. II, pp. 59 and 279 (1878); and also in *A List of Wills, Administrations etc. in the Public Record Office, 12th–19th Century*.

The Recovery Rolls in CP 43 (1583–1837) contain enrolments of transfer of property and include Roman Catholic deeds and wills. A list of CP 43 wills appears in *The Genealogist*, New Series Vol. III, pp. 122, 185 and 220 (1886).

Fig. 5 *The will of Simon Hyman Levy, a Jew, proved in 1789.* PROB 11/1184

Fig. 6 *The will of Dr. Daniel Phillips, a Quaker, proved 1748.* PROB 11/764

Fig. 7. *The will of the Reverend George Clayton, a Roman Catholic, proved in 1857.* PROB 11/2257

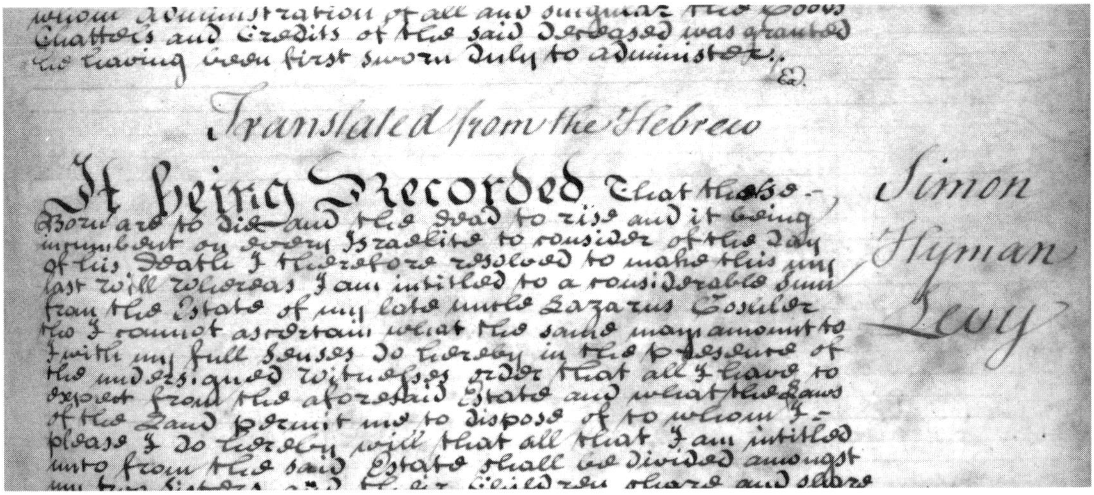

whom Administration of all and singular the Goods
Chattels and Credits of the said Deceased was granted
he having been first sworn duly to administer. Ex.
Translated from the Hebrew
It being Recorded That those
Born are to die and the dead to rise and it being
incumbent on every Israelite to consider of the day
of his Death I therefore resolved to make this my
last will whereas I am intitled to a considerable sum
from the Estate of my late uncle Lazarus Cosiler
tho I cannot ascertain what the same may amount to
I with my full senses do hereby in the presence of
the undersigned witnesses order that all I have to
expect from the aforesaid Estate and what the Laws
of the Land permit me to dispose of to whom I
please I do hereby will that all that I am intitled
unto from the said Estate shall be divided amongst
my two sisters and their children share and share
Simon Hyman Levy

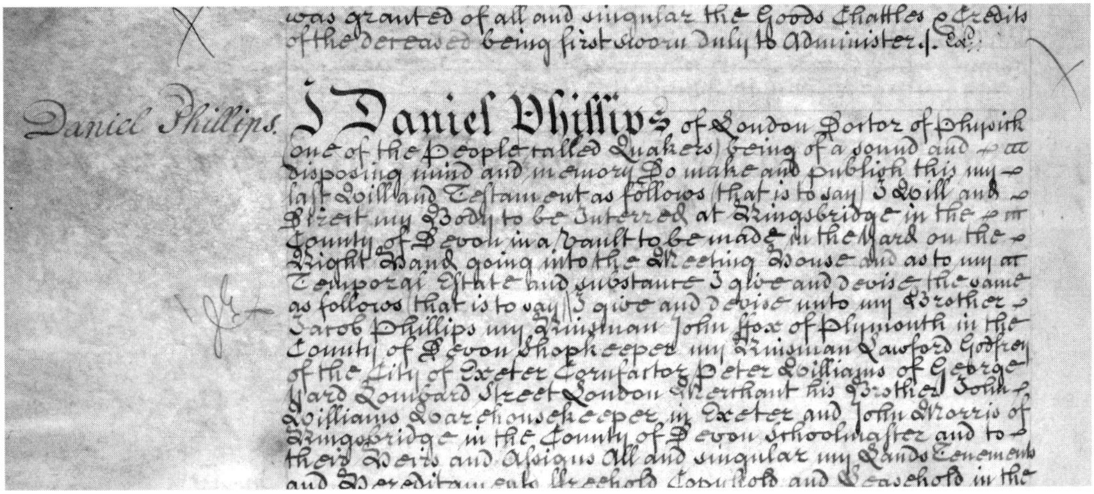

was granted of all and singular the Goods Chattles & Credits
of the deceased being first sworn duly to Administer. Ex.
Daniel Phillips.
I Daniel Phillips of London Doctor of Physick
one of the People called Quakers being of a sound and perfect
disposing mind and memory Do make and publish this my
last Will and Testament as follows (that is to say) I Will and
Direct my Body to be Interred at Kingsbridge in the
County of Devon in a Vault to be made in the Yard on the
Right Hand going into the Meeting House and as to my
Temporal Estate and substance I give and devise the same
as follows (that is to say) I give and devise unto my Brother
Jacob Phillips my Kinsman John Fox of Plymouth in the
County of Devon Shopkeeper my Kinsman Lawford Godfrey
of the City of Exeter Cornfactor Peter Williams of George
Yard Lombard Street London Merchant his Brother John
Williams Warehousekeeper in Exeter and John Morris of
Kingsbridge in the County of Devon Schoolmaster and to
their Heirs and Assigns All and singular my Lands Tenements
and Hereditaments Freehold Copyhold and Leasehold in the

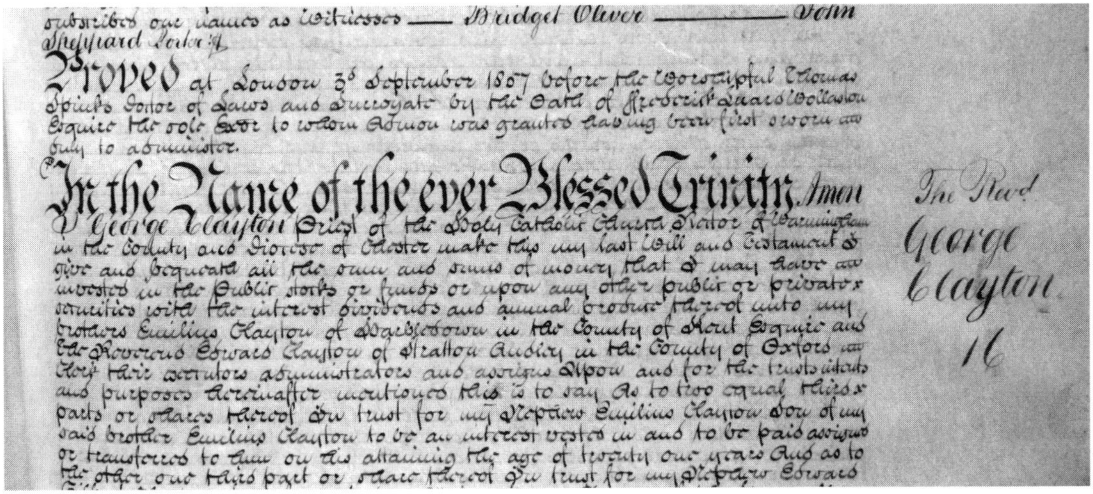

subscribed our names as witnesses — Bridget Oliver — John
Shepard Porter
Proved at London 3d September 1807 before the Worshipful Thomas
Stubbs Doctor of Laws and Surrogate by the Oath of Frederick Lewis Wollaston
Esquire the sole Exor to whom Admon was granted having been first sworn
duly to administer.
In the Name of the ever Blessed Trinity Amen
I George Clayton Priest of the Holy Catholic Church Rector of Warmingham
in the County and Diocese of Chester make this my last Will and Testament I
give and bequeath all the sum and sums of money that I may have
invested in the Public stocks or funds or upon any other public or private
securities with the interest dividends and annual produce thereof unto my
brothers Emilius Clayton of Wolverstone in the County of Kent Esquire and
the Reverend Edward Clayton of Stratton Audley in the County of Oxford [illegible]
Clerk their executors administrators and assigns Upon and for the trusts intents
and purposes hereinafter mentioned this is to say As to two equal third
parts or shares thereof In trust for my Nephew Emilius Clayton son of my
said brother Emilius Clayton to be an interest vested in and to be paid assigned
or transferred to him on his attaining the age of twenty one years And as to
the other one third part or share thereof In trust for my Nephew Edward
The Revd George Clayton
16

3.12 Extending your Search

If the most likely sources are exhausted and you still cannot find a will, there are other avenues to try. If you are fairly confident a will was written yet cannot find it among the records of the registered copy wills, extend your search for at least three years from the date of death of the testator. Although a straightforward will was proved within a few months of the date of death, a complicated or disputed estate could take several years.

If this fails:

- Look for the original will, rather than a registered copy. Probate courts required the executor to pay for the original will to be copied and not all executors did this, although it appears that the majority did.
- If the original will does not survive try the Probate Act Book instead. This is a record of all grants of probate made by the church courts (see 3.7.3).
- Try variant spellings of surnames as these can change over years and online indexes may have transcription errors.
- Try more unusual combinations, as some courts indexed titled people by title, rather than by name, and some of the indexes to wills are idiosyncratic. For example, you may find that the Bishop of Rochester is indexed under 'B' for 'Bishop'.
- Try death duties records.
- Did the person die in Scotland, Ireland or the Channel Islands? If so, see chapter 10.

It is always possible that no will was left, even though the individual was quite wealthy. This may be for one of the following reasons:

- The property was disposed of before death, making a will redundant
- The person whose will you are seeking did not own the capital he was living off, but merely a life interest
- He or she may have died suddenly at a relatively young age.

It is also possible that the person died without leaving a will (see chapter 4).

3.13 Case Studies

3.13.1 The will of an eccentric man

James Biddles died in 1834 and had his will proved in the Prerogative Court of Canterbury. Thanks to an obituary in *The Gentleman's Magazine,* it is possible to learn more about James Biddles. He is described as a rich, money-lending shoe-manufacturer of the City of London—and as mean in the extreme. Indeed, he reportedly often congratulated himself on not exceeding sixpence expenditure in a whole day. It was perhaps because of such thrift that he was able to leave money and property estimated to value more than £200,000, a sum that would be worth near to £10 million in today's money. The valuation of his personal estate contained in the Probate Act Book for 1834 (PROB 8/227), shown in Fig. 9, gives the much lower sum of £100,000, which a few months later was increased to £120,000. This figure is, however, based on the personal estate and excludes the valuation of freehold property belonging to Biddles.

Biddles's wealth was divided between 16 relatives and children, and his will showed generosity alongside the shrewdness for which he had earned such a reputation in his lifetime. He requested that the majority of his property not be sold for 10 years and that the interest only be paid out to the legatees, which ensured they would benefit from the expiry of leases on the properties. He left the sum of £200 to a young man who was his shopman and collected his rents, together with a request that he be permitted to reside on the premises two years rent-free. On 24 February an ailing Biddles added a codicil to his will leaving £50 to the wife of a neighbour who sat up with him. On 1 March, three days before he died, he added a second codicil, increasing this sum to £500.

Fig. 8 *The will of James Biddles, proved 14 March 1834, and an extract from his list of bequests.* PROB 11/1828

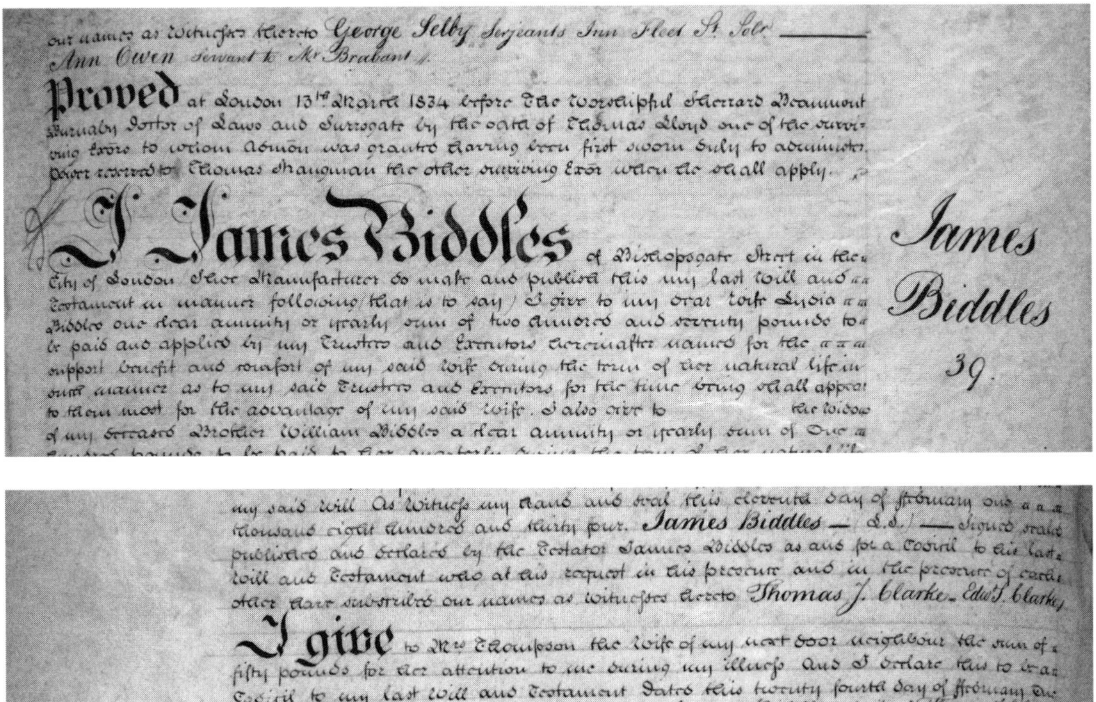

our names as witnesses hereto George Selby Serjeants Inn Fleet St. Solr ——
Ann Owen Servant to Mr Brabant.

Proved at London 13th March 1834 before the Worshipful Richard Beaumont Burnaby Doctor of Laws and Surrogate by the oath of Thomas Lloyd one of the surviving Exors to whom Admon was granted having been first sworn duly to administer. Power reserved to Thomas Shangman the other surviving Exor when he shall apply.

James Biddles 39.

I James Biddles of Bishopsgate Street in the City of London Shoe Manufacturer do make and publish this my last Will and Testament in manner following that is to say I give to my dear wife Lydia Biddles one clear annuity or yearly sum of two hundred and seventy pounds to be paid and applied by my Trustees and Executors hereinafter named for the support benefit and comfort of my said wife during the term of her natural life in such manner as to my said Trustees and Executors for the time being shall appear to them most for the advantage of my said wife. I also give to the widow of my deceased Brother William Biddles a clear annuity or yearly sum of One …

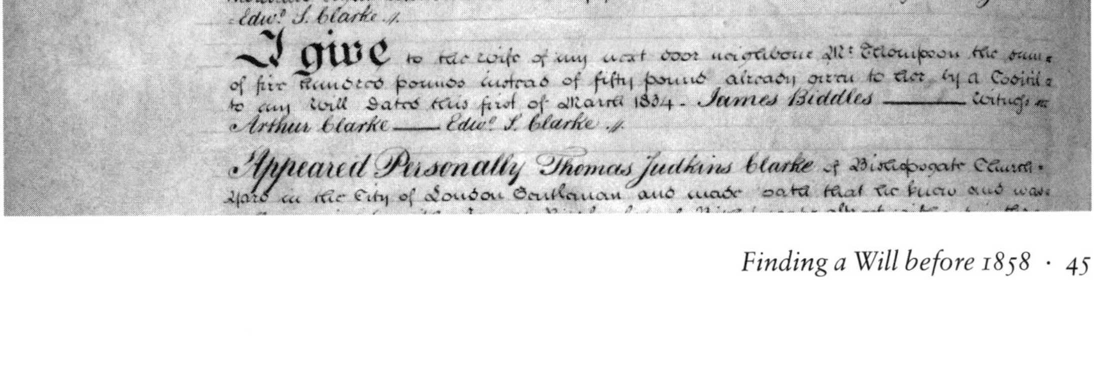

my said Will As witness my hand and seal this eleventh day of February one thousand eight hundred and thirty four. James Biddles — (L.S.) — Signed sealed published and declared by the Testator James Biddles as and for a Codicil to his last Will and Testament who at his request in his presence and in the presence of each other have subscribed our names as witnesses hereto Thomas J. Clarke — Edwd S. Clarke.

I give to Mrs Thompson the wife of my next door neighbour the sum of fifty pounds for her attention to me during my illness and I declare this to be a Codicil to my last Will and Testament dated this twenty fourth day of February One thousand eight hundred and thirty four. James Biddles. Witness Thomas J. Clarke Edwd S. Clarke.

I give to the wife of my next door neighbour Mr Thompson the sum of five hundred pounds instead of fifty pounds already given to her by a Codicil to my Will dated this first of March 1834 — James Biddles —— Witness Arthur Clarke —— Edwd S. Clarke.

Appeared Personally Thomas Judkins Clarke of Bishopsgate Church Yard in the City of London Gentleman and made oath that he knew and was …

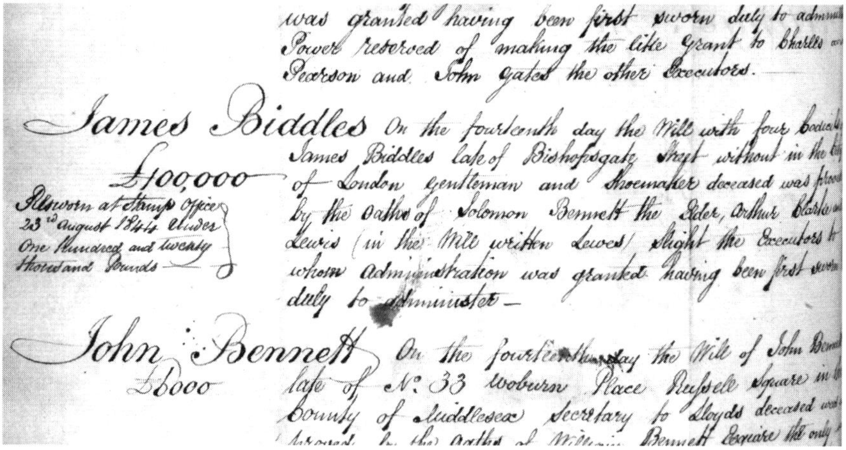
was granted having been first sworn duly to admin
Power reserved of making the like Grant to Charles
Pearson and John Yates the other Executors.
James Biddles On the fourteenth day the Will with four codicils
James Biddles late of Bishopsgate Street without in the
£100,000 of London gentleman and Shoemaker deceased was proved
Resworn at Stamp Office 23rd August 1844 Under One Hundred and twenty Thousand Pounds
by the Oaths of Solomon Bennett the Elder, Arthur
Lewis (in the Will written Lewes) Slight the Executors to
whom administration was granted having been first sworn
duly to administer —
John Bennett On the fourteenth day the Will of John
£6000 late of No 33 Woburn Place Russell Square in
County of Middlesex Secretary to Lloyds deceased

Fig. 9 *An entry from the probate act book for James Biddles showing the valuation of his personal estate at £100,000.* PROB 8/227

3.13.2 *A complicated probate*

The case of Lieutenant James Murray, which involved multiple grants and stretched over a long period of time, is a good example of a complicated probate. Murray was in the Royal Navy's Impress Service at Londonderry in Ireland, heading a press gang that conscripted men into military service. He died in 1804. His will bequeathed all his property to his children but named no executor, without which the church court could not automatically grant probate. In March 1806, as in any case where full probate could not be granted due to some complication, administration with will annexed was granted to the wife of a cousin, Charlotte Dick, until one of the children reached the age of majority, then 21. In December 1830, administration of unadministered goods was granted to Humphrey Donaldson, the attorney of the two children, both then resident in the East Indies. Donaldson, however, then died insolvent in Australia. A court case ensued in the Prerogative Court of Canterbury as it was alleged that Donaldson exploited part of the estate for his own use. It was not until May 1836 that administration with will annexed was granted to the two children, enabling them to take control of their inheritance. By this time the children must have been well beyond the age of majority, and the length of time it took for them to gain their inheritance is relatively unusual.

The 1830 and 1836 grants mentioned above are noted in small writing in the margin of the registered probate copy will of 1806 (PROB 11/1440)—the usual practice in these registers. Reference to the original grant to Charlotte Dick is given in the last paragraph of the text of the probate will.

4 ADMINISTRATIONS BEFORE 1858

4.1 Intestacy

In legal terminology a person who dies without leaving a will or whose will proves to be invalid is known as an *intestate*. When someone leaves a valid will, they are able to specify exactly what they want to happen to their personal estate, following payments to creditors. Both statute and common law govern the distribution of the personal estate of an intestate, which means that next of kin have little control over its distribution.

In instances of intestacy, not all estates before 1858 were subject to administration, as the process was time-consuming and costly. Next of kin were most likely to apply for a grant of administration if the estate was complicated or subject to dispute, or if it was necessary to establish a clear legal title to property. The estate may also have been settled prior to death. If no one applied for letters of administration, then there will be no formal record of the distribution of the personal estate.

Although grants of administration do not contain as much information as wills, they can be very valuable for family historians, as they often mention underage children and other next of kin. For local or economic historians, they can be helpful in that administrators were quite often creditors, trying to get back money owed them from various enterprises.

4.1.1 What was an administrator?

An *administration* (sometimes abbreviated to *admon*) is a grant, made by a relevant court, authorizing an appropriate person to administer the estate when no valid will has been left by the deceased. *Letters of administration* were usually granted to the widow, next of kin or to a creditor. They allow the *administrator* nominated by the court to collect rents and debts and to distribute the estate. The estate is distributed according to fixed rules under the supervision of the court. Sometimes administrations were granted after the granting of probate—for example, if an executor died and someone else was appointed to distribute the estate.

They were required to:

- Exhibit an inventory of the deceased's estate
- Collect any sums owed to the deceased
- Pay the deceased's debts and any legitimate expenses (such as medical bills, funeral costs, and the maintenance of the deceased's dependants) and submit an account of expenditure to the court
- Distribute the estate in accordance with the law of intestacy at the time.

The law required the administrator to compile an inventory of the personal estate within six months from the date of the grant of administration and an account within 12 months from the grant of administration.

It should be remembered that, as with wills, originally the ecclesiastical courts had jurisdiction only over the deceased's personal estate or moveable goods. Until the 1837 Wills Act they did not have complete authority over real estate.

4.1.2 *Who could administer the estate?*

When appointing administrators, the courts had to follow the order of precedence laid down by statute in 1529:

- Husband or wife
- Children
- Father or mother
- Brother or sister
- Next of kin (e.g. uncle or aunt)
- Creditor
- Others, at the discretion of the court.

4.1.3 *How was the estate distributed?*

In order to tighten procedures for administrators and force them to distribute the estate fairly, from 1670 the administrator was required to distribute one third of the personal estate to the widow of the deceased and the remainder to the deceased's offspring. The following provisos applied:

- If there were several children, the remainder would be shared among them equally
- If there were no children, half to the widow and the remainder equally to the remaining next of kin
- If there was no widow, then the remainder went to the children
- If there were no children, the administration was granted to someone with an interest in the estate (e.g. a creditor)
- If there were no next of kin and no one wished to claim administration, the estate would revert to the Crown (see 2.6).

Real estate descended to *the heir(s)-at-law*—normally to the eldest son or, if there were daughters only, then to all of them equally. Local custom in a manor could alter this; for example, where the custom of *Borough English* persisted (by which the youngest son inherited) or in those parts of Kent where *gavelkind* prevailed (by which all sons inherited equally). See 5.3.8.

Distribution of the estate could not take place until one year after the grant of administration was made, so that all debts were fully discharged.

4.2 The Records

The court kept copies of grants of administration in its administration act books, and it is these that are available in record offices. The original letters of administration rarely survive in archives unless the principal administrator revoked his or her right to administer the estate, or they were used as evidence in a lawsuit. In terms of information, letters of administration are fairly disappointing, as they normally simply state that a named individual was granted permission to distribute the estate. This may be accompanied by an administration bond providing slightly more information about the oath the administrator had to take before he or she could administer the estate. However, this extra information is likely to relate to the administrator (not always the next of kin), rather than the testator. It is possible to obtain additional information regarding the estate from the inventory, account or death duty records.

Administration act books normally give the following information:

- The date of the grant of administration
- The name of the intestate
- The parish of residence of the intestate
- The name of the administrator and his or her relationship to the intestate
- The dates by which the inventory and account had to be returned to the court.

For more complicated estates or later administrations, they may also include:

- The place of death of the intestate
- The marital status and/or occupation of the intestate
- The conditions limiting the grant (if applicable)
- The name of the special commissioner before whom the administrator was sworn
- Marginal notes referring to previous or subsequent grants.

Before 1733, except during the Interregnum (1651–1660), all administrations were written in Latin. Fig. 10 shows an example of a Latin administration (PROB 6/96, f. 97) translated into English. As the records are formulaic legal documents, this can be used as a basis for translating other Latin administrations.

You can find examples of original letters of administration at the National Archives in the records of the courts of Exchequer and Chancery, which are searchable using the Catalogue.

*Johannes Bayly**	*Tricesimo die Emanavit Commissio Elizabethae Bayly viduae Relictae Johannis Bayly nuper parochiae Sanctae Mariae Rotherhithe in Comitatu Surriae sed in Nave Regia Le Dreadnought defuncti habentis &c [dum vixit et mortis suae tempore bona jura sive credita in diversis diocesibus sive peculiaribus jurisdictionibus sufficientia ad fundandum jurisdictionem Curiae Praerogativae Cantuariensis] ad Administrandum bona jura et credita dicti defuncti De bene &c [et fideliter administrando eadem ad sancta Dei evangelia] juratae*	*ultimus [dies] Novembris* *ultimus [dies] Maij 1721*
John Bayly	On the thirtieth day a commission was issued to Elizabeth Bayly, widow relict of John Bayly formerly of the parish of St Mary Rotherhithe in the county of Surrey but in HMS Dreadnought deceased, having [while he lived and at the time of his death goods, rights or credits in different dioceses or peculiar jurisdictions sufficient to the foundation of the jurisdiction of the Prerogative Court of Canterbury], to administer the goods, rights and credits of the said deceased, having been sworn [on the holy gospels] to well [and faithfully administer the same].	last [day] of November last [day] of May 1721

* Letters omitted from the original text on account of abbreviations have been supplied underlined. Words omitted from the original—including those implied by &c (etc.)—have been supplied in square brackets.

The first date in the right-hand margin is the date by which the administrator was required to exhibit an inventory of the intestate's personal estate. The second date is the date by which the administrator was required to present an account of his or her administration of the estate.

Fig. 10 *The administration of John Bayly, granted May 1720.* PROB 6/96

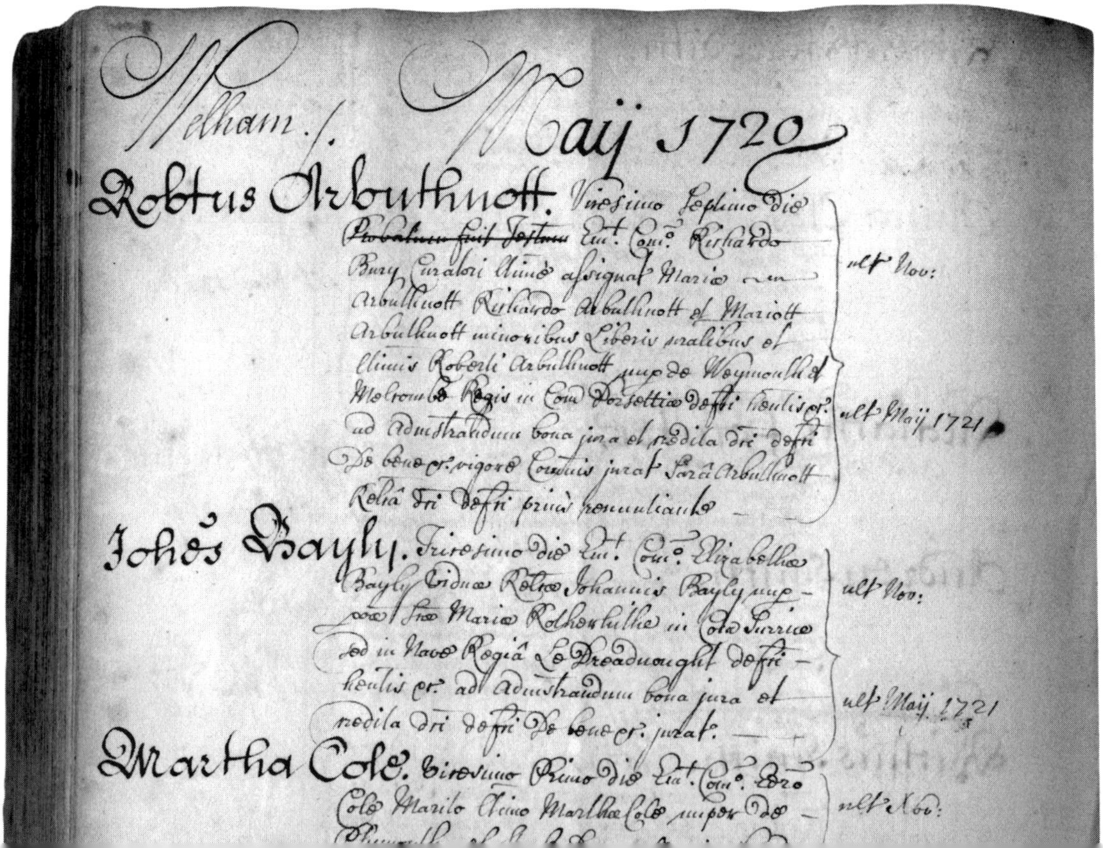

4.3 Finding an Administration

Administrations can be more difficult to find than wills as they provide less social and genealogical information; therefore indexing projects are less common. For many courts, a handwritten index arranged by the first letter of the intestate's surname may be the only means of locating the document. To identify the current location of an administration, use the table in section 3.2.1.

4.3.1 *Prerogative Court of Canterbury* (PROB 6 / *1559–1858*)

There is no single comprehensive index to PCC administrations and they are not included in DocumentsOnline. Instead, there is a combination of different personal-name indexes. To find an administration, you need to examine one of the many indexes, in different formats for different periods, listed below (some of which cover both administrations and wills):

1559–1660	Published indexes, in several date sequences
1661–2	Calendars in PROB 12, arranged annually
1663–4	Typescript indexes
1665–1700	Calendars in PROB 12
1701–49	Index compiled by Friends of The National Archives
1750–1852	Calendars in PROB 12 and a card index covering 1750–1800 available at the National Archives and the Society of Genealogists
1853–8	Two alphabetical calendars in PROB 12.

The indexes to administration acts supply:

The calendar year of grant
The month of grant
The place of residence of the deceased.

Early published indexes give a folio number (each folio has a recto and a verso, so the folio number relates to both sides of the page), which corresponds to a small handwritten number in the act book. Before 1719, if there is no folio number you will need to make a note of the month of the grant given in the index and search through the particular month in the act book. After 1719, administrations are arranged by seat (see below).

4.3.2 *PCC seat system* (*1719–1858*)

From 1719 to 1858, the PCC divided the business of granting probate and administration between five 'seats', each with its own distinct geographical area of responsibility. The seat sections usually appear in the following order: Registrar's seat, Surrey seat, Welsh seat, Middlesex seat, and London seat. Each seat is arranged in calendar order, and the entry should appear in alphabetical order by the initial letter of the intestate's surname. The administrative areas of the five seats were as follows:

Registrar's seat	Testators or intestates dying overseas or at sea, except in cases where the grant was made to the widow and she lived in an area within the jurisdiction of one of the other seats, in which case probate or administration was granted at that seat. Such entries are indicated by 'pts' (in partibus transmarinis—meaning died abroad) or ser or serv (in servitio regis—in the service of the Crown). Testators or intestates living outside the province of Canterbury. Estates that might be, or were, subject to litigation within the PCC. (If, however, a subsequent grant of probate or administration was made, it was issued at the seat that would have been responsible had there been no litigation.)
Surrey seat	Cornwall, Devon, Dorset, Hampshire, Somerset, Surrey, Sussex, Wiltshire.
Welsh seat	Berkshire, Derbyshire, Gloucestershire, Herefordshire, Leicestershire, Northamptonshire, Oxfordshire, Rutland, Shropshire, Staffordshire, Warwickshire, Worcestershire, Wales.
Middlesex seat	Bedfordshire, Buckinghamshire, Cambridgeshire, Essex, Hertfordshire, Huntingdonshire, Kent, Lincolnshire, Middlesex (except parishes listed below), Norfolk, Suffolk.
London seat	The city of London, including the following parishes and administrative areas (some of them in Middlesex or partly in Middlesex and partly in London): Charterhouse; Furnivall's Inn; Glasshouse Yard; Gray's Inn; Holy Trinity Minories; Liberty of the Rolls; Liberty of the Tower of London; Lincoln's Inn; Old Artillery Ground; Precinct of Norton Folgate; Precinct of St Katherine by the Tower; Precinct of the Savoy; St Andrew Holborn; St Anne Soho; St Botolph Aldersgate; St Botolph without Aldgate; St George Bloomsbury; St George the Martyr Holborn (Queen Square); St Giles Cripplegate; St Giles in the Fields; St James Clerkenwell; St James Westminster; St John Clerkenwell; St John the Evangelist Westminster; St John Wapping; St Leonard Shoreditch; St Luke Old Street; St Margaret Westminster; St Mary le Strand; St Mary Matfelon Whitechapel; St Sepulchre.

A number of PCC series are arranged in this way. It is also necessary when using the seat system to bear in mind the following anomalies:

If the place of residence is given as Middlesex and it is not possible to tell whether the deceased lived in an area subject to the Middlesex seat or the London seat, you may need to search both.

The city of Bristol was partly in Somerset (Surrey seat) and partly in Gloucestershire (Welsh seat). It may therefore be necessary to search both.

In some act books the term 'walk' is used, rather than seat.

4.3.3 *Other sources*

The initial application for a grant of administration (these are in PROB 14, 1657–1858) bears the administrator's signature and gives an approximate date of the intestate's death. If the court took over the distribution of the estate, details of this can be found in the Muniment Books in PROB 16 (1610–1858).

Administrators were required to enter into a bond to ensure the proper administration of the estate. See 4.5.

Estates of intestates may have been subject to death duties during the period from 1796–1858. See 7.1 for more information.

Administrators were required to produce an inventory and account of the distribution of the estate. See Chapter 6 for more information.

• PREROGATIVE COURT OF YORK (1502–1858) Administrations are included in the PCY probate act books. As mentioned in 3.7.3, from 1502 grants of probate and administration were entered into the act books of the various rural deanery courts. The earliest surviving act book of the Prerogative Court is dated 1587; before that date, prerogative business is in the act books of York City Deanery, held at the Borthwick Institute. There are gaps in the probate act books series during the sixteenth and seventeenth centuries.

4.4 Additional Information from Administrations

Records that reflect variations to the normal process of the granting of administrations include:

Grants of administration of goods not administered (*administratio de bonis non administratis*, often abbreviated to *admon dbn*). These occurred following the death or refusal or inability to act of the initial administrator, and are found in the administration act books in the normal way.

Grants where the administration was granted to a creditor.

Grants relating to minors (*administratio durante minore aetate*). Where an estate was administered in the name of a minor (under 21), the name of the minor is given.

Grants that were disputed. If an entry in the administration index is prefixed by the abbreviations *dec* (by decree), *int dec* (interlocutory decree) or *sent* (sentence), then the estate was the subject of litigation (see Chapter 8).

4.5 Administration Bonds

From 1529, administrators—including those responsible for administrations with will annexed (see 4.7)—were required to enter into a bond for a sum of money, with two or more guarantors, whereby they undertook to

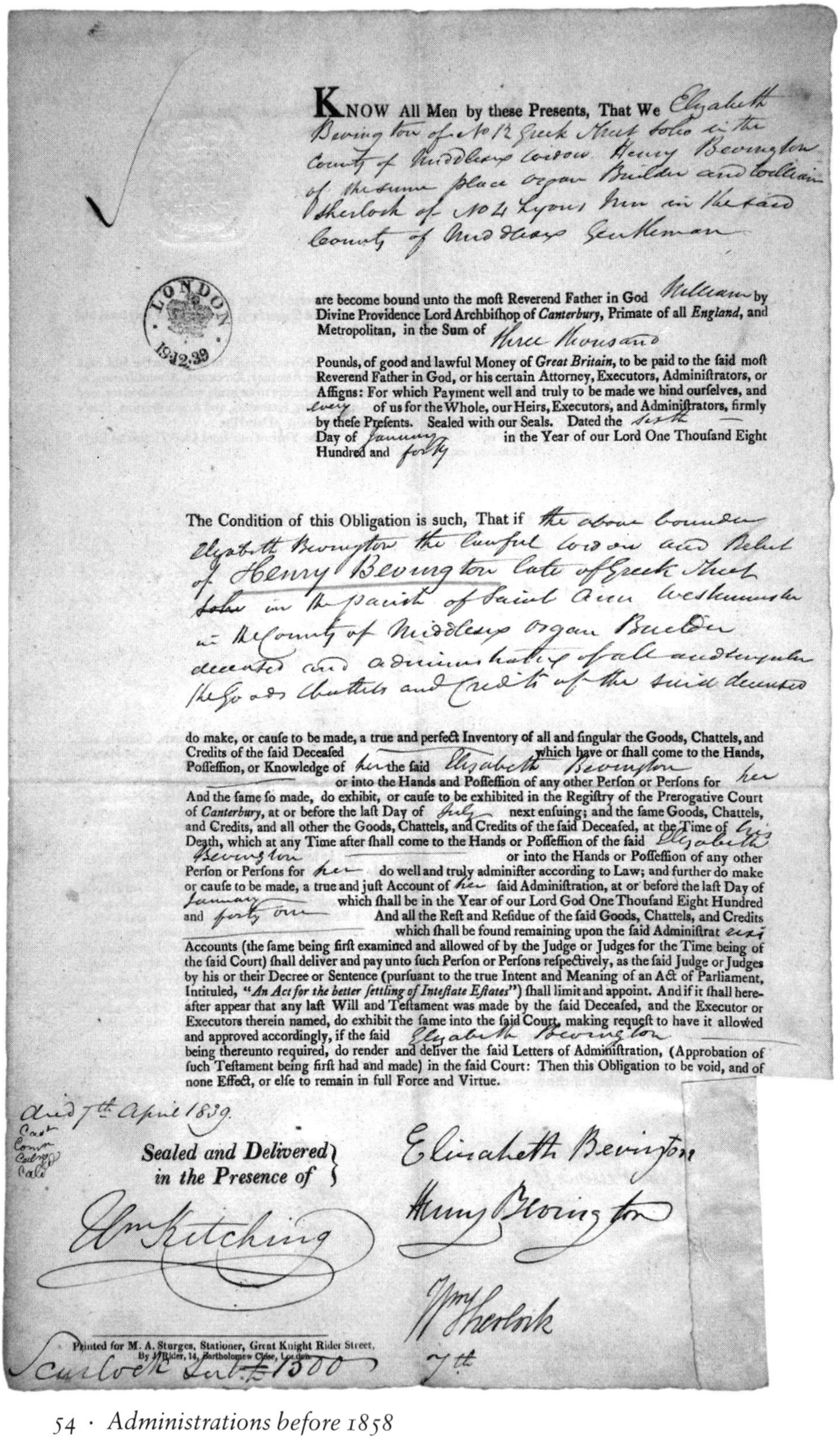
KNOW All Men by these Presents, That We Elizabeth Bevington of No 12 Greek Street Soho in the County of Middlesex widow Henry Bevington of the same place Organ Builder and William Sherlock of No 4 Lyons Inn in the said County of Middlesex Gentleman

LONDON 1932.39

are become bound unto the most Reverend Father in God William by Divine Providence Lord Archbishop of *Canterbury*, Primate of all *England*, and Metropolitan, in the Sum of Three thousand Pounds, of good and lawful Money of *Great Britain*, to be paid to the said most Reverend Father in God, or his certain Attorney, Executors, Administrators, or Assigns: For which Payment well and truly to be made we bind ourselves, and every of us for the Whole, our Heirs, Executors, and Administrators, firmly by these Presents. Sealed with our Seals. Dated the sixth Day of January in the Year of our Lord One Thousand Eight Hundred and forty

The Condition of this Obligation is such, That if the above bounden Elizabeth Bevington the lawful widow and Relict of Henry Bevington late of Greek Street Soho in the parish of Saint Ann Westminster in the County of Middlesex Organ Builder deceased and administratrix of all and singular the Goods Chattels and Credits of the said deceased do make, or cause to be made, a true and perfect Inventory of all and singular the Goods, Chattels, and Credits of the said Deceased which have or shall come to the Hands, Possession, or Knowledge of her the said Elizabeth Bevington or into the Hands and Possession of any other Person or Persons for her And the same so made, do exhibit, or cause to be exhibited in the Registry of the Prerogative Court of *Canterbury*, at or before the last Day of July next ensuing; and the same Goods, Chattels, and Credits, and all other the Goods, Chattels, and Credits of the said Deceased, at the Time of his Death, which at any Time after shall come to the Hands or Possession of the said Elizabeth Bevington or into the Hands or Possession of any other Person or Persons for her do well and truly administer according to Law; and further do make or cause to be made, a true and just Account of her said Administration, at or before the last Day of January which shall be in the Year of our Lord God One Thousand Eight Hundred and forty one And all the Rest and Residue of the said Goods, Chattels, and Credits which shall be found remaining upon the said Administratrix Accounts (the same being first examined and allowed of by the Judge or Judges for the Time being of the said Court) shall deliver and pay unto such Person or Persons respectively, as the said Judge or Judges by his or their Decree or Sentence (pursuant to the true Intent and Meaning of an Act of Parliament, Intituled, "*An Act for the better settling of Intestate Estates*") shall limit and appoint. And if it shall hereafter appear that any last Will and Testament was made by the said Deceased, and the Executor or Executors therein named, do exhibit the same into the said Court, making request to have it allowed and approved accordingly, if the said Elizabeth Bevington being thereunto required, do render and deliver the said Letters of Administration, (Approbation of such Testament being first had and made) in the said Court: Then this Obligation to be void, and of none Effect, or else to remain in full Force and Virtue.

Died 7th April 1839.

Sealed and Delivered in the Presence of

Wm Kitching

Elizabeth Bevington

Henry Bevington

Wm Sherlock

7th

Printed for M. A. Sturges, Stationer, Great Knight Rider Street, By J. Rider, 14, Bartholomew Close, London.

Sherlock Sub £1500

Fig. 11 *Administration Bond for Henry Bevington (January 1840). The personal estate is recorded as £3,000—twice its value.*
PROB 46/893

perform faithfully the tasks assigned to them by the probate court. This was to ensure that the estate was administered properly. The appropriate ecclesiastical court would keep a copy of the bond, and another copy was given to the administrator.

Administration bonds usually include the following:

The place of residence of the administrator
The places of residence of his or her guarantors
The signature (or mark) of the administrator
The signatures (or marks) of the guarantors.

The value of the bond is often double the valuation of the personal estate and may be annotated (formally noted) in the administration act books. Sometimes the value of the bond was less than double, though it was usually greater than the value of the personal estate. A second bond was sometimes entered into if the original valuation was inaccurate.

Although administration bonds provide a rough estimate of the value of an individual's estate, a more accurate indicator would be either the death duty or the inventory and account. Bonds can supply additional information about an estate, but their genealogical value is normally limited to providing details about the administrator rather than the intestate.

Before 1601 Prerogative Court of Canterbury bonds are in PROB 51 which is searchable by name on the Catalogue. The earliest bonds in this series predate the earliest surviving administration act book (PROB 6), which begins from December 1559. PCC bonds from 1601 to 1713 are in PROB 54, though a catalogue for these records is not available. The bonds from 1714 to 1858 are in PROB 46, arranged by the month of the grant and by seat (see 4.3.2). PROB 46 is stored off-site, so allow three working days for the document to arrive.

Generally, bonds for the Prerogative Court of York (and other ecclesiastical courts) are found together with the administration itself.

4.6 Special or Limited Administrations

Sometimes the court limited the grant of administration to a particular part of the deceased's estate or to a specified period of time. Instances include administrations granted during the absence (usually abroad) of the obvious administrator and those limited to the payment of seamen's wages.

From 1810 to 1858, limited administrations granted by the Prerogative Court of Canterbury are in PROB 7, arranged by seat (see 4.3.2). Before that date, they are in PROB 6, preceding the relevant monthly section. Cross-references in PROB 6 to entries in PROB 7 are identifiable by the term '*entered at length*' in the administration act book.

Limited administrations granted by the Prerogative Court of York and minor church courts are with the main administration.

4.7 Administrations Granted as Part of Probate

In certain cases, an administrator was appointed (instead of an executor) to administer a testator's estate. The two main examples of these are *letters of administration with will annexed* and *administration with will annexed of goods not administered*. Although the same procedure was followed as for the administration of an intestate's estate, the record of the grant is copied into the probate act book and not the administration act book.

Such PCC grants are annotated (formally noted) in the name indexes to wills. Prior to 1781, letters of administration with will annexed and letters of administration of goods not administered issued by the PCC were recorded in the ordinary Probate Act Books (PROB 8) 1526–1858. From 1781, such grants are in PROB 9 (1781, 1800, 1802–1858). Administrators of such estates were required to enter into bonds for the proper administration of the estate (see 4.5). PROB 8 and PROB 9 are arranged by seat (see 4.3.2).

4.7.1 *Administration with will annexed*

These grants relate to valid wills where probate was not granted because the executor refused to act or was unable to do so. In such situations, an administrator is appointed by the court, usually the next of kin (under the same laws as intestacy), but the distribution of the estate follows the terms of the will and not the various intestacy laws. The Latin name for this is *administratio cum testamento annexo*, often abbreviated to *AW*.

Situations of this kind would occur when:

The nominated executor failed to respond to the summons asking him to prove the will
The nominated executor renounced the right to administer
The nominated executor died before the testator
The testator failed to nominate an executor in the will.

Before 1733, except during the Interregnum (1651–1660), all grants of administration with will annexed were written in Latin. Fig. 12 shows an example of a Latin administration (PROB 8/113, f. 97), translated into English.* As the records are formulaic legal documents, this can be used as a basis for translating other such documents.

* Letters omitted from the original text on account of abbreviations have been supplied underlined. Words omitted from the original—including those implied by &c (etc.)—have been supplied in square brackets.

The first date in the right-hand margin is the date by which the administrator was required to exhibit an inventory of the intestate's personal estate. The second date is the date by which the administrator was required to present an account of his or her administration of the estate.

Rogerus Pocock	*Decimo Septimo die Emanavit Commissio Gulielmo Sussex Legatario Principali nominato in Testamento Rogeri Pocock nuper de Felfam in Comitatu Sussexiae Clerici defuncti habentis &c [dum vixit et mortis suae tempore bona jura sive credita in diversis dioceses-ibus sive peculiaribus jurisdictionibus sufficientia ad fundandum jurisdictionem Curiae Praerogativae Cantuariensis] ad administrandum bona jura et credita dicti defuncti juxta tenorum et effectum Testamenti ipsius defuncti (Eo quod Rebecca Collier executrix et Legataria residuria in dicto Testamento nominata oneri Execucionis ejusdem expresse renuntiaverit) De bene &c [et fideliter administrando eadem ad sancta Dei evangelia] jurato*	*ultimus [dies] Novembris* *ultimus [dies] Maij 1721*
Roger Pocock	On the seventeenth day a commission was issued to William Sussex, principal legatee named in the will of Roger Pocock formerly of Felpham in the county of Sussex, clerk, deceased, having [while he lived and at the time of his death goods, rights or credits in different dioceses or peculiar jurisdictions sufficient to the foundation of the jurisdiction of the Prerogative Court of Canterbury], to administer the goods rights and credits of the said deceased according to the wording and effect of the said will of the deceased (since Rebecca Collier executrix and residuary legatee named in the said will shall have expressly renounced the burden of the execution of the same), having been sworn [on the holy gospels] to well [and faithfully administer the same].	Last [day] of November Last [day] of May 1721

Fig. 12 *An entry in the Probate Act book for Roger Pocock, dated 1720.* PROB 8/113

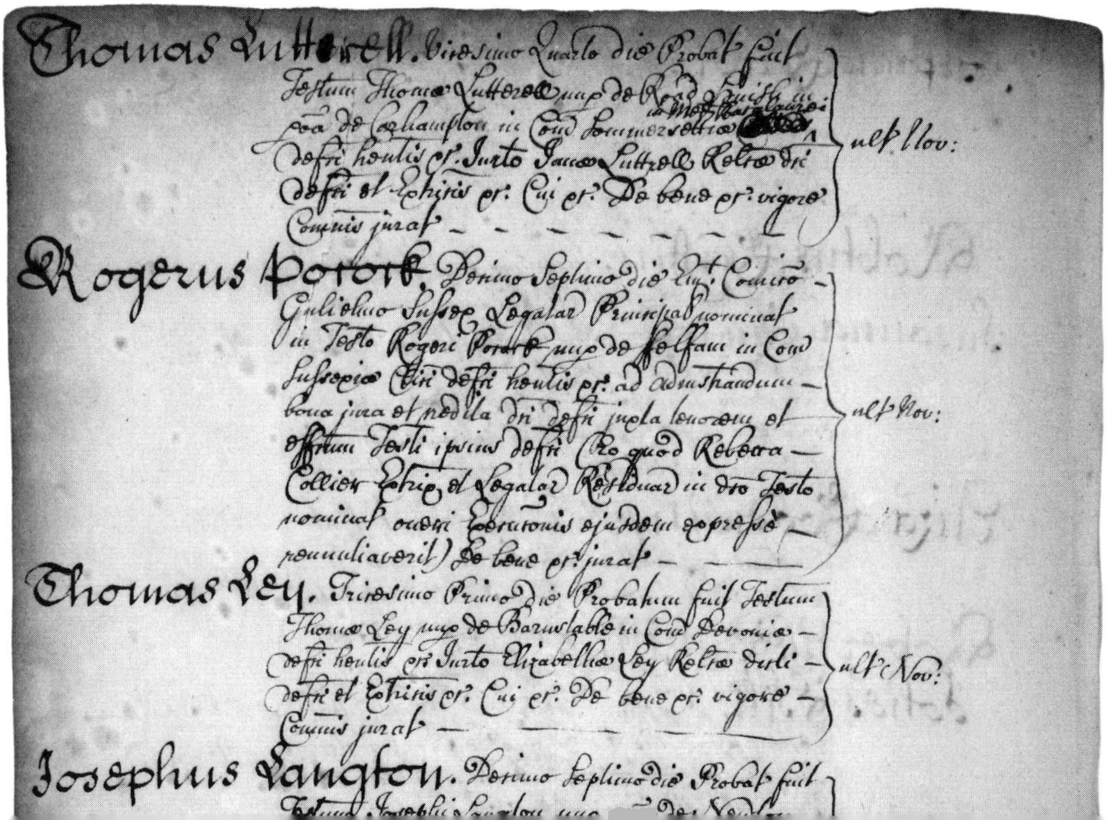

4.7.2 *Administration with will annexed of goods not administered*

A second or further grant of administration—called *administratio de bonis non administratis* (often abbreviated to *admon dbn*)—was issued when the administration of the estate was incomplete.

Grants of this kind were made when:

The executor died or renounced his or her executorship before the administration of the estate was complete
The previous executor had died
The grant had been revoked by the court
The grant was issued during the minority of the next of kin, which had since expired
The residuary legatee or next of kin was inaccessible because abroad and the executor was dead.

If a former grant was made, it was recorded—usually annotated with the year and month of the previous grant, which will help to identify other references to the same estate. Some estates were subject to a large number of grants, sometimes years after the first grant.

5 INTERPRETING WILLS

5.1 Drafting a Will

During the medieval period, wills progressed from oral statements of intent to written documents. However, because the ability to read and write was relatively uncommon, very few people wrote their own wills. Traditionally such clerical work was the province of the parish priest, but over time it became common practice for scribes, lawyers, doctors and other professionals to undertake the task.

It was the responsibility of the scribe to translate the wishes and requirements of the testator into a legible, formal legal document. Sometimes numerous revisions were made before a satisfactory version was produced. Often, after completing the will, the scribe was called back in order to add codicils—especially since child mortality rates were high—and frequently alterations or substitutions were made.

A good scribe was expensive, but it was essential to find someone reliable and competent. Mistakes in the drafting of a will could prove very costly in terms of litigation and disputes after the testator's death. Also, it was important that the person employed to write the will was trustworthy, especially if some of the bequests—or omissions—were controversial.

Books of pro forma wills were available for consultation, and were used as a basis for drafting a straightforward will. Wills were written on any material, although paper or parchment are normal. They were written in any hand (for example, Secretary, Roman or Court hand) or language.

5.2 How were Wills Recorded?

- In the testator's own hand Also known as holographic. Historically, because literacy was rare, wills of this kind were unusual. In order for a will in the testator's own hand to be valid, it was signed by at least two credible witnesses.
- Scribe This was the normal method of drafting a will.
- Oral will Also known as a nuncupative will or a spoken will. This

usually occurred when the testator had left the drafting of a will to the last minute and was on his deathbed. It was necessary for at least two witnesses to be present when the words were spoken, and for them to be aware that the testator was making his will. The words were written down and signed as soon as possible, normally following the death of the testator.

In order to prevent fraud and give sufficient time for any other wills to be declared, probate would not be granted for this type of will until at least 14 days after the death of the testator. The ecclesiastical courts specified no precise form that nuncupative wills should take, but required that the meaning of the bequests be clear and free from ambiguity or obscurity. In 1676, the Act for Prevention of Fraud and Perjuries stipulated that if the estate totalled more than £30 a nuncupative will would no longer be acceptable unless at least three witnesses were present. Nuncupative wills

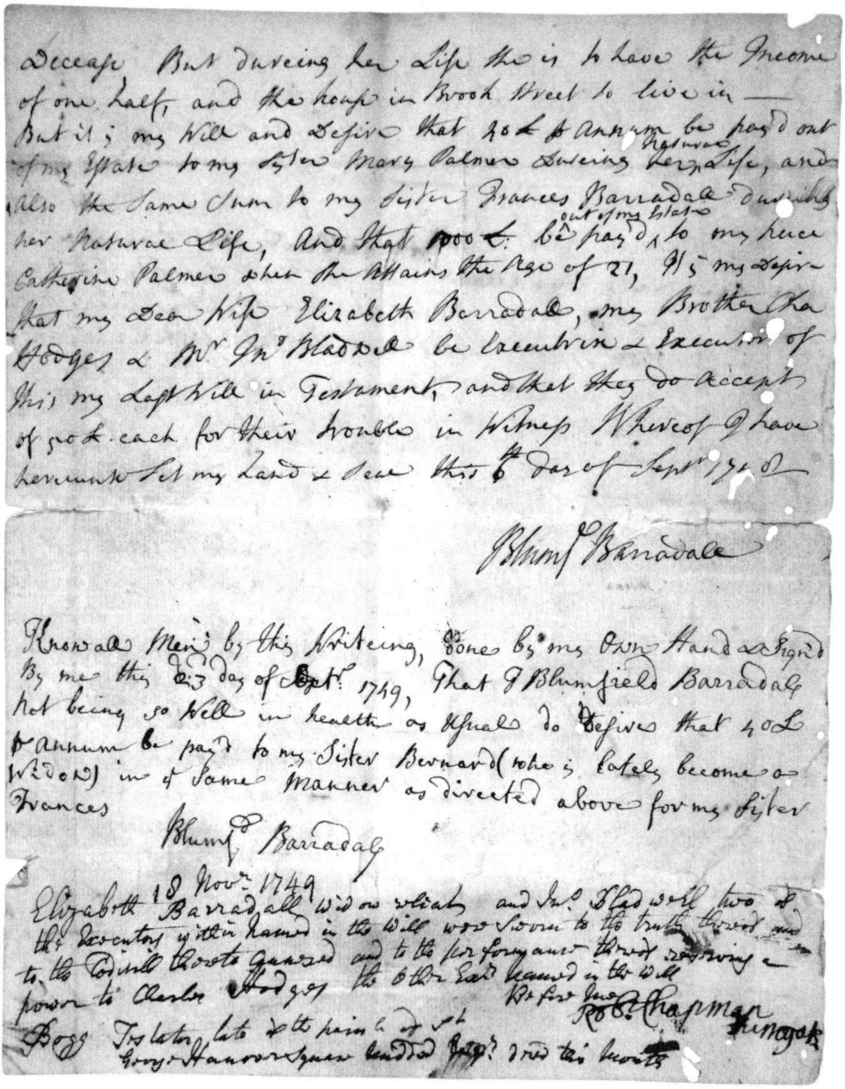

Deceace But dureing her Life she is to have the Income
of one half, and the house in Brook Street to live in —
But it is my Will and Desire that 40£ p Annum be pay'd out
of my Estate to my Sister Mary Palmer dureing her natural Life, and
Also the Same Sum to my Sister Frances Barradall dureing
her Natural Life, And that 1000£ be pay'd out of my Estate to my Neice
Catherine Palmer when she Attains the Age of 21, It is my Desire
that my Dear Wife Elizabeth Barradall, my Brother Cha
Hodges & Mr Jno Bladwell be Executrix & Executors of
this my Last Will in Testament, and that they do accept
of 50£ each for their trouble in Witness Whereof I have
hereunto Set my Hand & Seal this 6th day of Septr 1748

Blumfd Barradall

Know all Men by this Writeing, done by my Own Hand & Sign'd
By me this 23 day of Septr 1749, That I Blumfield Barradall
not being so Well in health as Usual do Desires that 40£
p annum be pay'd to my Sister Bernard (who is lately become a
Widow) in ye Same Manner as directed above for my Sister
Frances

Blumfd Barradall

18 Novr 1749
Elizabeth Barradall Widow relict and Jno Bladwell two of
the Executors within named in the Will were sworn to the truth thereof and
to the Codicill thereto annexed and to the performance thereof reserving
power to Charles Hodges the other Exor named in the Will
Before me
Robt Chapman
[illegible]

Fig. 13 *The holograph will of Blumfield Barradall featuring a sadly prescient codicil, added in September 1749.*
PROB 10/2067

are easily identifiable, as they usually begin with the word 'Memorandum'.

Following the Wills Act of 1837, nuncupative wills were declared invalid unless made by soldiers or sailors on active service.

The National Archives has a series of nuncupative wills (PROB 20), ranging from 1623 to 1838, where the Prerogative Court of Canterbury was asked to rule on authenticity.

5.3 Likely Contents of a Will

The will would include some or all of the following:

5.3.1 *The name, place of residence and occupation of the testator*

People from all strata of society, from the highest (the titled gentry) to the lowest, even paupers, could leave wills. They were more common among wealthy people because they were more likely to have complicated estates and financial matters that needed putting in order prior to death. Also, they were more likely to be able to afford the often complained-about fees of the ecclesiastical courts. Having less to dispose of, the poor had less need to make a will.

If you think your ancestor's occupation was too lowly for him or her to have left a will, you may be encouraged by the range of testators whose wills were proved by the lower courts. In the eighteenth century, the archdeaconry court in Berkshire proved wills of brewers, bricklayers, broadweavers, collar makers, cordwainers, drapers, gardeners, grocers, harness makers, labourers, servants, tanners and waggoners.

Other occupations mentioned in old wills include baker and gingerbread baker, barrister, innkeeper, surgeon, merchant and tailor. Often men are simply described as gentleman, and women as widow or spinster.

5.3.2 *A statement of health*

Early wills often include a statement that the testator is of 'sound mind' but 'sick in body'. This reference to soundness of mind was to satisfy the legal requirement that testators were in control of their senses and free from coercion. As the majority of old wills carry some kind of declaration of poor health, it can be assumed that testators tended to leave the making of a will until they were close to death or dangerously ill. However, some people made wills much earlier in life—often following marriage or the birth of children, during an illness, before embarking on a long or hazardous journey or following an inheritance.

5.3.3 *A statement of Christian faith (more likely in early wills)*

There has been much debate and research regarding the religious preamble with which early wills begin. In medieval times religion formed a central part of people's lives, and it is not known to what extent these religious statements were a matter of personal belief or simply a formulaic insertion by the scribe. However, given that the scribe was supposed to read the will back to the testator before it was signed, it is likely that the religious statement would have broadly reflected the views of the testator, even if the words were not his or her own.

One aspect of a will that may provide evidence of a moral or religious outlook is the number and type of charitable bequests. Following the Reformation, preambles were often phrased to reflect a Protestant bias (Catholics were more likely to mention saints and the Virgin Mary). It is therefore sometimes possible to determine the denomination of a testator from the wording of the introduction.

5.3.4 *A statement of mental capability*

Those proved not to be in full possession of their senses at the time the will was written risked their will being declared void by the ecclesiastical courts. Within this category were the dumb or deaf (the court would grant probate only if it could be proved they had understanding and a desire to leave a will), drunks, lunatics and idiots. The blind could make nuncupative wills provided they followed the normal legal requirements.

5.3.5 *Details of bequests—personal estate*

The terms *bequest* or *legacy* are used to describe the personal estate left by a testator. A beneficiary or legatee is someone who inherits. Items such as jewellery, plate, furniture and clothes, etc., are the most frequent types of bequest. Farm stock (sheep, cows, oxen, pigs, etc.) often feature as bequests in less wealthy early estates. Individual items may be mentioned, although this is more common in female wills. Many bequests were in the form of cash, and are therefore quite a good gauge of the value of the testator's personal estate.

Personal estate included leasehold houses and land, where the lease ran for a finite period. It also included personal possessions such as furniture and other household effects, and any farm animals or equipment. It might also encompass debts due to or by the testator. Executors (or, if there was no will, administrators) were appointed by the probate court before debts could be collected by lawsuit.

It is primarily this type of property that wills are dealing with—though there was a great incentive to minimize the amount of personal estate bequeathed by will, since duty on its value had to be paid to the church.

A bequest may be bequeathed 'absolutely' (in its entirety, without conditions) or 'conditionally' (provided that certain conditions are adhered to or fulfilled). As mentioned earlier, a will is a statement of intent rather than an accurate indicator of the testator's wealth. So, when a testator lists a large series of bequests, it should not necessarily be assumed that at his death he had sufficient funds to pay them or that they were in fact paid. A more accurate indication of wealth can be obtained from the inventory and accounts (if they survive), or from the death duty registers for estates between 1796 and 1903.

5.3.6 *Details of real estate*

Real estate is land-based property, as opposed to personal estate (goods and chattels). It is *devised* by will and not bequeathed. Real estate encompassed both the land and the buildings on it, together with the associated land rights. It might be held by freehold—which gave the holder the right to sell the property—or by *copyhold*, a type of tenancy whereby the land returned at intervals to the disposal of the lord of the manor.

Older wills are unlikely to mention real estate. However, the absence of any reference to it does not mean the land was not passed on. Real estate largely fell beyond the terms of the will. It had its own regulation through the manorial courts and common law courts. The heir-at-law (usually the eldest son) would inherit the land automatically. Only in 1540 (under the Statute of Wills) was the disposal of some types of real estate by will approved by statute. From 1837, all kinds of real estate could be disposed of by will.

For a long time there were severe restrictions on the willing of land, as land transfer was governed by strict rules—initially to protect the Crown's rights to feudal and other dues. Before 1540, *freehold land* could not be left by will. Instead, it descended by the laws of inheritance, usually to the eldest son. A man wishing to vary the strict rules of land inheritance (to provide for younger sons, for example) had to set up a kind of trust called a *use* that transferred ownership of the land to trustees who would hold the land for the purposes specified in his will. Henry VIII tried to block this, but eventually, in 1540, he had to give way and allow at least some land to be

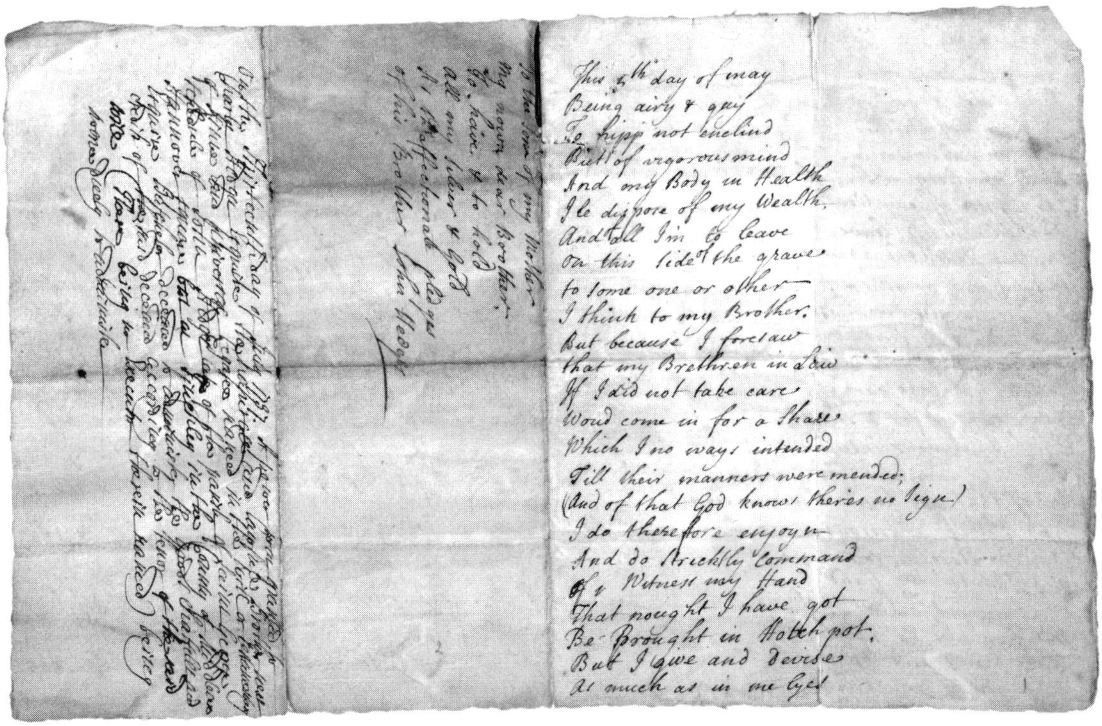
This 5th day of may
Being airy & gay
To hypp not enclin'd
But of vigorous mind
And my Body in Health
I'le dispose of my Wealth.
And all I'm to leave
On this side the grave
to some one or other
I think to my Brother.
But because I foresaw
that my Brethren in Law
If I did not take care
Wou'd come in for a Share
Which I no ways intended
Till their manners were mended;
(And of that God knows there's no sign)
I do therefore enjoyn
And do strictly Command
Of Witness my Hand
That nought I have got
Be brought in Hotchpot,
But I give and devise
As much as in me lyes

Fig. 14 *The will of John Hedges was written in verse in 1737.*
PROB 10/1850

devisable by will, under the Statute of Wills of that year.

A testator could set up a trust or trusts to settle property the way he or she wished. The trustees would be bound by the wishes of the original holder of the property, often (but not always) expressed in his or her will. Such trusts were often used to protect the interests of dependants; but they were flexible and could be used to protect property, too.

Leases of land did not count as real estate but as personalty and so could be bequeathed by will. Land held by copyhold tenure (manorial land held by copy of court roll) was not transferable by will until 1926.

See *An Introduction to English Legal History* by J. H. Baker (OUP, 4th edn 2002) for more information.

5.3.7 *Provision for the widow*

Older wills often mention widows' 'thirds'. This refers to a widow's entitlement, for life or until remarriage, to one third of her husband's property settled on her as dower at the time of their marriage. Sometimes the widow had already been provided for at the time the will was written, and so it may not state the details. Often a husband's bequests to his widow were on condition that she did not remarry. This was because before the Married Women's Property Act of 1882 a woman's goods and property were forfeit to her husband on marriage.

You should not assume that the widow is necessarily the mother of all of the deceased's children. It was not uncommon for a man to remarry following the death of his wife.

5.3.8 *Provision for the children*

Usually the greater part of the estate went to the eldest son (or heir-at-law, see 5.3.6). However, this may not be stipulated in the will, such provision being already recorded on deeds. Married daughters may have already received their marriage portion and therefore be omitted from the will. Particular attention should be paid to phrases like 'when he reaches the age of...'—although they do not give the person's age, they are helpful as they confirm that he or she was under a certain age at the time that the will was written. Some testators used their will as an opportunity to exact revenge on their offspring. Philip Thickness, whose will was proved in 1793, requested that 'my right hand be cut off after my death to my son Lord Audley and I desire it may be sent to him in hopes that such a sight may remind him of his duty to God after having so long abandoned the Duty he owed to a father who once affectionately loved him' (PROB 11/1228).

For more about guardianship of children, see 8.13.

5.3.9 *Instructions for burial*

A testator would often state where he or she wanted to be buried. This information is particularly rewarding as records of burials can be difficult to trace. Registers are held in many different locations and there is no comprehensive index to them. Some testators had strange burial requests, for

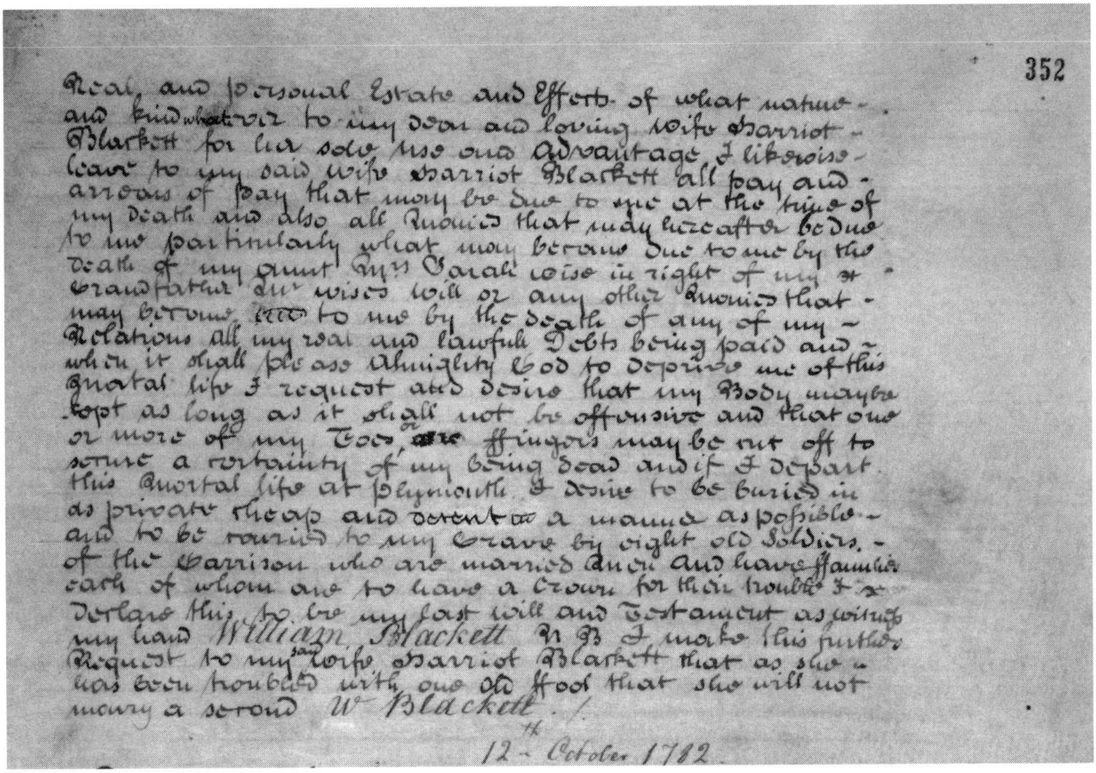
352
Real and personal Estate and Effects of what nature
and kind whatsoever to my dear and loving wife Harriot
Blackett for her sole use and Advantage, I likewise
leave to my said wife Harriot Blackett all pay and
arrears of pay that may be due to me at the time of
my death and also all Monies that may hereafter be due
to me particularly what may become due to me by the
death of my Aunt Mrs Sarah wise in right of my
Grandfather Sir wises will or any other Monies that
may become due to me by the death of any of my
Relations all my real and lawful Debts being paid and
when it shall please Almighty God to deprive me of this
mortal life I request and desire that my Body may be
kept as long as it shall not be offensive and that one
or more of my Toes or ffingers may be cut off to
secure a certainty of my being dead and if I depart
this mortal life at Plymouth I desire to be buried in
as private cheap and decent a manner as possible
and to be carried to my Grave by eight old Soldiers
of the Garrison who are married men and have ffamilies
each of whom are to have a Crown for their trouble &
declare this to be my last will and Testament as witness
my hand William Blackett N B I make this further
Request to my said wife Harriot Blackett that as she
has been troubled with one old ffool that she will not
marry a second W Blackett. /
12th October 1782.

Fig. 15 *The will of William Blackett, proved in 1782, which includes a startling bequest.*
PROB 11/1095

example the the will of William Blackett proved in 1782. He requested that 'my body may be kept as long as it shall not be offensive and that one or more of my toes or fingers may be cut off to secure a certainty of my being dead and if I depart this mortal life at Plymouth I desire to be buried in as private cheap and decent a manner as possible' (PROB 11/1095).

5.3.10 *The testator's signature*

The will was signed at the end by the testator or by some person in the testator's presence or under his or her direction. The testator, in the presence of witnesses, would acknowledge the signature, and they would sign the will in his or her presence. Sometimes a will was signed at the bottom of every page, or at the foot of the final page with the loose pages sewn together at the top or along the side. Modern wills are often drawn up by a solicitor or on printed forms with the blanks filled in.

5.3.11 *Names of witnesses*

The role of a witness is to authenticate the document and to prevent concealment of the will or fraudulent substitution by a third party. Historically, two witnesses were generally considered sufficient. Following the Act for the Prevention of Frauds and Perjuries in 1676, three to four credible witnesses were required for nuncupative wills. However, if there was no question that the will was either written or dictated by the testator, witnesses were not always necessary, although the court would probably take affidavits from relatives or acquaintances familiar with the testator's handwriting as a precaution. Witnesses could be either male or female. The following were not allowed to act as witnesses: criminals and perjurers, children, idiots and lunatics and those who might be biased.

Before 1858, it was considered acceptable for a witness to act even if he or she benefited from the will, although there had to be another witness to corroborate that bequest. After 1858, witnesses were not allowed to benefit from the estate.

In order to validate a holographic will, at least two credible witnesses were needed.

5.3.12 *Appointment of executor(s)*

An executor could be anyone except those barred from will-making. He or she was seen as someone who would act as the testator would and who would carry out his or her wishes as stipulated. There was therefore effectively a moral agreement between the executor and the testator to see the distribution of the estate and the payment of the debts through to its conclusion, although this was not enforceable in law.

The testator was allowed to revoke his will at any time during his life, thus removing the executor from his or her obligation. Similarly, the executor was free to renounce his right to administer the estate.

An executor could be appointed either simply (without any requisites) or conditionally (e.g. for a certain period of time or to administer a certain part of the testator's estate). There was no limit to the number of executors that could be named in a will, and particular executors could be charged with dealing with particular aspects of the estate.

A testator who failed to name an executor ran the risk of being treated as having died intestate. The administration of the estate would then fall to the next of kin as prescribed in the various intestacy laws. If the executor died before the administration of the estate was complete, an administrator for the goods left unadministered was appointed. This was known as an *administration with will annexed*.

5.3.13 *Date of will*

The dating of a will was crucial as it could be voided in its entirety if there was found to be a later one.

5.3.14 *Codicil*

Changes or revisions to a will could be made by adding a codicil (see Fig. 13). This was an attachment to the original will that avoided the need to submit a new document. There was no restriction on the number of codicils that could be made, and the addition of the codicil could be made either in writing or orally. The court granting probate was supposed to treat codicils as part of the original will.

5.3.15 *Probate clause*

Originally, the probate clause was attached to the will by seal following the grant of probate by the ecclesiastical court. Later, instead, the confirmation of probate was annotated (formally noted), usually on the last page of the will. Probate clauses are formulaic and merely confirm that probate was granted on a particular day. As a result, they provide little in the way of personal information about the testator and his or her family. Before 1733 —except during the Interregnum (1651–1660)—probate clauses were written in Latin, as shown in Fig. 16 and transcribed here:

Probatum fuit hujusmodi Testamentum apud London coram Venerabili viro Roberto Wood Legum Doctore Surrogato Venerabilis et Egregij viri Johannis Bettesworth Legum etiam Doctoris Curiae Praerogativae Cantuariensis Magistri Custodis sive Commissarij legitime constitui Vicesimo Secundo die Mensis Februarij Anno Domini Millesimo Septingentesimo Decimo nono Juramento Thomae Willisee Executoris unici in dicto Testamento nominati Cui commissa fuit Administratio omnium et Singulorum bonorum jurium et creditorum dicti defunci De bene et fideliter administrando eadem ad Sancta Dei Evangelia Jurato. Examinatur.

This will was proved at London before the worshipful Robert Wood LLD [Doctor of Laws], surrogate of the worshipful and wise John Bettesworth, also LLD, Master Keeper or Commissary of the Prerogative Court of Canterbury, lawfully constituted on the twenty-second day of the month of February 1719 by the oath of Thomas Willisee, named sole executor in the said will to whom administration of all and singular the goods rights and credits of the said deceased was granted being sworn on the holy gospels to administer the same well and faithfully. Examined.

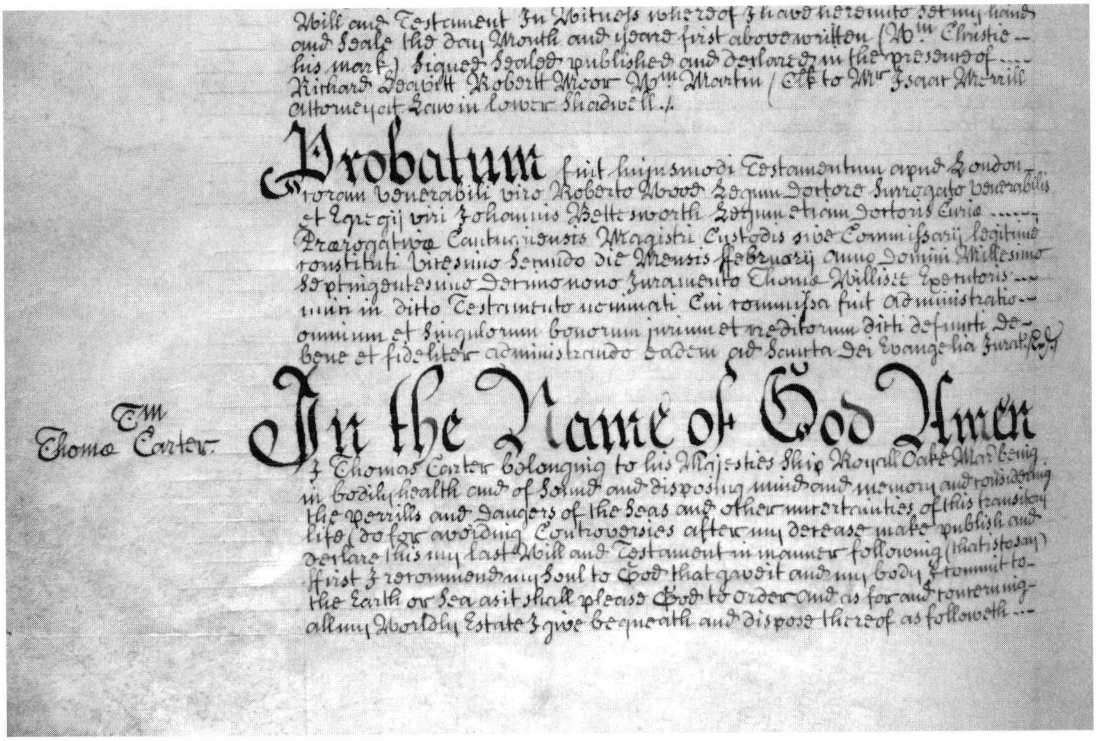
Will and Testament In Witness whereof I have hereunto set my hand and Seale the day Month and yeare first abovewritten (Wm Christie – his mark) Signed Sealed published and declared in the presence of ... Richard Leavitt Robert Moor Wm Martin / Clk to Mr Isaac Merrill Attorney at Law in Lower Shadwell.

Probatum fuit hujusmodi Testamentum apud London coram Venerabili viro Roberto Wood Legum Doctore Surrogato Venerabilis et Egregij viri Johannis Bettesworth Legum etiam Doctoris Curiae Praerogativae Cantuariensis Magistri Custodis sive Commissarij legitime constituti Vicesimo Secundo die Mensis Februarij Anno Domini Millesimo Septingentesimo Decimo nono Juramento Thomae Willisee Executoris unici in dicto Testamento nominati Cui commissa fuit administratio omnium et Singulorum bonorum jurium et creditorum dicti defuncti De bene et fideliter administrando eadem ad Sancta Dei Evangelia Jurat.

Tm Thomas Carter

In the Name of God Amen

I Thomas Carter belonging to his Majesties Ship Royall Oake being in bodily health and of Sound and disposing mind and memory and considering the perrills and dangers of the Seas and other uncertainties of this transitory life do for avoiding Controversies after my decease make publish and declare this my last Will and Testament in manner following (that is to say) First I recommend my Soul to God that gave it and my body I commit to the Earth or Sea as it shall please God to order And as for and concerning all my Worldly Estate I give bequeath and dispose thereof as followeth ---

Fig. 16 *A typical example of a Latin probate clause, from the will of William Christie dated 1719.* PROB 11/572

5.4 Validity

A will could be declared void, either fully or in part, if:

- The will was made by a testator who was legally exempt from making a will
- Bequests were jointly owned
- The form of the disposal was unlawful
- The executor was incapable of acting as such
- The will was made in fear (the testator had been coerced into making a will)
- The will was fraudulent
- There was an error regarding either the person, name or suitability of an executor or legatee, or an item bequeathed
- There was uncertainty regarding either an executor or a legatee, or an item or items bequeathed, or the date of the will
- The quality and legibility of the will were imperfect.

5.5 People Unable to Leave a Valid Will

The following categories of people were either unable to leave a valid will or only able to do so if certain conditions were fulfilled:

- Traitors (abolished under the Forfeiture Act of 1870—until then those convicted of treason forfeited all goods and property to the Crown, so any will left by a traitor would be declared void)
- Felons
- Usurers
- Libellers
- Suicides (abolished under the Forfeiture Act of 1870)
- Slaves (slaves and their goods considered to be the property of their master and so were their goods and therefore unable to make wills)
- Excommunicates (abolished in 1813—until then their wills were declared void)
- Heretics
- Apostates (those who did not believe in baptism).

5.5.1 *Married women*

Before 1882, a married woman could make a will only with her husband's consent (which he could revoke at any time—even after her death, but before probate). Widows and spinsters, however, could leave wills in their own right.

From 1882, the Married Women's Property Act allowed women to leave wills in their own right.

5.5.2 *Children*

Boys from the age of 14 and girls from the age of 12 could make wills. A girl's will would be declared void once she married, unless it was made with the consent of her husband. However, in 1540, the Statute of Wills forbade the devise of land by anyone under the age of 21, and in 1837 this was extended to all bequests. Under the Wills Act of 1837, the minimum age for leaving a will became 21.

5.6 Reading Wills

5.6.1 *Handwriting*

There are a number of steps you can take to make it easier to read and understand a will, or other document. For example:

- Try using a photocopier to enlarge the document. Sometimes enlarging even a small section can help. Be careful not to make the copy too large, as that may lead to distortion.
- Number the lines of the document, then take a fresh piece of lined paper (to serve as a worksheet for transcription) and number the lines to match those of the document. It is advisable to 'double-space' your worksheet, for clarity.

Remember the following if you get stuck:

- You can 'get your eye in' by starting with words you can read and leaving blanks in your worksheet to come back to later. Once you have become used to the handwriting you may find that you can decipher words that seemed incomprehensible at first.
- Reading a sentence aloud may help put a word that you could not otherwise read in context.

There is an excellent palaeography tutorial on the National Archives website (*www.nationalarchives.gov.uk/palaeography*). It explains how to read old documents and uses an old will as a practical example. Also on DocumentsOnline (*www.nationalarchives.gov.uk/documentsonline/wills-sample.asp*) there are examples of wills from different dates which demonstrate the differences in style and handwriting. There are numerous books on palaeography available from reference libraries and bookshops. See further reading on p.155 for some suggestions.

If you find a document impossible to read, you could ask an expert researcher for help. Details of such researchers are on the National Archives website, at *www.nationalarchives.gov.uk/irlist/*.

5.6.2 *Interpreting wills*

The terminology of wills can be misleading. *Father*, *brother* and *son*, *mother*, *sister* and *daughter* may be used to refer to in-laws as well as blood relatives. The term *cousin* was often used, indiscriminately, for all types of kin. Omissions of family members may indicate that they were out of favour or dead. Or, as already mentioned, a previous settlement may have been made.

Wills can also provide a certain amount of 'hidden' information.

- It may be possible to deduce whether a daughter was married (for example, if she is referred to by a different surname). This may narrow the range of a marriage register search to before the date the will was written.
- Make notes regarding legatees who are not directly connected to the family. If the wills of these individuals have survived, they may provide a cross-reference back to the original family.
- References may be made to individuals who were unmarried when the will was made but who later married. Information of this kind can narrow down searches in the marriage registers.
- Indirect reference may be made to people who died before the will was written (for example, 'To the children of my deceased sister...'). Such references provide an indication of the latest possible date of death.

5.6.3 *Spelling*

Deciphering wills is made more difficult by the number of abbreviations and other devices employed by scribes in order to speed up the process of writing, thus saving time and money. Some of the standard abbreviations are described below.

- A small letter positioned above the line (superscript) indicates an abbreviation. For example, yr (your), wt (with) and wtout (without).
- Often, the letter 'x' (Greek *chi*) stands for Christ—particularly at the beginning of the will in phrases such as 'xian burial'.
- The scribe may miss out a letter and place the mark '~' over the top. The letters 'm' or 'n' are often omitted.
- If the letter 'p' has a curly tail or the downstroke is crossed, it is serving as an abbreviation for per, par, pro, pri or pre. Thus 'pish' with a curly or crossed 'p' stands for parish.
- 'u' and 'v' are often used interchangeably—as in 'vnto'.
- 'i' and 'j' are often used interchangeably, especially in inventories and accounts—for example, iiij is commonly used for 4.
- Scribes often used 'is', 'ys' or just 's' in place of 'es' at the end of a word.
- Often the letter 'y' was substituted for 'i'—for example, 'contaynyng', 'syke' and 'payed'—to make the handwriting easier to read.

6 INVENTORIES AND ACCOUNTS

6.1 What are Inventories?

Inventories are detailed lists of articles such as goods and chattels found in the possession of a person at the time of their decease. Parcels of land are also sometimes included. The production of an inventory as part of the process of probate and administration was required in ecclesiastical law from 1342—following a canon by John Stratford, Archbishop of Canterbury—although there is documentary evidence of inventories in existence before then. The bulk of surviving inventories, for estates of both testators and intestates, date from after 1529, when this requirement was laid down in statute.

The reason for the production of an inventory as part of the probate and administration process was to identify the value of the deceased's personal estate and make it public, and to facilitate payment of the deceased's outstanding debts. Once the court had accepted that a legitimate inventory was produced and the deceased's debts paid off, the executor was required to distribute the balance of the estate to the next of kin. This measure was adopted to prevent dishonesty by the executor or administrator.

6.1.1 *Procedure and appraisal*

The inventory was usually compiled within a few days of the death of the testator or intestate, generally by someone with an interest in the estate such as the next of kin or a legatee or creditor. It was supposed to list all personal estate or moveable assets—but not real estate, as this was outside the jurisdiction of the ecclesiastical courts. Personal estate included furnishings and other household items, clothing, leasehold property, livestock and crops.

The law stipulated that the appraisal of the deceased's goods was to take place openly and in the presence of witnesses. The goods included in the inventory were to be valued and priced by someone 'honest and skilful to their correct value', or to what they would fetch at auction at the time. Often the executor or administrator (usually the widow) would call in a neighbour to undertake the valuation; or if there were specialist items such

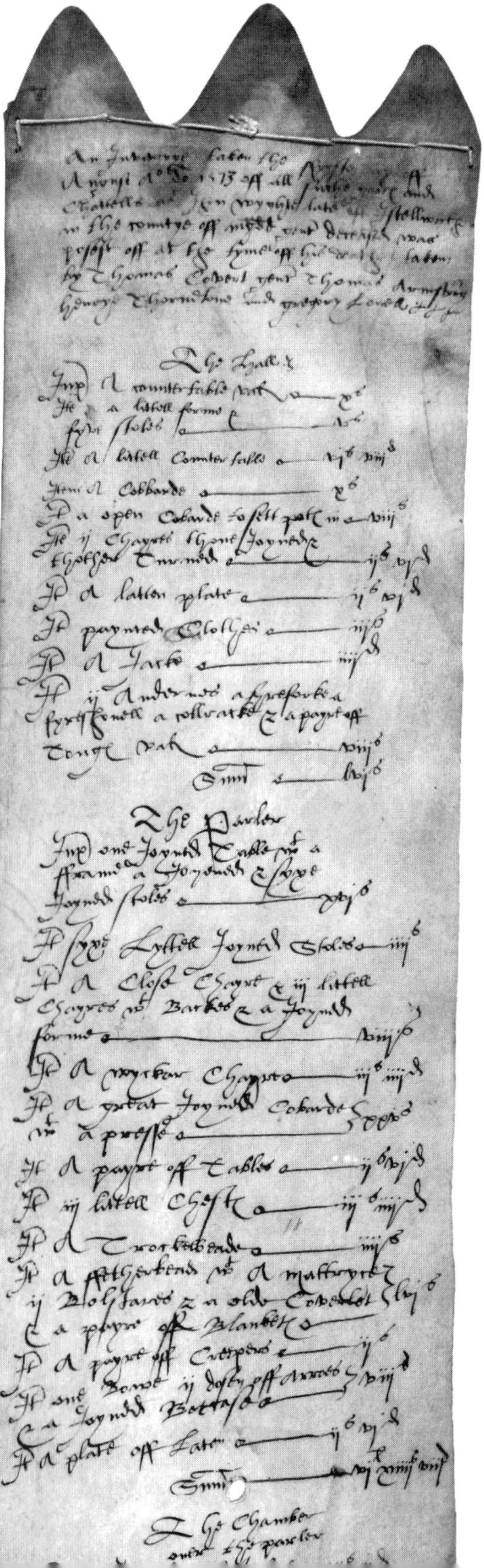

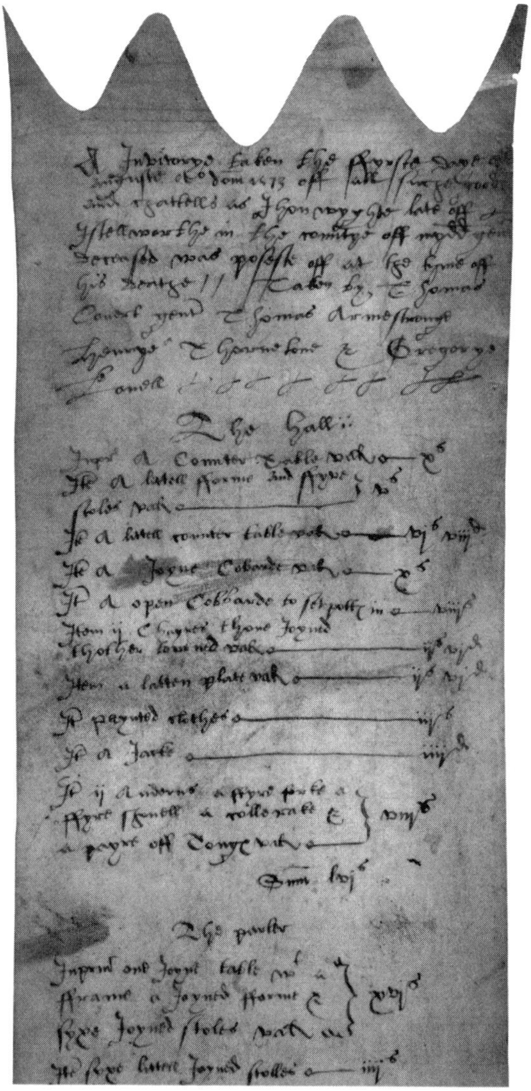

Fig. 17 *A rare example of both copies of an inventory from 1573. One was usually returned to the executor.*
PROB 2/396;
PROB 2/395

as shop goods, an expert might be called in. These appraisers might be paid for their services, which could be claimed back from the estate.

The executor or administrator swore a solemn oath when the inventory was submitted and declared that it was an accurate and true evaluation of the estate. Anyone wishing to state that items were missing from the inventory had to prove this was the case before an ecclesiastical judge, otherwise the inventory would be accepted as it stood.

6.1.2 *Valuation*

It is difficult to know whether the prices stated in an inventory accurately reflect the value of the items. It was possible for the appraiser to either overestimate or underestimate the value of the goods, either accidentally or intentionally. But as the inventory was submitted in court, appraisers were aware of the risk of deliberately giving a false valuation. Corrupt executors could and were brought to account by legatees or creditors and by the ecclesiastical courts.

Overvaluing of goods might occur because there were goods in the deceased's house that belonged to someone else or the value of goods such as crops had fallen between the date of the valuation and the date they were sold.

6.1.3 *What goods were contained within the inventory?*

The inventory was, by law, supposed to cover everything due to the deceased at the time of his or her death, including: goods (moveable and immoveable), chattels, wares and merchandise, leases, crops growing above the ground, items attached to freehold property, debts and rent (see Fig. 18).

Inventories were not supposed to include: grass, trees, glass in windows and root vegetables (such as carrots, parsnips and turnips). Leases and tenements were classed as immoveable goods.

Under civil law, a widow's *bona paraphernalia*—personal items such as her apparel (clothes), bed, jewels and ornaments—were to be excluded from the inventory. But the church courts generally interpreted *bona paraphernalia* as comprising her apparel only.

6.1.4 *Inventories as sources*

The documents concentrate primarily on those people in the middle and upper classes of society. However, despite these limitations, they are invaluable for understanding social and economic history in the sixteenth to eighteenth centuries. They provide information, not easily obtainable from other sources, about people's furniture, clothing, agriculture, crafts and lifestyles to show how they lived. They can therefore be used to build up a picture of the social and economic structure of a community for much of the early modern period.

Inventories provide a list and statement of an individual's personal estate. They do not list debts, and therefore on their own cannot be used as an accurate indicator of the wealth of the deceased. A more accurate picture can be obtained when used in conjunction with the account and will.

6.1.5 *Format*

As inventories are formal legal documents, the information contained in them is laid out in a formulaic way, although their exact nature varies from one church court to another. A detailed inventory may include:

- The name, and occasionally place of residence and occupation, of the appraiser(s)
- A detailed room-by-room listing and valuation of the contents of the home
- Stock from shops
- Agricultural equipment, crops and livestock
- The signature(s) of the appraiser(s)
- Credits owed to the deceased.

6.1.6 *Survival*

Unfortunately the survival of inventories is erratic, but the additional information they can provide makes them worth searching for. Prerogative Court of Canterbury inventories survive from 1417 to 1858; however, from 1710 inventories were only required in cases of litigation. Few Prerogative Court of York inventories survive before 1688.

6.1.7 *Declaration (in lieu of inventory)*

In some cases it was not possible to produce an inventory, so a document called a declaration was submitted instead. This often took the form of a sworn statement giving the reasons for the lack of inventory. These documents can be as detailed as an inventory or simply a statement by the executor(s) stating what, if any, of the deceased's property was in his or her (or their) control. A declaration was often used in lieu of an inventory when some time had elapsed since the death of a testator.

6.1.8 *Inventories by commission*

An executor was not always in a position to go to court to exhibit the inventory or account. The court had power to grant commissions or licences to local clergymen to administer appropriate oaths to executors or administrators. The clergyman would then return the appropriate document to court.

6.2 What are Accounts?

The executor was required to declare what goods and chattels belonged to the testator, declare what debts and legacies she or he had paid for and provide proof of every payment made.

Fig. 18 *An example of a pro forma inventory from* The Ecclesiastical Law *by Robert Burn (Vol. IV, 1842).*

The ecclesiastical court would examine the account and check that it had been properly calculated, how much was distributed, and what expenses were claimed. If the account was accurate, the executor was released from

Form of an Inventory.

A true and perfect inventory of all the goods, chattels, and personal estate of A. B., late of C., in the county of ——, and diocese of ——, yeoman, deceased, made by us whose names are hereunto subscribed, the —— day of ——, in the year of our Lord ——.

	£	s.	d.
His purse and apparel	15	0	0
Horses and furniture	20	0	0
Horned cattle	27	0	0
Sheep	20	0	0
Swine	0	13	0
Poultry	0	2	4
Plate and other household goods	18	0	0
One lease of, &c.	30	0	0
Rent in arrear	25	0	0
Corn growing at the time of his death	12	0	0
Hay and corn	10	0	0
Ploughs and other implements of husbandry	6	10	0
Debts	100	0	0
Total	284	6	4
Other debts, supposed to be desperate	25	2	6

Debts owing by the deceased 250l.

Appraised by us, the day and year above written,

A. B.
C. D.

Form of a Will of Lands and Goods (*y*) [*since Jan.* 1, 1838.]

In the name of God, Amen. I, A. B., of ——, Esquire, do make and declare this my last will and testament in manner following.

First, I give and devise to my younger son, B. B., all that my whole freehold messuage and tenement, situate, lying, and being at ——, to

(*y*) [*Vide supra*, 226, 268.—Ed.]

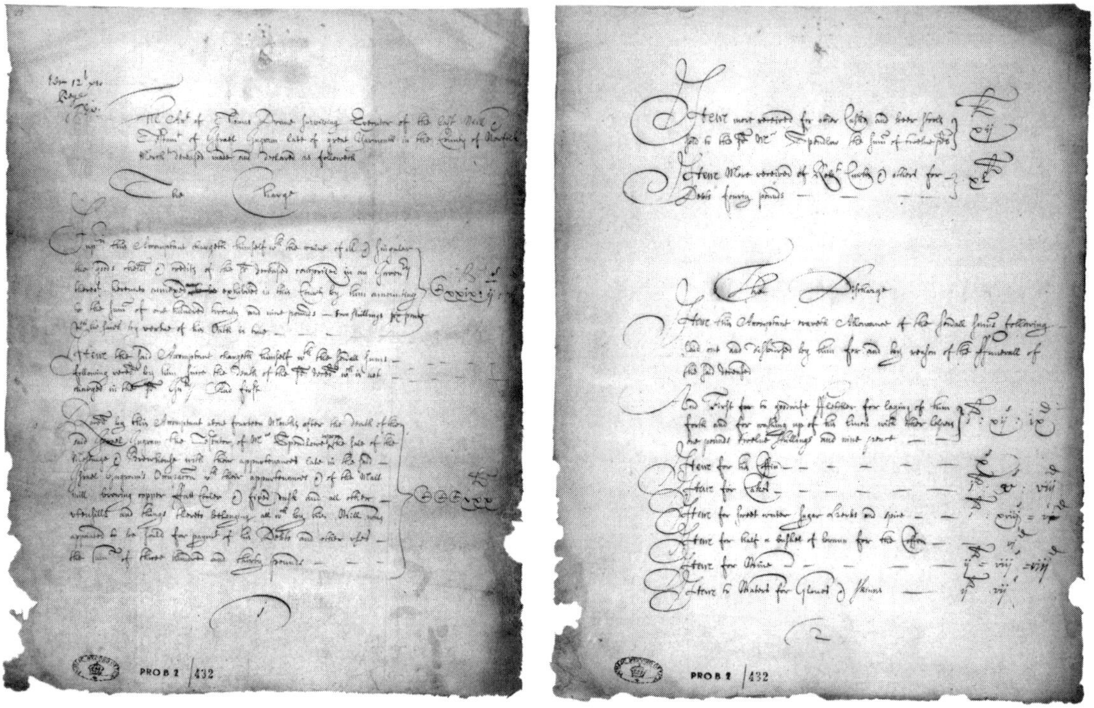

Fig. 19 *An inventory showing the charge and discharge of the estate of Israel Ingram (1652).*
PROB 2/432

any further obligation and could not be called to further account.

If the distribution of the estate took longer than a year, the court could send an official known as an apparitor to chase the executor or administrator. As the court would reclaim any costs thus incurred from the value of the estate, it was not in the interests of the executor or administrator to delay.

Submitting the account served to:

Make the affairs of the testator public
Demonstrate that all debts had been paid
Confirm the residue available for distribution.

The account reiterated the value of the personal estate as stated in the inventory. This was known as the charge. The account also gives the disbursements (what had been paid out) or discharge. The charge is usually formulaic and generally gives little more than an overview of the value of the estate. The final valuation may differ from that cited in the inventory—for example, because:

Sale prices had been either overestimated or underestimated
Items had been omitted from the inventory that were subsequently included.

Probate accounts are either filed as a separate document attached to the inventory, or copied at the end of the inventory.

6.2.1 *Format*

An account may include some or all of the following information:

- The executor or administrator's name
- The relationship (if any) of the executor or administrator to the deceased
- The executor or administrator's place of residence
- The name of the accountant (usually one, but sometimes more), and whether acting as an executor or administrator
- The 'charge'—the value of the deceased's goods based on the inventory
- The 'discharge'—monies paid out by the executor or administrator, including legal fees and funeral costs
- The date when the account was presented in court (ecclesiastical courts seem to have followed legal terms and sat four times a year)
- The total expenditure deducted from the charge to produce the final amount to be distributed.

Accounts can provide a fascinating insight into daily life and are therefore useful for both financial and social historians, especially when used in conjunction with the inventory and the will. Some accounts state expenditure as a lump sum, others give annual expenditure. The account can also flesh out a will, by providing details of family members not given in the will itself.

6.2.2 *Survival*

It is estimated that only 5 per cent of probate accounts survive in relation to wills. They survive from around 1521 to 1685. From 1685 (An Act for the Reviveing and Continuance of Severall Acts of Parlyament), administrators of intestates' estates were no longer required to produce an account of the deceased's moveable goods unless either the next of kin or a minor or creditor specifically requested it. However, an inventory of the deceased's estate was still required. From this date, the numbers of surviving accounts for both estates of testates and intestates drop dramatically (in some jurisdictions more so than others), and their survival compared with inventories is poor. Accounts are more likely to survive if there was a court case.

6.2.3 *Charge*

The charge is the total value of the personal estate as cited in the inventory. Additions were made at this stage if extra goods had been sold or the inventory had been either undervalued or overvalued. An inventory was overvalued if the debts owed to the deceased could not be collected. 'Desperate debts' were normally included in the charge, even if they were thought not to be collectable. Debts are often totalled, without itemizing individual creditors.

6.2.4 *Discharge*

The discharge lists the expenditure incurred in settling the deceased's estate. This document can add an extra layer of information not obtainable

Fig. 20 *The inventory of George Roberts, dated 1802–5, which names his livestock.* PROB 37/257

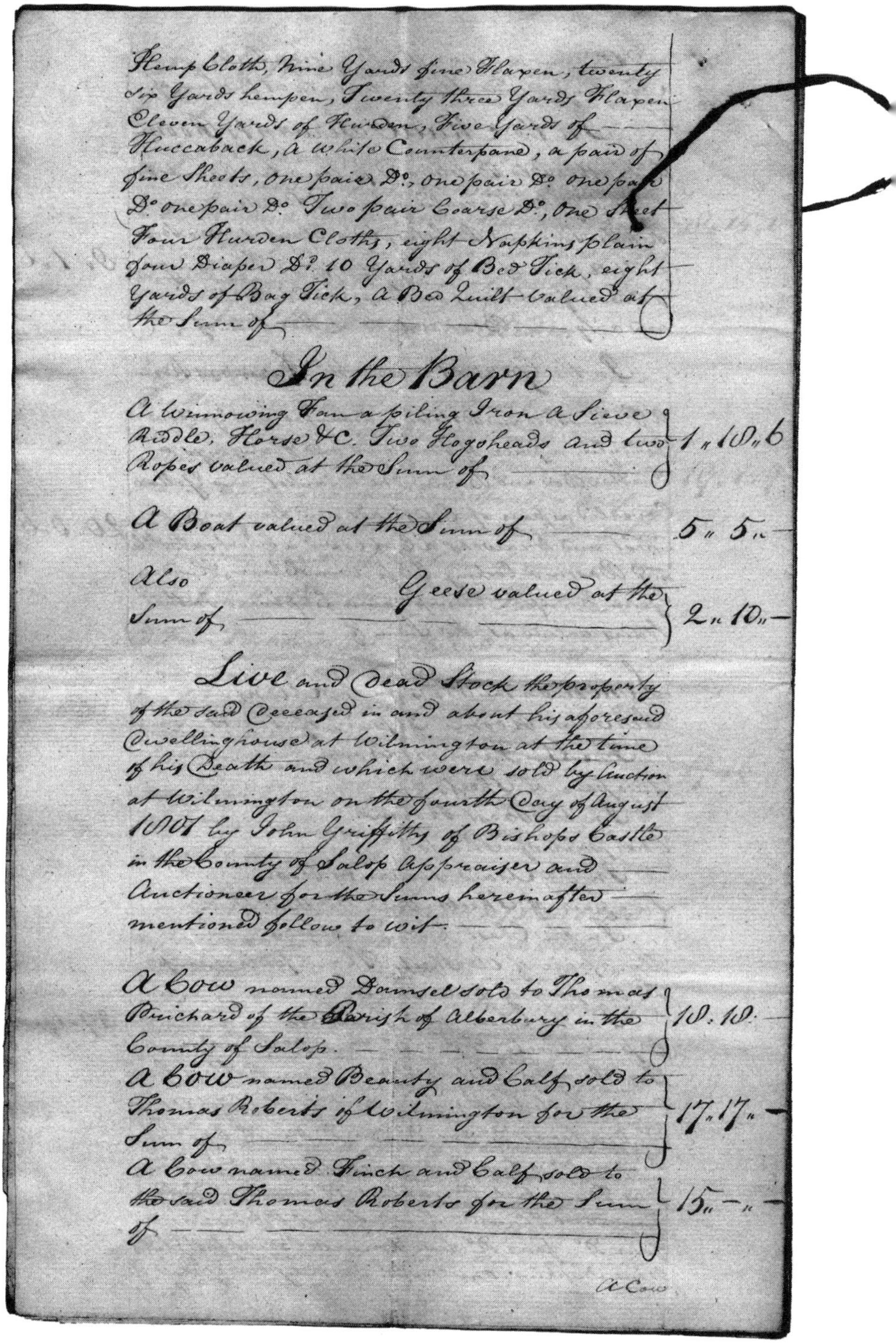

Hemp Cloth, Nine Yards fine Flaxen, twenty six Yards hempen, Twenty three Yards Flaxen Eleven Yards of Hurden, Five Yards of Huccaback, a White Counterpane, a pair of fine Sheets, one pair Do., one pair Do. one pair Do. one pair Do. Two pair Coarse Do., One Sheet Four Hurden Cloths, eight Napkins plain four Diaper Do. 10 Yards of Bed Tick, eight Yards of Bag Tick, a Bed Quilt valued at the Sum of

In the Barn

A Winnowing Fan a piling Iron a Sieve Riddle, Horse &c. Two Hogsheads and two Ropes valued at the Sum of — 1,, 10,, 6

A Boat valued at the Sum of — 5,, 5,, –

Also Geese valued at the Sum of — 2,, 10,, –

Live and Dead Stock the property of the said Deceased in and about his aforesaid Dwellinghouse at Wilmington at the time of his Death and which were sold by Auction at Wilmington on the fourth Day of August 1801 by John Griffiths of Bishops Castle in the County of Salop Appraiser and Auctioneer for the Sums hereinafter mentioned follow to wit

A Cow named Damsel sold to Thomas Prichard of the Parish of Alberbury in the County of Salop — 10. 10.

A Cow named Beauty and Calf sold to Thomas Roberts of Wilmington for the Sum of — 17,, 17,, –

A Cow named Finch and Calf sold to the said Thomas Roberts for the Sum of — 15,, –,, –

A Cow

from the will or inventory. It may detail such expenditure as:

- Funeral costs
- Medical expenses during the deceased's last illness
- Administrative costs during probate (the drawing up of the inventory, the fee payable to the court for the granting of probate, payment for writing up the account, and court fees for the final presentation of the account)
- Maintenance of the estate (for example, feeding and maintenance of livestock and payment of wages, rent and taxes)
- Court costs
- Debts owed by the estate
- Maintenance of household expenditure for the deceased's family.

6.3 Litigation

'Disputed accounts' were called for either during the course of a court case or at the end. In such cases several accounts might be produced, especially when a minor suing was an accountant (via a guardian) or an adult was suing an accountant. In either event, the account would concentrate on specific aspects of the executor's or administrator's expenditure.

Ecclesiastical courts had no power to enforce payment of money owed, and in such circumstances the case was heard by an equity court such as Chancery (see 8.7).

6.4 Debt

The executor or administrator was required to pay the debts of the deceased before any money could be distributed to the legatees. He or she was responsible for the maintenance of dependants (children, next of kin, apprentices) and the children's debts (lodgings, clothes, food, education, etc.). The estate could not be wound up until all the children had come of age.

Debts owed to the testator were included in the inventory, but debts incurred by the testator were not. Debts were often divided into two categories:

- Sperate debt (debts that were believed to be recoverable)
- Desperate debt (hopeless debts that could not be recovered).

6.5 Finding Inventories and Accounts

6.5.1 *Prerogative Court of Canterbury (1417–1858)*

Inventories at the National Archives are in the following series:

TNA series	Date
PROB 2	1417–1668
PROB 3	1701–1782
PROB 4	1660–c.1720
PROB 5	1643–1836
PROB 28	1641–1722
PROB 31	1722–1858
PROB 36	1653–1721
PROB 37	1783–1858

All these series are searchable on the Catalogue by name. However, as they were catalogued in different ways, you will need to type into the search box the surname and first name and if this is unsuccessful the first name and surname (e.g. Smith John and then try John Smith). Remember to try variants of spelling, particularly for older inventories. Try using the keyword 'inventory' if you need to reduce the number of hits. See 8.5.1 for more information about the series PROB 31.

6.5.2 *Prerogative Court of York (1427–1858)*

The arrangement of Prerogative Court of York inventories differs from that of the Prerogative Court of Canterbury. Whereas the various kinds of PCC probate records are divided into separate series, PCY inventories—and the same applies to those in many local archives—are kept with the relevant will or administration, along with any other testamentary paperwork in the probate file. Very few probate files survive for the Prerogative Court of York before 1630. The best survival rate is between 1680 and 1770.

6.6 Reading Inventories

Medieval and early modern scribes used Roman numerals when calculating inventories. Some of the most common financial abbreviations are:

li (librae)	=	pounds
s (solidi)	=	shillings
d (denarii)	=	pence

These abbreviations are used as a heading for columns of figures, for example (for the sum of three pounds, eight shillings and two pence):

li	s	d	
xxx	viij	ij	(three pounds, eight shillings and two pence)

In early handwriting the letters 'i' and 'j' were used interchangeably, but perhaps most often in figure work. For example, j is 1, xj is 11, and cj is 101.

A raised (superscript) xx indicates a score (20). For example, the combination iij^{xx} means 60.

Roman numerals

I or j	=	1
II or ij	=	2
III or iij	=	3
IV or IIII or iiij	=	4
V	=	5
VI or vj	=	6
VII or vij	=	7
VIII or viij	=	8
IX or viiij	=	9
X	=	10
XI or xj	=	11
XIX	=	19
XX	=	20
XXX	=	30
XXXX or XL	=	40
L	=	50
LX	=	60
LXXX or iiij^{xx}	=	80
LXXXX or XC	=	90
XCIX or iiij^{xx}xix	=	99
C	=	100
CI or cj	=	101
CC	=	200
CCC	=	300
CCCC or iiij^{c}	=	400
D	=	500
DC	=	600
M or MI	=	1,000
MM or MIMI	=	2,000

7 DEATH DUTY REGISTERS, 1796–1903

7.1 Introduction to 'Death Duties'

The term 'death duties' encompasses a range of taxes levied on estates left by will or administration. Although generally referred to as death duty registers, the records relate to the payment of three different taxes: Legacy Duty, Succession Duty and Estate Duty.

The death duty registers—which contain brief details of the estate and to whom it was left—are to be found in the National Archives series IR 26. They extend from 1796 to 1903, with some gaps in the 1890s caused by a fire.

Before 1805 the registers cover about a quarter of all estates; but from 1857 there should be an entry for all estates except those worth less than £20. However, unless the assets were valued at £1,500 or more, the taxes were often not collected—and so not all the details were entered in the register.

During the period 1796–1903, death duties were not levied on the estates of people who lived abroad or who died in the service of their country. Also, until 1894, no death duties were payable on overseas property belonging to people resident in Britain. From 1894, Estate Duty was levied on the personal estate (excluding leasehold property) held abroad of people resident in Britain at the time of their death.

After 1903, the death duty registers were discontinued and an individual file system was introduced. Under this new system, the individual files were retained for a minimum of 30 years following closure of a file and were then destroyed. The only surviving files are the ones for well-known people and others who were prominent in public life in the series called Selected Death Duty Accounts (IR 59) see 7.8.

7.2 Short Cuts to Wills and Administrations

Between 1797 and 1857 (as well as before) wills were proved and administrations granted in more than 200 church courts, with no union index. However, the National Archives series IR 27 consists of indexes to the death duty registers that show where the will was proved or the grant of administration issued—thus providing a very helpful short cut to finding the actual will or administration.

In addition, the National Archives has digitized all the 'country court' IR 26 death duty register entries (i.e. those deriving from courts other than the Prerogative Court of Canterbury) for the years 1796 to 1811 and they are available on DocumentsOnline. Find My Past (*www.findmypast.com*) provides charged online access to the death duty indexes 1796–1903.

It should be stressed that not all wills and administrations figure in IR 27, as not all estates were subject to death duties. So the absence of an entry in IR 27 does not necessarily mean that no will or administration exists—simply that you will have to go the long way round to find it.

7.3 Death Duty Registers as Sources

The information provided by death duty registers is not the same as the information given in probate records. Indeed, the details can be especially rewarding if you find the entry for an intestate, as most administrations give scant information. The administration entries normally list all the family members entitled to be included in the distribution of the estate. The registers can be difficult to read and use, as they are roughly written and use many abbreviations.

7.3.1 *Information about people*

The registers in IR 26 can give:

- The name of the deceased with address and last occupation
- The date of the will (and, from 1889, date of death)
- The place and date of probate
- The names, addresses and occupations of executors or administrators
- Details of estates, legacies, trustees, legatees and annuities, and the duty paid
- Information about the people who received bequests (beneficiaries) or who were the next of kin (such as the exact relationship to the deceased).

Tax was not payable on bequests of personal estate to people within a closely defined family circle, and as a result the family relationship was often noted in the registers. In 1796 tax was not payable on bequests to offspring, spouse, parents and grandparents. In 1805 the exemption was

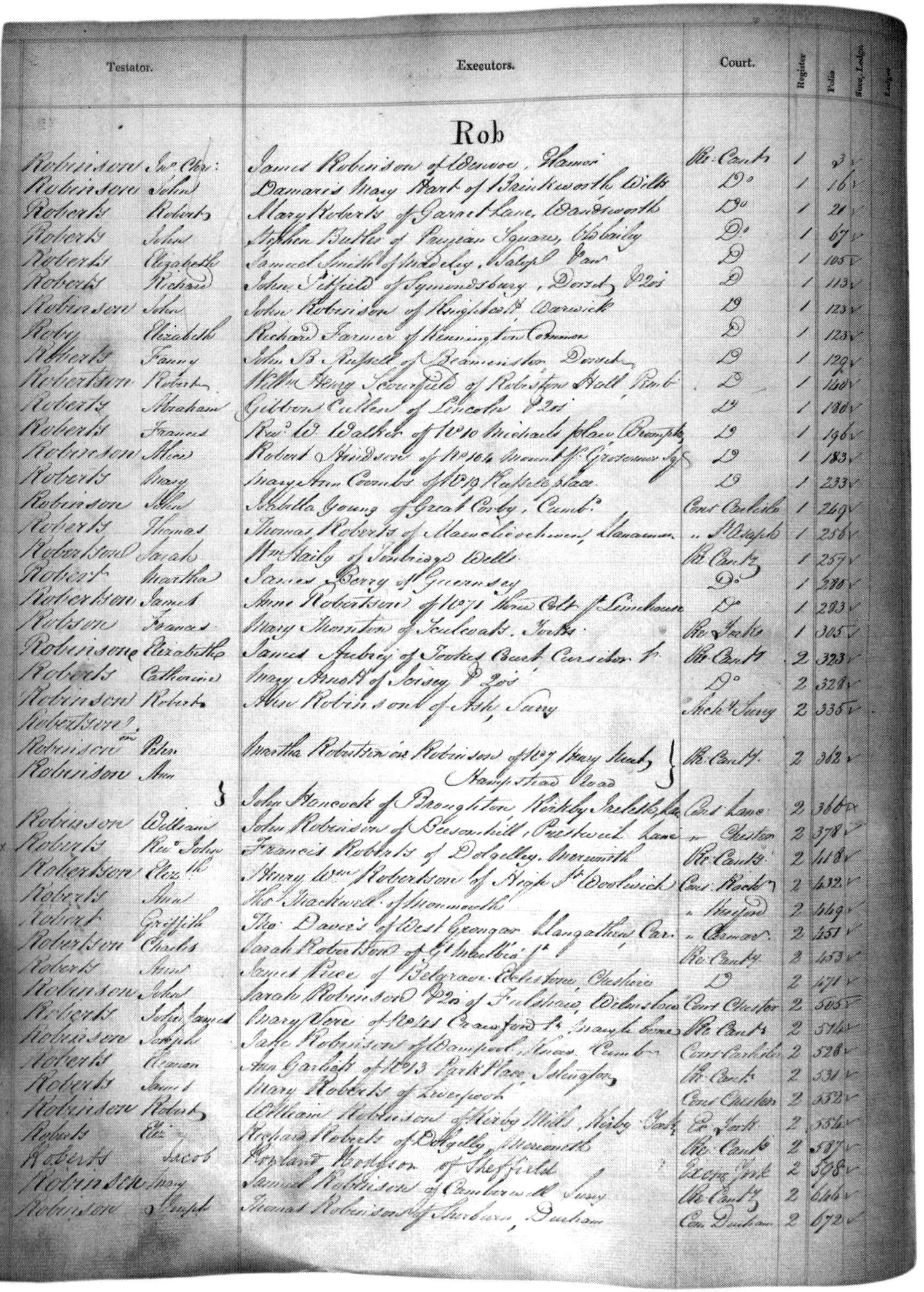

Testator.		Executors.	Court.	Register	Folio	Succ. Ledger	Ledger
		Rob					
Robinson	Jno. Chr:	James Robinson of Denver, Glamor	Pr: Cant^y	1	3	✓	
Robinson	John	Damaris Mary Hart of Brinkworth Wilts	D^o	1	16	✓	
Roberts	Robert	Mary Roberts of Garret Lane, Wandsworth	D^o	1	21	✓	
Roberts	John	Stephen Butler of Paragon Square, Old Bailey	D^o	1	67	✓	
Roberts	Elizabeth	Samuel Smith of Madeley, Salop Esqr	D^o	1	105	✓	
Roberts	Richard	John Pitfield of Symondsbury, Dorset & 2 os	D^o	1	113	✓	
Robinson	John	John Robinson of Knightcott Warwick	D^o	1	123	✓	
Roby	Elizabeth	Richard Farmer of Kennington Common	D^o	1	125	✓	
Roberts	Fanny	John B. Russell of Beaminster Dorset	D^o	1	129	✓	
Robertson	Robert	Willm Henry Scourfield of Robeston Hall Pemb	D^o	1	140	✓	
Roberts	Abraham	Gibbons Cullen of Lincoln & 2 os	D^o	1	180	✓	
Roberts	Frances	Revd W. Walker of N° 10 Michaels place Brompton	D^o	1	196	✓	
Robinson	Alice	Robert Hudson of N° 164 Mount St Grosvenor Sq	D^o	1	183	✓	
Roberts	Mary	Mary Ann Coombs of N° 19 Russell place	D^o	1	233	✓	
Robinson	John	Isabella Young of Great Corby, Cumb^d	Cons Carlisle	1	249	✓	
Roberts	Thomas	Thomas Roberts of Maenclochog, Llanarmon	" St Asaph	1	258	✓	
Robertson	Sarah	Wm Haily of Tunbridge Wells	Pr: Cant^y	1	257	✓	
Robert	Martha	James Berry of Guernsey	D^o	1	280	✓	
Robertson	James	Anne Robertson of N° 71 Three Colt St Limehouse	D^o	1	283	✓	
Robson	Frances	Mary Thornton of Sculcoats. Yorks	Pr: Yorks	1	305	✓	
Robinson	Elizabeth	James Aubrey of Tookes Court Cursitor S^t	Pr: Cant^y	2	323	✓	
Roberts	Catherine	Mary Arnott of Jersey & 2 os	D^o	2	328	✓	
Robinson	Robert	Ann Robinson of Ash, Surry	Arch^d Surry	2	335	✓	
Robertson or Robinson	Peter	Martha Robertson or Robinson of N° 7 Mary Street, Hampstead Road	Pr: Cant^y	2	362	✓	
Robinson	Ann	John Hancock of Broughton Kirkby Ireleth, Lanc	Cons Lanc	2	366	✗	
Robinson	William	John Robinson of Besomhill, Prestwich Lanc	" Chester	2	378	✓	
Roberts	Revd John	Francis Roberts of Dolgelley. Merioneth	Pr: Cant^y	2	418	✓	
Robertson	Eliz^th	Henry Wm Robertson of High St Woolwich	Cons: Roch^r	2	432	✓	
Roberts	Anne	Thos Mackwell of Monmouth	" Hereford	2	449	✓	
Robert	Griffith	Thos Davies of West Georgia Llangathen Car	" Carmar	2	451	✓	
Robertson	Charles	Sarah Robertson of G^t Marlbro' S^t	Pr: Cant^y	2	453	✓	
Roberts	Anne	James Price of Belgrave Eccleston, Cheshire	D^o	2	471	✓	
Robinson	John	Sarah Robinson & 2 os of Fulshaw, Wilmslow	Cons Chester	2	505	✓	
Roberts	John James	Mary Vere of N° 41 Crawford St Marylebone	Pr: Cant^y	2	[illegible]	✓	
Robinson	Joseph	Jane Robinson of Wampool, Abbey Holme, Cumb	Cons Carlisle	2	528	✓	
Roberts	Herman	Ann Garlick of N° 13 Park Place, Islington	Pr: Cant^y	2	531	✓	
Roberts	Saml	Mary Roberts of Liverpool	Cons Chester	2	552	✓	
Robinson	Robert	William Robinson of Kirby Mills, Kirby York	Ex. York	2	556	✓	
Roberts	Eliz	Richard Roberts of Dolgelly, Merioneth	Pr: Cant^y	2	587	✓	
Roberts	Jacob	Rowland Hodgson of Sheffield	Exchq York	2	598	✓	
Robinson	Mary	Samuel Robinson of Camberwell Surry	Pr: Cant^y	2	646	✓	
Robinson	Joseph	Thomas Robinson of Sherburn, Durham	Cons Durham	2	672	✓	

Fig. 21 *A page showing the entry for Robert Robinson in the death duty index for 1821.*
IR 27/178

restricted to spouse and parents; and from 1815 only bequests to the spouse were exempt from tax.

Because the registers could be annotated with additional information for many years after the first entry, they can include details such as:

The date of death of spouse
The dates of death or marriage of beneficiaries
Births of posthumous children and grandchildren
Changes of address
References to lawsuits
Cross-references to other entries in IR 26.

If any of the estate was left in trust before 1852, look at the reversionary registers as well, as trusts were set up to last for a long time. Between 1853 and 1894 you may need to look at two series of registers to find all the entries relating to a person's estate—the Legacy Duty registers for personal estate and the Succession Duty registers for real estate.

From 1882 all wills proved and administrations granted are included in the indexes, regardless of any potential death duty: if there was no liability, the index reference will either be *NE* (no entry) or left blank. From 1889, the date of death of the deceased will be included.

7.3.2 *Evidence of value of the estate*

The death duty register entries include a valuation of the deceased's estate. However, this figure should be treated with caution, for the following reasons:

Before 1853 it relates to the deceased's personal estate only and excludes freehold property—whereas from 1853 it should take into account both personal and real estate.
It does not take into account the deduction of debts and expenses.
Part of the personal estate may not have been taken into account, as the valuation figure only provides a record of the bequests as described in the will.
The value placed on bequests may not be accurate.
The valuations are expressed as an amount linked to the relevant tax band, and the tax bands were periodically changed by legislation. (From 1804 to 1815, a 'sum sworn under £10,000' means between £7,500 and £10,000.)

From 1853 to 1893 there may be both a Legacy Duty register entry (personal estate) and a Succession Duty entry (real estate), so the two valuations need to be added together.

7.4 Legacy Duty (from 1796)

7.4.1 *Legacy Duty Act*

Although Legacy Duty was introduced by an Act of Parliament in 1780, there are no registers for the pre-1796 period. Under the Legacy Duty Act of 1796, which applied to the whole of Britain, duties were payable on legacies and residues of personal estate but were restricted to certain types of bequest. The amount of duty payable was based on rates that varied according to degree of blood relationship (consanguinity) to the deceased. Spouses, children, parents and grandchildren were exempt.

During this period of British history the French Revolutionary Wars were causing considerable strain on state finances. However, this form of inheritance tax was very unpopular and it resulted in a number of disputes in the central courts at Westminster, particularly in the Court of Chancery and the Court of Exchequer.

Subsequently, the taxation net was widened by a series of further Acts. First the Legacy Duty Act of 1805 and then the Stamp Act of 1815 extended Legacy Duty to cash legacies and residues that were to be generated by the sale of real estate. Legacy Duty continued until 1949, but from 1894 to 1903 you will need to look at the Estate Duty registers.

7.4.2 *Legacy Duty records*

Between 1796 and January 1858, the registers and indexes reflect the existence of many probate courts involved in the registration of estates for Legacy Duty. Each court had its own index of estates left by will between 1796 and 1811, and its own administration index for 1796 to 1857.

The table below provides a quick guide to which part of the IR 27 and IR 26 series lists you will need to look at to identify the index or register you need. Please note microfilm copies are held at the National Archives.

Date range	Category/ content	Indexes IR 27	Registers IR 26	Form and access
	TESTATORS			
1796–1811	PCC testators	1–16	1–178	DocumentsOnline (see 3.1.2) Microfilm
1796–1811	Country courts testators	67–93	287–437	DocumentsOnline (see 3.1.2) to the year 1811 and Microfilm
1812–81	Testators	140–419	535–3292	Microfilm to 1860 and then original documents at the National Archives

Date range	Category/ content	Indexes IR 27	Registers IR 26	Form and access
	INTESTATES			
1796–1857	PCC intestates	17–66	179–286	Microfilm
1796–1857	Country courts intestates	67–139	287–534	Microfilm
1858–63	Intestates	420–429	3293–3316	Microfilm to 1860 and then original documents at the National Archives
1864–81	Intestates	No indexes	3317–3433	Original documents at the National Archives
	BOTH TESTATORS AND INTESTATES			
1882–94	All testators and intestates	430–531	3434–4855	Original documents at the National Archives
	LONG-RUNNING ENTRIES (E.G. FOR TRUSTS)			
1812–52	Reversionary registers	No indexes	4856–4867	Original documents at the National Archives

The indexes can be a bit tricky. In particular, you should note that:

The date given in the index entry is the date of probate or issue of grant of administration, not the date of death.

Abbreviations such as *SP* (of the same place), *NE* (no entry), *& ors* (and others) and *& anor* (and another) are often used. The index entry will normally give you a folio reference to the corresponding register. Look at the IR 26 series list to convert the reference.

An index entry without a folio reference means that no tax was payable, as does *NE* (no entry).

A reference such as RR/41/J/12 is to the reversionary registers. It gives the year (e.g. 41), initial letter of surname (e.g. J) and folio (e.g. 12), and needs to be converted using the IR 26/4856–4867 part of the series list.

Before 1812, the registers include abstracts of wills. After 1812, copy wills were made, but these have largely been destroyed. However, those from the major local probate courts in Cornwall, Devon and Somerset were sent to the respective record offices to fill some of the gaps in local probate records caused by enemy action during the Second World War. David Hawkings' *Index of Somerset Estate Duty Office Wills and Letters of Administration 1805–1811* (Weston-super-Mare, 1995) can be consulted at the National Archives.

7.5 Succession Duty (from 1853)

The next significant date in the history of death duties is 1853, when under the Succession Duty Act the transmission of a family's main land holdings to the next heir—or to anyone else—became taxable for the first time.

Duty was now payable where a person became beneficially entitled to or interested in property upon the death of another (described as 'gratuitous acquisition of property'). The relevant registers are as follows:

Date range	Category/ content	Indexes IR 27	Registers IR 26	Form and access
1853–94	Testators and intestates	None	4868–6262	Original documents at the National Archives
1853–78	Succession Arrears (outstanding claims)	None	6263–6282	Original documents at the National Archives

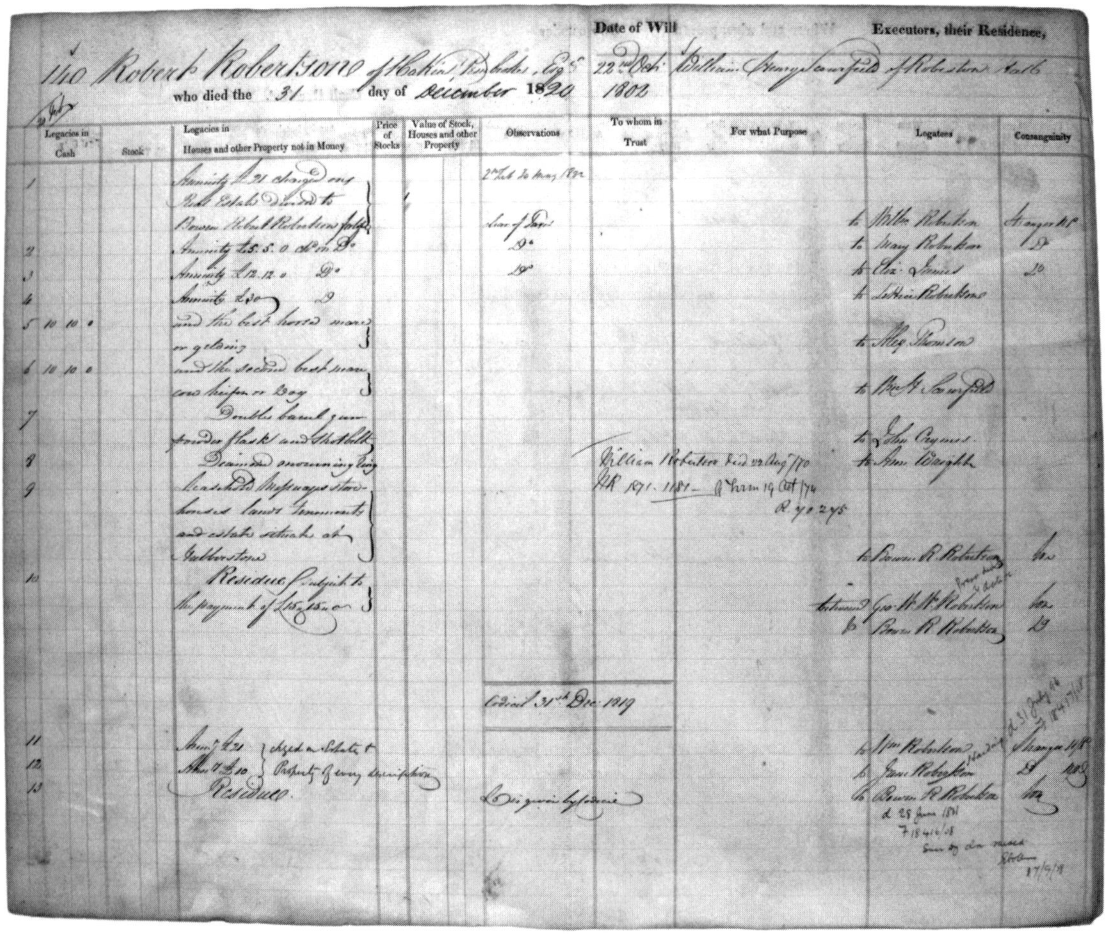

Fig. 22 *Robert Robinson's entry in the death duty register for 1821.* IR 26/875

In the Succession Duty registers, entries can relate to wills proved many years before the date of the register—for example, a register for 1865 could contain an entry relating to a will proved in 1830. The Succession Duty registers provide details of duty payable on intestate estates between 1858 and 1881; after 1881, details for intestates may be found in the will and administration registers for 1881–94 and the Estate Duty registers for 1894–1903.

Due to a fire, eleven of the Succession Duty registers for 1894 have not survived. Although Succession Duty continued to 1949, between 1894 and 1903 you will need to look at the 'Old Duty' registers.

There is an extra column in the IR 27 indexes 1889–99 giving the folio number in the corresponding Succession Duty registers. For other years the Legacy Duty register entries refer to Succession Duty register entries, often abbreviated to Succ. Reg. followed by a folio number.

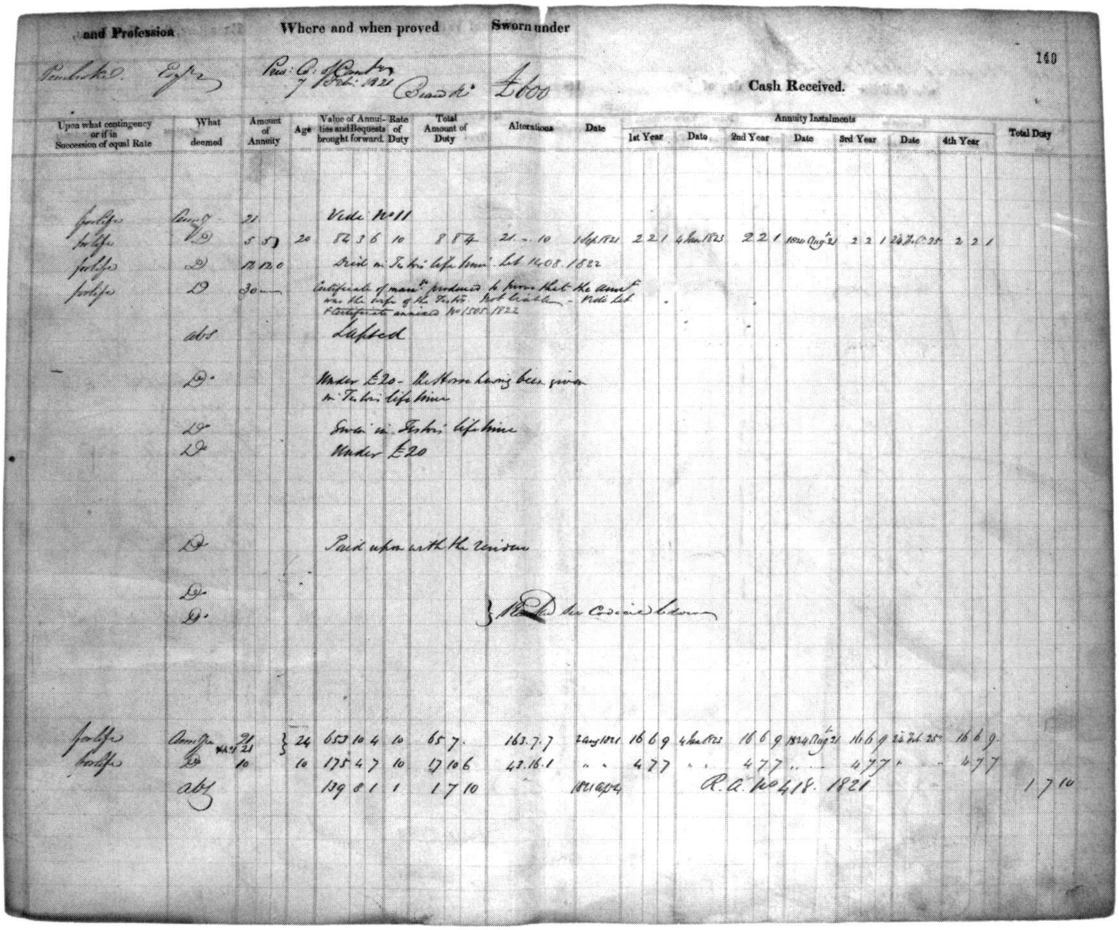

7.6 Estate Duty (from 1894)

Introduced by the Finance Act of 1894, Estate Duty was payable on all property (both real and personal estate) passed on at death. This duty continued through to modern times, being finally replaced by Capital Transfer Tax in 1975.

After 1894, Legacy Duty and Succession Duty became known as 'Old Duty' and any property liable to these two duties was exempted from Estate Duty. The relevant registers are as follows:

Date range	Category/ content	Indexes IR 27	Registers IR 26	Form and access
1894–1903	Testators and intestates	532–605	6283–8690	Original documents at the National Archives
1895–1903	Old Duty registers	None	8691–8743	Original documents at the National Archives

The index entry will give you a folio reference to the corresponding register. You then need to look at the IR 26 series list to convert the reference.

Approximately 500 Estate Duty registers (many of them relating to the period 1894–8) have not survived, mainly because of a fire in the Estate Duty Office building that housed the records.

7.7 The Layout of the Registers

7.7.1 *Up to and including 1811*

Before 1812, the registers are reasonably simple. An entry for the estate of a particular person occupies two facing pages and is divided into columns. Each column contains a specific piece of information, defined by a printed column heading, and has its own abbreviations.

7.7.2 *From 1812*

From 1812, an entry for the estate of a particular person still extends over two facing pages and is divided into columns. Each entry is separated from the next by a ruled line and each now has two sets of headings. The first of these is printed at the very top of the page. Here you will find the name of the deceased, the date of the will and approximate value of the estate, details of the executors, the date of probate, and the name of the court where the will was proved. Equivalent information is given for an administration. The information given under this first set of headings is ruled off from the rest of the entry. The second set of headings are printed immediately below the first set of headings at the top of the page—and give the details of the will or administration.

7.7.3 *What do the headings and abbreviations mean?*

Below, to serve as a guide, we show what the various headings mean in a register dating from 1837 and what you can expect to find in each column. However, as the registers changed over time, you will find that the headings and the content of the columns vary a little, depending on the date of the register you are looking at.

FIRST SET OF COLUMN HEADINGS

Column	Heading	
1–2	Name and address, date of death	
3	Date of will/administration	
4	Executors/administrator	
5–6	Residence	Residence of executors/administrator.
7–8	Description	Occupation/rank of executors/administrator.
9–13	Where and when proved	Name of court where grant of probate or administration was made and date on which the grant was made. SAMPLE OF ABBREVIATIONS USED: *ArchCt/Totnes/archd'on* = Archdeaconry Court of Totnes *BishCt/Lichfield/* = Bishop's (Consistory) Court of Lichfield *ConCt/London* = Consistory Court of London *ConstEpic/Wells* = Episcopal Consistory Court of Bath and Wells *Deans/Lichfield* = Dean and Chapter of Lichfield *Ecclesi/St Albans* = Archdeaconry of St Albans *ExCt/York* = Exchequer Court of the Archbishop of York *PC/Cant.y* = Prerogative Court of Canterbury *PecuC/Biggleswade* = Peculiar Court of Biggleswade *RuralD/Chester* = Rural Dean of Chester
14	Sum sworn under	Approximate value of estate.

SECOND SET OF COLUMN HEADINGS

Column	Heading	
1	Legacies	
2	Observations	Notes on the legacies or other information for the purposes of estimating duty payable.
3	To whom in trust	To whom estate is entrusted (e.g. the executors).

Column	Heading	
		The date of codicils in which legacies are bequeathed. ABBREVIATIONS USED: *exors* = executors
4	For what purpose	What is to be done with the legacy. Into how many portions it is to be divided. Upon what conditions legatees are entitled to it. Whether the legacies have to be converted into certain forms for payment, etc.
5	Legatee	To whom the legacies are due. ABBREVIATIONS USED: *Resy Legatee* = residuary legatee (i.e. the legatee who receives the remainder of the estate once the claims of the other legatees have been satisfied)
6	Consanguinity	Relationship of legatees to the deceased (for the purposes of calculating the rate of duty payable on the legacy). ABBREVIATIONS USED: See table below.
7	Upon what contingency or, if in succession, of equal rate	Upon what conditions the legacies are bequeathed and the procedure to be followed when the legatee dies (i.e. does the legacy pass to the legatee's heirs or to other defined persons?). ABBREVIATIONS USED: See table below.
8	What deemed	The form of the bequest. Whether an absolute gift or an annuity, and whether there are any contingency clauses to the bequest. ABBREVIATIONS USED: *abs* = absolute legacy (i.e. unconditional) *abs & int* = absolute and interest *abswp* = absolute legacy with a proviso (conditional grant) *anny* = annuity *anny wp* = annuity with a proviso (conditional annuity) *dwp* = ditto (usually absolute) with a proviso *in deft of appt eqy amg them* = in default of apportionment equally among them
9	Age of annuitant	Age of annuitant (given in some cases only).
10	Value of annuities and bequests	Value of bequests received by legatees; or total value of annuities as computed for paying duty.
11	Rate of duty	Percentage of bequest or annuity to be paid as duty, according to degree of consanguinity.
12	Date of payment	Date when payments of duty were made.

13	Annuity instalments	Value of instalments of duty paid on annuities (there were usually four such payments).
14	Total duty	Total duty paid on legacy.

Note: Columns 9–14 sometimes contain no information, presumably because duty was never paid or because there were insufficient assets to pay for legacies. In place of such information, there is often a reference such as RA 767/46 1 LD, which refers to a residuary account. Most residuary accounts have been destroyed, although a few still survive in IR 19 and IR 59 (see 7.8).

ABBREVIATIONS USED IN COLUMN 6 OF THE SECOND SET OF HEADINGS (CONSANGUINITY)

BF = brother of a father (i.e. uncle)
BM = brother of a mother (i.e. uncle)
Child or *Ch* = child of deceased
DB = descendant of a brother (niece, nephew, etc.)
DS = descendant of a sister (niece, nephew, etc.)
DBF = descendant of a brother of a father (i.e. cousin)
DBM = descendant of a brother of a mother (i.e. cousin)
DSF = descendant of a sister of a father (i.e. cousin)
DSM = descendant of a sister of a mother (i.e. cousin)
DBGF = descendant of a brother of a grandfather
DBGM = descendant of a brother of a grandmother
DSGF = descendant of a sister of a grandfather
DSGM = descendant of a sister of a grandmother
G child = grandchild
GG child = great-grandchild
G daughter = granddaughter
G son = grandson
SF = sister of a father (i.e. aunt)
SM = sister of a mother (i.e. aunt)
Str or *Stra* or *Strag* = stranger in blood
Stra BL = stranger, brother-in-law
Stra DL = stranger, daughter-in-law
Stra NC = stranger, natural child (i.e. illegitimate)
Stra ND = stranger, natural daughter (i.e. illegitimate)
Stra NS = stranger, natural son (i.e. illegitimate)
Stra NC (of a daughter) = stranger, illegitimate child of a daughter
Stra NC (of a son) = stranger, illegitimate child of a son
Stra (sent) = stranger, servant of deceased
Stra SL = stranger, sister-in-law *or* stranger, son-in-law
Stra or *'son'* = stranger, natural son (i.e. illegitimate)
Stra or *'daughter'* = stranger, natural daughter (i.e. illegitimate)

ABBREVIATIONS USED IN COLUMN 7 OF THE SECOND SET OF HEADINGS (CONTINGENCY)

Amg = among
attn = attain
contingency = condition of bequest
dividds = dividends
eqy = equally

Est = estate
Int = interest
int durg miny prinl when 21 = interest on bequest payable during minority of legatee, and principal when legatee attains 21 years of age
Pble = payable
P or *princl* = principal
reversion = bequest reverts to another legatee upon a certain condition (e.g. upon the death of the first beneficiary)
Ring etc. = mourning ring and other bequests
SER or *suc of equal rate* = succession of equal rate after death of legatee (i.e. equal division of the bequest among the heirs of the legatee)
*until she att*ns *21 or marr* = legacy not operable until the beneficiary reaches the age of 21 or marries
*when 21 with accum*ls = legatee to receive principal and accumulated interest when he/she attains 21 years of age
with bent of survp = with benefit of survivorship (e.g. if a bequest is distributed between a group of legatees and one dies, the rest will be entitled to share out the legacy equally among themselves within six months)

ABBREVIATIONS FOUND IN VARIOUS COLUMNS OF THE REGISTERS

*de bonis non/15*th *Oct 1851/* = date of later grant of administration
*in res*d = in residue
not liable = no duty payable (on bequests to relatives closely related to the deceased)
not subject to Duty = no duty payable (on legacies to be paid out of the profits from real estate sales, prior to 1805)
P E = personal estate
Qy = query
RA/1448–1837/ = Residuary Account RA 1448 1837. Reference to a residuary account (see 7.8). Most residuary accounts have now been destroyed, although a few remain in IR 19 and IR 59
R E = real estate

7.8 Related Records at the National Archives

7.8.1 *Residuary accounts*

Examples of residuary accounts (1796–1903) can be found in IR 19. Unfortunately, this series has been heavily weeded, so you may, for example, find that only accounts for surnames beginning with the letters A to G have been preserved for a particular year. However, copies of death duty accounts can sometimes be found among family papers. In IR 59 there are residuary accounts, ranging from 1805 to 1993, for famous people—including Jane Austen, Charles Dickens, Friedrich Engels, Benjamin Disraeli, William Gladstone, Florence Nightingale and Percy Bysshe Shelley. The more modern accounts are closed for 75 years.

Residuary accounts are identified in death duty register entries by a reference number preceded by the initials RA. They supplement the death duty registers by providing a detailed breakdown of the residuary part of the estate. This is shown as listings with valuations—with one side of the

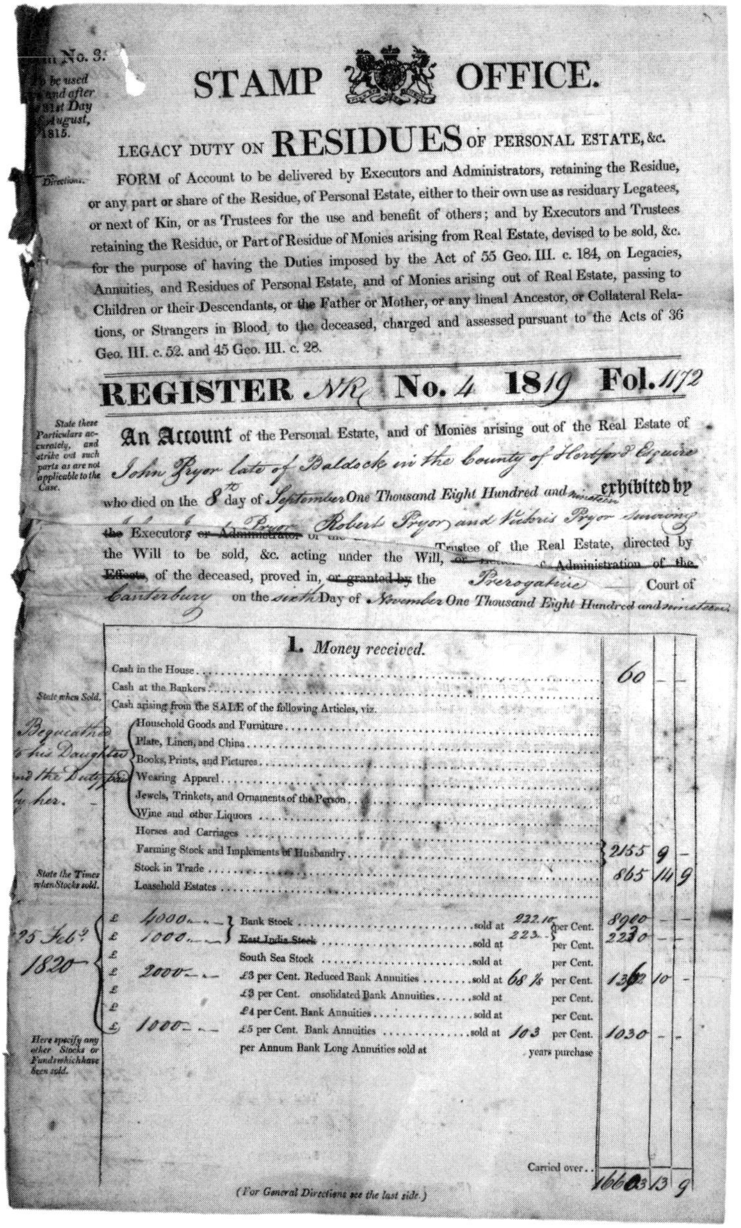
No. 3. To be used on and after the 31st Day of August, 1815.

STAMP OFFICE.

LEGACY DUTY ON RESIDUES OF PERSONAL ESTATE, &c.

Directions. FORM of Account to be delivered by Executors and Administrators, retaining the Residue, or any part or share of the Residue, of Personal Estate, either to their own use as residuary Legatees, or next of Kin, or as Trustees for the use and benefit of others; and by Executors and Trustees retaining the Residue, or Part of Residue of Monies arising from Real Estate, devised to be sold, &c. for the purpose of having the Duties imposed by the Act of 55 Geo. III. c. 184, on Legacies, Annuities, and Residues of Personal Estate, and of Monies arising out of Real Estate, passing to Children or their Descendants, or the Father or Mother, or any lineal Ancestor, or Collateral Relations, or Strangers in Blood, to the deceased, charged and assessed pursuant to the Acts of 36 Geo. III. c. 52. and 45 Geo. III. c. 28.

REGISTER NR No. 4 1819 Fol. 1172

State these Particulars accurately, and strike out such parts as are not applicable to the Case.

An Account of the Personal Estate, and of Monies arising out of the Real Estate of John Pryor late of Baldock in the County of Hertford Esquire who died on the 8th day of September One Thousand Eight Hundred and nineteen exhibited by ~~the~~ Robert Pryor and Vickris Pryor surviving Executors ~~or Administrator~~ ... Trustee of the Real Estate, directed by the Will to be sold, &c. acting under the Will, ~~or ... Administration of the Effects~~ of the deceased, proved in, ~~or granted by~~ the Prerogative Court of Canterbury on the sixth Day of November One Thousand Eight Hundred and nineteen

1. Money received.

		£	s.	d.
	Cash in the House			
	Cash at the Bankers	60	–	–
State when Sold.	Cash arising from the SALE of the following Articles, viz.			
Bequeathed to his Daughter and the Duty paid by her.	Household Goods and Furniture			
	Plate, Linen, and China			
	Books, Prints, and Pictures			
	Wearing Apparel			
	Jewels, Trinkets, and Ornaments of the Person			
	Wine and other Liquors			
	Horses and Carriages			
	Farming Stock and Implements of Husbandry	2155	9	–
State the Times when Stocks sold.	Stock in Trade	865	14	9
	Leasehold Estates			
25 Feb. 1820	£ 4000 Bank Stock sold at 222.10 per Cent.	8900	–	–
	£ 1000 ~~East India Stock~~ sold at 223 per Cent.	2230	–	–
	£ South Sea Stock sold at per Cent.			
	£ 2000 £3 per Cent. Reduced Bank Annuities sold at 68 1/8 per Cent.	1362	10	–
	£ £3 per Cent. Consolidated Bank Annuities sold at per Cent.			
	£ £4 per Cent. Bank Annuities sold at per Cent.			
	£ 1000 £5 per Cent. Bank Annuities sold at 103 per Cent.	1030	–	–
Here specify any other Stocks or Funds which have been sold.	per Annum Bank Long Annuities sold at years purchase			
	Carried over	16603	13	9

(For General Directions see the last side.)

Fig. 23 *The death duty account for John Pryor, dated 1821.* IR 19/35

account for assets (including cash, stocks and shares, and household furniture) and the other for liabilities, including debts. Most wealthy men left the major part of their fortunes as residuary estate. Sometimes letters from the executor or administrator and affidavits are attached to the accounts.

7.8.2 *Correspondence and reports on contentious cases*

Although the death duty registers contain numerous references to correspondence, most of it has not been preserved. Nevertheless, letters relating to 'contentious cases', 1812–36, survive in IR 6. This description is in fact misleading, as all communications between the Legacy Duty Office and executors or administrators were described as 'contentious'. Correspondence of this kind can be revealing—for example, it may explain why there was a delay in the payment of the duty by the executor or administrator. The IR 26 registers give the year and number of the letter.

Further material on contentious cases are in the following series:

IR 49	Reports on contentious cases	1800–25
IR 50	Reports on contentious cases	1825–33
IR 67	Case books	1853–66
IR 98	Board of Inland Revenue Officers' and Counsels' Opinions (subject to 75 years closure)	1853–1959
IR 99	Solicitors' Opinions and Reports (subject to 75 years closure). Need to be ordered three working days in advance.	1855–1964

Unlike the letters in IR 6, these include only a small number of cases.

IR 62 contains Estate Duty Board Papers, 1869–1975. Among them are a number of files relating to cases where exemption or postponement of Estate Duty was claimed for paintings and manuscripts and other works of art. These files are mostly closed for 75 years; others can be viewed at the National Archives, but need to be ordered three working days in advance.

7.9 Case Study

7.9.1 *Death duties paid*

Robert Robinson, a farmer, died on 31 December 1820 leaving a will dated 22 October 1802. This was proved in the Prerogative Court of Canterbury on 7 February 1821. As there was a residue left on his estate, it was liable for legacy duty. As a consequence there is an entry for him in the death duty index (see Fig. 21), which leads to one in the death duty registers for 1821 (see Fig. 22). The latter is a good example of the valuable information that this source can offer family historians. The top of the entry conveniently gives all of the dates mentioned above along with a personal estate valuation figure expressed as the top limit of the relevant tax band.

The death duty register also confirms the various annuities and other legacies left by Robinson, including 10 guineas to buy the best horse, mare or gelding that he possessed and another for 10 guineas to buy the second-best mare, cow, heifer or dog. However, there is one small difference, which serves as an example of the insight that can be gained from a careful comparison of death duty register and will. In his will five guineas were left to a named servant in case she was still in his service at the time of his demise. As she does not appear in the death duty register, it can be assumed that she did leave the household before his death.

As is to be expected, particularly where complicated trusts were concerned, the death duty register entry includes the dates of death for Robinson's sons and daughter. These had to be reported to and recorded by the Legacy Duty Office because of the effect on the payment of the annuities. One of the intended beneficiaries, Elizabeth James, is recorded as dead in the lifetime of the testator. This is followed by the reference 'Let 1408.1822'. The number 1408 is the number given to the letter and 1822 the year. This relates to a letter that was sent into the Legacy Duty Office by the executor of the will to report the death. As the correspondence survives for this period in the series IR 6, the relevant letter can be consulted.

At the bottom of the second page of the death duty entry the number RA 418 1821 is given. This leads to the death duty accounts in the series IR 19. Luckily, the completed death duty or residuary account form survives for Robert Robinson (IR 19/35) with an attached sheet giving an estimate of the leasehold property and a letter from an auctioneer listing and giving the value of the goods of the deceased that remained unsold. The residuary account form mentions how much cash Robert Robinson had in his house and at the bankers, and gives the amount of funeral expenses.

In addition, in the middle of the first page, next to the date of death of one of Robert Robinson's sons, William, both the year and folio reference of his death duty register entry, plus the year and number for his residuary account, are given.

8 LITIGATION

8.1 People at their Worst, Records at their Best

The records relating to disputes over wills and the estates of intestates (people who failed to leave a will) can be the most interesting of probate records, sometimes encompassing the records of both ecclesiastical and non-church courts. They represent only a small proportion of all testators and administrators, but certainly justify the effort involved in undertaking a search for a dispute. They also provide a high percentage of female litigants.

The depositions provide wonderful details about families and communities. The animosity and greed of individuals are often cruelly exposed. Charles Dickens referred to this as 'hatred pursued beyond the grave'. There can sometimes be 20 or more witnesses in a case. Deponents (witnesses) had to give their age, occupation and address (the seventeenth-century and early-eighteenth-century depositions also record place of birth, annual income, and when the deponent last took the sacrament). Every character involved as a witness can therefore be quickly placed in context. These witnesses may be family members, who would need to state their relationship to the deceased; and often they were domestic servants, who might provide intimate details of what took place in a household.

There is information about illnesses and medical practices; about the strange behaviour of the deceased, since insanity of the deceased was often the grounds for questioning the legality of a will; and about drinking habits (as drunkenness was also frequently cited as the reason why the deceased was not in a fit state to make a will), together with vivid scenes from local public houses.

The varied nature of the types of cases brought before a church court can be illustrated by looking at just one year. In 1752, for example, one case at the Prerogative Court of Canterbury involved the violent conduct of the wife; in another case, a will was set aside on the grounds of fraud and failure of proof; and in another, forgery of a will failed to be established.

Intestacy cases produce much information about marriage customs. It was common for children or other close relatives to dispute the widow's claim to marriage, to try to prevent her gaining administration of the estate. Typically, they would attempt to blacken her name.

Disputes can be found in all levels of church courts. With the exception of the Prerogative Court of Canterbury, they were also dealing with the spiritual discipline of parishioners and their moral behaviour—including matters such as defamation, heresy, marriage and tithes.

8.2 Disputes brought before Church, Equity and Common-Law Courts

Different types of disputes about wills—or the absence of wills—were presented at one of three different types of courts. Church courts mainly dealt with disputes regarding:

The validity of a will
The authenticity of a document produced as a will
The mental capacity of the deceased when making a will
Rival claims to be next of kin in cases of intestacy
The conduct of executors and administrators in distributing the deceased's estate.

Equity courts, the most important of which was the Court of Chancery, dealt with cases relating to the interpretation of wills and matters arising out of their content. The records are held at the National Archives.

Common-law courts—the two largest being the Court of King's Bench and the Court of Common Pleas—dealt with disputes concerning freehold property and other issues that were heard under the common law. These included matters such as the deceased's state of mind (also dealt with by the church courts, under ecclesiastical law). The relevant records are held at the National Archives (see 8.7).

8.2.1 *In which church courts were disputes heard?*

Disputes were heard at all levels of the church courts, from the lowest (archdeaconry courts) to the highest (the Prerogative Courts of Canterbury and York). Sometimes disputes that were normally handled by the lower courts were heard by the Prerogative Courts—especially that of Canterbury, because of its prestige. The records of disputes are usually held in the same archives as the associated wills and administrations.

The records of the Prerogative Courts of Canterbury and York are described in 3.5 and 3.6. Those of the lower courts tend to follow the same arrangement as the Prerogative Court of York—with individual files of case documents and act books, which recorded the daily business of the courts.

The pleadings, including allegations, answers and depositions (the written statements of witnesses), were mainly in English. However, before 1733 the records of the proceedings are in Latin—except for the Interregnum, 1651–1660.

You may find that a case relating to a will or administration commences a generation or more after the grant of probate or administration, especially in disputes over legacies or trusts affecting the children or grandchildren of the deceased. Also, when there is more than one case concerning a will or administration, the parties may be different.

8.3 Disputes in the Prerogative Court of Canterbury

8.3.1 *Online catalogues*

You may find references to disputes over wills or administrations—including Court of Chancery cases—by searching the Catalogue by name. For example, if you search for the name Leonard Potter, you will find 'William Potter and Agnes Potter v Margaret Potter widow: personal estate of Leonard Potter, deceased, of Kendal, Westmorland 1648' given under the Chancery Proceedings document reference C 10/1/88. Finding the phrase 'the estate of' is always a clue to an inheritance dispute.

Allegations in the series PROB 18 (1661–1858) are searchable by name on the Catalogue. Although not all disputes generated allegations, they are easy to search and therefore eliminate as a source. See 8.5.1 for more information.

Descriptions of many of the case files for the various bishop and archdeacon courts are given on Access to Archives (A2A) at *www.nationalarchives.gov.uk/a2a/* (see 3.1.3). Some records are searchable by the name of the testator and/or parties. Others are described in more general terms—for example, for Worcestershire Record Office, within the Diocesan Central Registry records, one file of consistory court papers dating from the eighteenth and nineteenth centuries is described as consisting of 'papers relating to testamentary and miscellaneous causes'.

8.3.2 *Sentences*

If you find references to a 'sentence' in court records, this indicates that the judge delivered a final judgment in a disputed case. Until 1803 the sentences or judgments of the Prerogative Court of Canterbury were filed in the probate registers (PROB 11), and they are now on DocumentsOnline. The published indexes to wills from 1383 to 1700 and those for later wills also contain references to sentences among the alphabetical listings of the registered copy wills (see 3.7.2).

The yearly indexes to wills and administrations (PROB 12) contain not only references to 'by sentence' (often abbreviated to 'by sent') but also annotations next to entries indicating that the judge had granted an 'Interlocutory Decree' (usually abbreviated to 'Int Dec' or simply to 'Decree'). This was less final and commonly used in administration cases, where someone could appear after a judgment was given and prove that they were the true next of kin, as a result of which the original decree would have to be revoked.

8.3.3 *Other PCC sources*

A marginal note against the grant in the PCC probate act books (PROB 8) and administration act books (PROB 6) shows the existence of a judgment

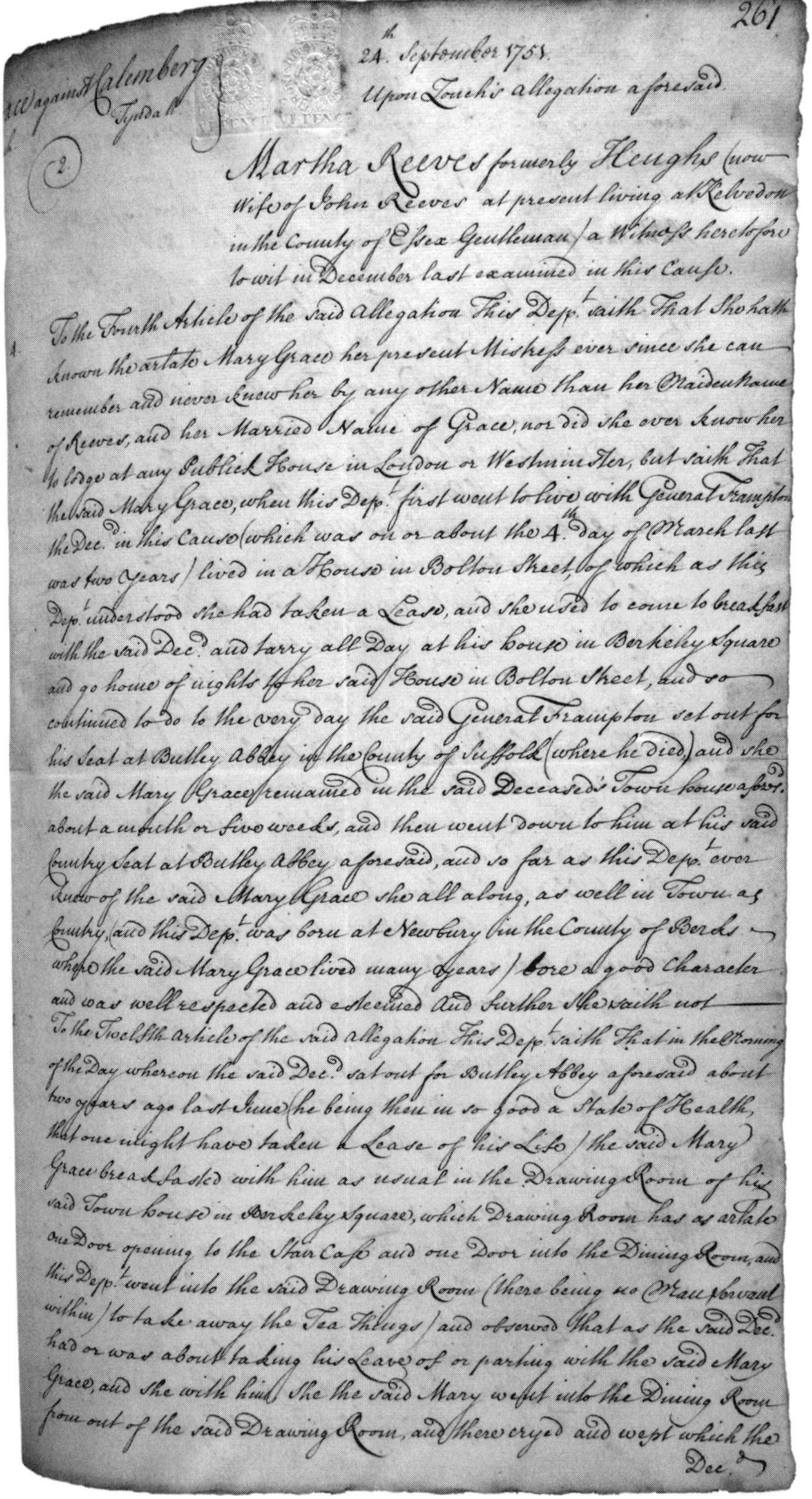

261

W against Halemberg
Tyndall

24th September 1751.
Upon Zouch's allegation aforesaid.

(2)

Martha Reeves formerly Heughs (now Wife of John Reeves at present living at Kelvedon in the County of Essex Gentleman) a Witness heretofore to wit in December last examined in this Cause.

4. To the Fourth Article of the said allegation This Depont. saith That She hath known the articulate Mary Grace her present Mistress ever since she can remember and never knew her by any other Name than her Maiden Name of Reeves, and her Married Name of Grace, nor did she ever know her to lodge at any Publick House in London or Westminster, but saith That the said Mary Grace, when this Depont. first went to live with General Frampton the Deced. in this Cause (which was on or about the 4th day of March last was two Years) lived in a House in Bolton Street, of which as this Depont. understood she had taken a Lease, and she used to come to breakfast with the said Deced. and tarry all Day at his house in Berkeley Square and go home of nights to her said House in Bolton Street, and so continued to do to the very day the said General Frampton set out for his Seat at Butley Abbey in the County of Suffolk (where he died) and she the said Mary Grace remained in the said Deceased's Town house afores. about a month or five weeks, and then went down to him at his said Country Seat at Butley Abbey aforesaid, and so far as this Depont. ever knew of the said Mary Grace she all along, as well in Town as Country, (and this Depont. was born at Newbury in the County of Berks where the said Mary Grace lived many Years) bore a good Character and was well respected and esteemed And further She saith not

To the Twelfth article of the said allegation This Depont. saith That in the Morning of the Day whereon the said Deced. sat out for Butley Abbey aforesaid about two Years ago last June (he being then in so good a State of Health, that one might have taken a Lease of his Life) the said Mary Grace breakfasted with him as usual in the Drawing Room of his said Town house in Berkeley Square, which Drawing Room has as articulate one Door opening to the Stair Case and one Door into the Dining Room, and this Depont. went into the said Drawing Room (there being no Man Servant within) to take away the Tea Things and observed that as the said Deced. had or was about taking his Leave of or parting with the said Mary Grace, and she with him, She the said Mary wept into the Dining Room from out of the said Drawing Room, and there cryed and wept which the

Deced.

Fig. 24 *Deposition of Martha Reeves, a witness in the case of the disputed will of General Frampton in 1751.*
PROB 24/76

or a revoked administration. Death duty register entries may indicate a Court of Chancery case and sometimes give the Chancery action number.

For information relating to inventories/exhibits (PROB 31) and exhibits indexes (PROB 33) see 8.5.1. For information relating to acts of court books (PROB 29) and acts of court (PROB 30) see 8.5.1.

8.4 Signs of a Probate Dispute or Problem

If you find that probate was granted more than a few months after death, the delay may indicate that there was a dispute. However, a more likely reason is that there was a procedural problem with probate. Examples of this type include:

- AUTHENTICITY AND VALIDITY One of the most frequent subjects of dispute was the question of whether a will was genuine. A church court could declare that a will was a forgery, or that it was invalid because the testator was drunk or insane when making the will.
- PROOF OF PEDIGREE Proof of pedigree cases—or 'interest cases', as they were also known—arose when the legal interest of a person purporting to be the next of kin was denied on grounds of illegitimacy or lack of evidence supporting their claim. Such cases could be concerned with determining the right to administer the goods of someone who died without leaving a will. In cases involving a will, the main proceedings would be suspended until questions of pedigree had been resolved.
- INVENTORY AND ACCOUNT Any person having an interest in an estate, whether as a legatee, beneficiary, creditor or next of kin, could ask the court to order the executor or administrator to produce an inventory and account. This happened in the event of failure to pay a legacy or legacies, or where fraud was suspected. The church courts had no power to compel payment of legacies, but an action 'in inventory and account' did enable a beneficiary to determine the amount of assets in the estate before bringing a separate action to enforce payment in the Court of Chancery.
- SUBTRACTION OF LEGACY This is where the intended recipient of a legacy brought proceedings against an executor or administrator because payment of the legacy was either deferred beyond the legal period or refused. The legatee would have first ascertained that there were sufficient assets to cover payment of the legacy—usually by forcing the executor or administrator to produce an inventory and account.

8.5 Contentious and Non-Contentious Business

The contentious (contested) business of the courts—also called the testamentary business—comprised cases that involved disputes over wills or administration. They could involve simply one person against another, or more than one person or party on either side. By contrast non-contentious (non-contested) business involved procedures invoked where probate was not straightforward.

8.5.1 *The litigation process and PCC records*

The main method of bringing an action before a church court was by a *citation* (summons). These documents contain the name of the judge, the plaintiff (sometimes referred to as the *promoter*) and the defendant (sometimes referred to as the *ministrant*), along with the cause of the action and time and place of appearance. The party cited might either appear in person or be represented by a *proctor* (attorney), who was appointed by an instrument called a *proxy*.

The process of litigation was sometimes commenced by the issuing of a *caveat*. This was a formal notice, usually entered by a proctor on behalf of a party that had an interest in the estate of the deceased, restraining the court from making a grant of probate or letters of administration without first giving notice to the issuer of the caveat. The proctor entering the caveat was then 'warned' by the party claiming representation as an executor or administrator—meaning that the proctor had to appear in court if he intended to continue with the case. Both parties were then 'assigned' by order of court to set out their respective claims. At this point the suit or action would commence to try the validity of the will or the right to administration, as appropriate, either under intestacy or with 'will annexed'.

• PLEADINGS The *pleadings*—the written case made by each side in a dispute—are also sometimes referred to as *proceedings*. They consist of a statement of the facts that the parties are relying on and propose to prove, the grounds of the action, and the defence. Both the first plea and subsequent pleas are called *allegations*. These are similar to *bills* and *answers* in the Court of Chancery. Each contains a statement of facts, but unlike Chancery bills and answers they are broken down into *articles*—the facts being arranged under separate heads, often numbered, according to subject matter or the order in which they occurred. In church courts, the defendant's responses to the allegations are called *answers*.

RELEVANT SERIES AT THE NATIONAL ARCHIVES

TNA series	Content and date range	Indexes
PROB 18	Allegations, 1661–1858	Searchable by name on the Catalogue
PROB 25	Answers, 1664–1854	
PROB 28	Cause papers, 1642–1722	
PROB 37	Cause papers, 1783–1858	Searchable by name on the Catalogue

The next stage in the litigation process was the examination of witnesses.

Fig. 25 *The answers of Mary Grace in response to the allegations by Henrietta Calemberg over General Frampton's will.* PROB 25/15

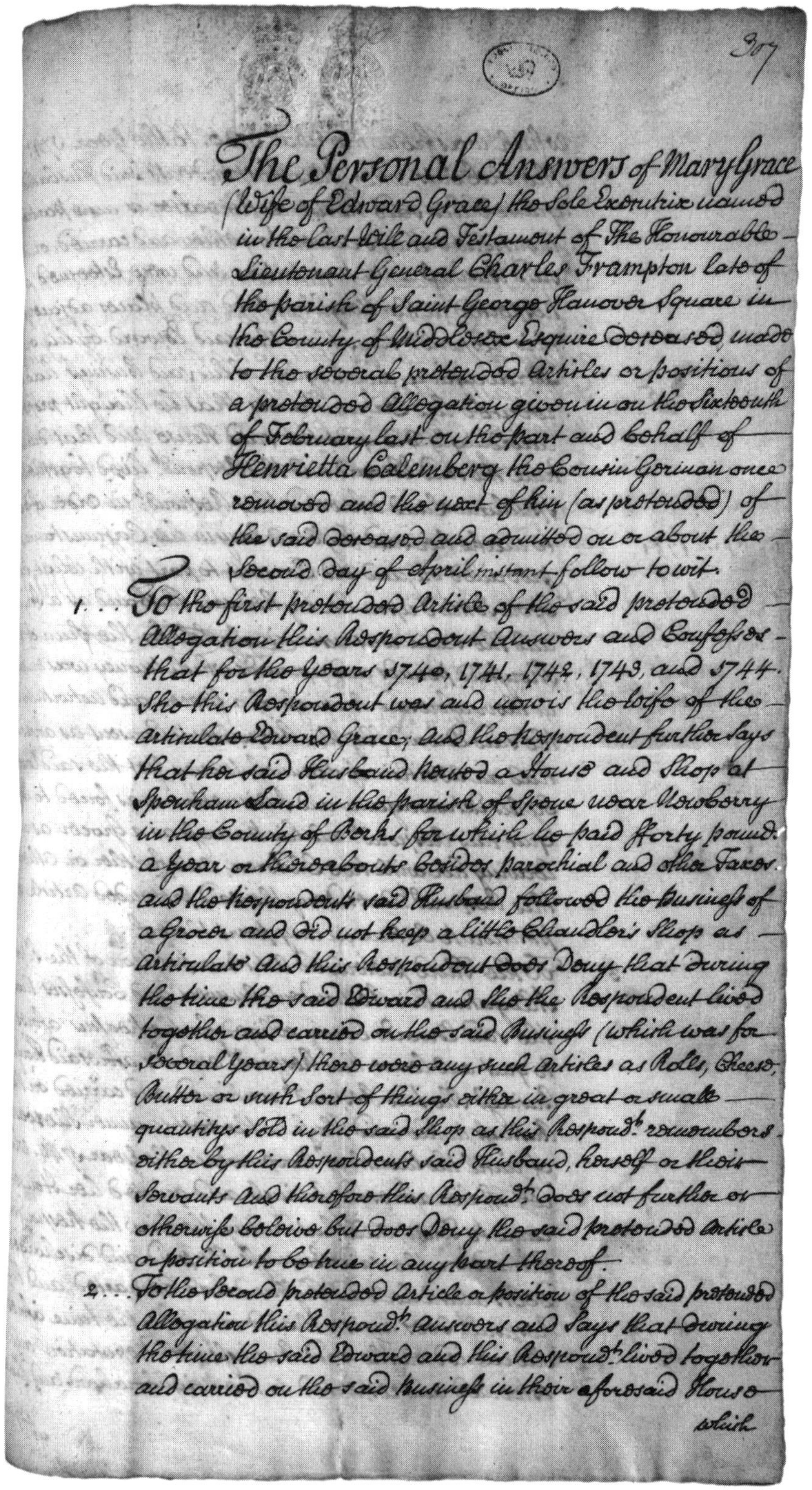

307

The Personal Answers of Mary Grace (Wife of Edward Grace) the Sole Executrix named in the last Will and Testament of The Honourable Lieutenant General Charles Frampton late of the parish of Saint George Hanover Square in the County of Middlesex Esquire deceased made to the several pretended Articles or positions of a pretended Allegation given in on the Sixteenth of February last on the part and behalf of Henrietta Calemberg the Cousin German once removed and the next of kin (as pretended) of the said deceased and admitted on or about the Second day of April instant follow to wit.

1... To the first pretended Article of the said pretended Allegation this Respondent Answers and Confesses that for the years 1740, 1741, 1742, 1743, and 1744 She this Respondent was and now is the wife of the articulate Edward Grace, And the Respondent further says that her said Husband rented a House and Shop at Speenham Land in the parish of Speen near Newberry in the County of Berks for which he paid fforty pounds a year or thereabouts besides parochial and other Taxes and the Respondents said Husband followed the Business of a Grocer and did not keep a little Chandler's Shop as articulate And this Respondent does Deny that during the time the said Edward and She the Respondent lived together and carried on the said Business (which was for several years) there were any such Articles as Rolls, Cheese, Butter or such Sort of things either in great or small quantitys sold in the said Shop as this Respondt. remembers either by this Respondents said Husband, herself or their Servants And therefore this Respondt. does not further or otherwise believe but does Deny the said pretended Article or position to be true in any part thereof.

2... To the Second pretended Article or position of the said pretended Allegation this Respondt. answers and Says that during the time the said Edward and this Respondt. lived together and carried on the said Business in their aforesaid House which

They were examined on written interrogatories—a series of questions submitted by the proctors, regarding any articles in an allegation that contained facts within their knowledge. (Confusingly, these interrogatories were also sometimes referred to as 'articles'.)

Either the witnesses were brought to London to be examined or, if it was inconvenient for them to attend, they were examined by commission—that is, a suitable person was commissioned to question them—near their place of residence. Witness statements taken in London were known as town depositions, those taken outside London as country depositions.

The town depositions were taken in private by examiners (before 1691 by a deputy registrar) of the court. The relevant allegation was delivered to the examiner, who after studying the document devised questions based on each article of the allegation, which were then put to the witnesses.

The cross-examination, a series of questions put to the witnesses of the opposing side, was conducted by interrogatories. The witness was given a copy of the interrogatories, after they were sworn, so that he or she could study them before being examined.

The deponents (witnesses) were required to give their age, occupation, place of residence, and sometimes former places of residence and place of birth. Ages given are often imprecise (a common problem for genealogists).

TOWN DEPOSITIONS

TNA series	Date range	Indexes and search facilities
PROB 24	1657–1809	Paper catalogue index to deceased and to details of deceased and parties given (such details as yet not included in the Catalogue).
PROB 26	1809–58	Indexed by name of testator or intestate, plaintiff and parties to dispute.
PROB 37	1810–58	See below.

COUNTRY DEPOSITIONS

TNA series	Date range	Indexes and search facilities
PROB 26	1826–58	Indexed by name of testator or intestate, plaintiff and parties to dispute.
PROB 28	1660–*c.*1722	Indexed by name of testator or intestate, plaintiff and parties to dispute.
PROB 31	1722–*c.*1780	See below.
PROB 37	1783–1858	See below.

• EXHIBITS These are documents produced in court as evidence. The range of exhibits is illustrated by PROB 31, which covers the years 1722 to 1858. These include inventories, declarations in lieu of inventory (which can be as detailed as inventories in listing the effects of the deceased), and accounts of executors and administrators. In addition, there are various copies of wills, including both 'authentic' and 'bogus' wills. The exhibits also include certificates of burial from parish registers, private diaries, account books, newspapers including death announcements, and bibles.

TNA series	Date range
PROB 31	1722–1858
PROB 32	1666–1717
PROB 35	1529–86
PROB 36	1662–1720
PROB 37	1783–1858
PROB 49	1686–1849

All of the above series are searchable by name on the Catalogue with the exception of PROB 35.

If you find information in the series PROB 31 this establishes that there were exhibits in a case. The Catalogue only lists inventories from this series so you should need also to also check the indexes to this series in PROB 33, either in hard-copy form or on microfilm.

• THE HEARING All the court papers in a case were delivered to the judge. The hearings took place in open court, and proceedings were opened by the counsel on both sides stating the points of law and fact on which they were basing their arguments. The evidence was then read in court, unless the judge indicated that he had already read it, though certain passages might be read again for clarification.

The case was then discussed and argued by counsel. Finally, the judgment was given by the judge in open court, including the reasons for the decision. The question of costs, claimed by the successful side in order to recover the amount spent on fighting the case, was mainly at the discretion of the judge. Reasons for granting or refusing costs were given when the judgment was delivered.

• COURT BOOKS AND ACTS OF COURT The progress of a case can be traced through court books and similar records. These include the orders of the judge and petitions of the parties (requesting, for example, that a particular witness be examined). Up to 1733, apart from 1651–60, during the Interregnum, the records are in Latin. At the National Archives these records are in two series: acts of court books (PROB 29) and bundled acts of court documents (PROB 30). These provide the only evidence relating to all disputed cases.

Some of the entries will resemble disputed cases, but are in fact *Proofs in Solemn Form*—wills that were proved by witnesses (unlike the vast majority of wills, which are proved in *Common Form*). Nuncupative (oral) wills were often proved in this way, because objections were frequently anticipated. This type of process also generated records similar to those you would normally find in a disputed case.

TNA series	Content and date range	Indexes
PROB 29	Acts of court books, 1536–1819	
PROB 30	Acts of court, 1740–1858	Many of the volumes are internally indexed.

8.5.2 *Other PCC record series relating to disputes*

There are a number of other series of PCC records that, although they generally give less information than the series already described, can fill gaps in the records of a case and supply details regarding the case's progress:

- Caveat books 1666–1858 (PROB 40) This series contains a sample of the entry books in which caveats were recorded. They are all internally indexed by the name of the deceased. The first three volumes (1666, 1774 and 1776) give the name of the person entering the caveat, normally the plaintiff in the case. Thereafter the caveats are entered under the name John Thomas—a name (among a few others) often used in legal documents up to the nineteenth century, though more typically for fictitious disputes invented as a legal contrivance in order to transfer freehold land from one person to another.

- Court caveat books 1678–1857 (PROB 41) These record the next step after the entry of the caveat, the summoning of the party into court. These volumes are useful in covering for the paucity of caveat books (see above) and gaps in the act of court books (PROB 29).

- Citatory mandates 1666–1857 (PROB 48) This series consists of files and bundles of citatory mandates summoning the parties and witnesses to attend court. Often a brief outline of a case is given—usefully filling gaps in the act of court books (PROB 29).

- Assignations 1665–1858 (PROB 43) As well as assignation books, PROB 43 includes draft acts. The assignation books contain entries noting appointments for court hearings and give a brief summary of the proceedings in each case. The draft acts, which are usually on a single sheet of parchment, also provide a brief summary of the proceedings.

- Muniment books 1611–1858 (PROB 16) These books contain the registration of some exhibits produced in court and, before the nineteenth century, orders and decrees.

- Instruments from other courts, Commonwealth to George III (PROB 44) These include legal-process documents relating to Prerogative Court of Canterbury cases referred to the High Court of Delegates, plus a few injunctions from the common-law courts stopping proceedings in the PCC deemed prejudicial.

- Supplementary wills, Series II 1623–1857 (PROB 22) This series contains copy wills that were made for exhibiting in other courts.

8.6 Appeals

The entering of an appeal automatically suspended the execution of the final judgment. There could be several levels of appeal, each one being referred to a higher court. There were different appeal paths for courts under the jurisdiction of the two Prerogative Courts. A case could start in an archdeacon's court, be appealed to the bishop's diocesan court, and then be appealed to the relevant archbishop's court. A case could be referred to the Court of Arches for the province of Canterbury, or the Chancery Court (not be confused with the non-ecclesiastical Court of Chancery in Westminster) for the province of York. Above them was the High Court of Delegates.

8.6.1 *Court of Arches and equivalent courts*

The records of the Court of Arches are held by Lambeth Palace Library. For details of these records, consult *Index to the cases in the records of the Court of Arches at Lambeth Palace Library 1660–1913* (British Record Society, Index Library, Vol. 85, 1972). The records of the Chancery Court for the province of York (see 8.9) are held at the Borthwick Institute of Historical Research.

At one time the provinces of Canterbury and York each had a Court of Audience, the status of which was similar to that of the Court of Arches. In 1660, the Court of Audience for the province of Canterbury merged with the Court of Arches. The records for the province of Canterbury are held by Lambeth Palace Library, those for the province of York by the Borthwick Institute. Few pre-1660 records survive for either of these courts.

8.6.2 *Papal Court in Rome*

Until 1533 the final appeal from church courts in England and Wales was to the Papal Court in Rome. There are published calendars giving translations of the Papal Registers in: *Calendar of Entries in the Papal Registers to Great Britain and Ireland: Papal Letters*, 1198 to 1492 (14 volumes, Public Record Office, 1893 to 1960) and 1492-1521 (4 volumes, Irish Manuscripts Commission, 1978–2005). The original documents are held by the Vatican Archives, but copies can be seen at the National Archives.

8.6.3 *High Court of Delegates*

The High Court of Delegates developed from 1533 to take over the appeal function from the Papal Court (and from 1834 that of the Judicial Committee of the Privy Council). The delegates consisted of a number of judges, from different types of court, appointed by the Lord Chancellor.

TNA series	Content	Date range
DEL 1	Processes (copies of the proceedings) in the lower courts	1609–1834
DEL 2	Miscellaneous papers, including country depositions	c.1600–1834
DEL 3	Personal answers and London depositions	1564–1735
DEL 4	Act books	1539–1818
DEL 5	Sentences	1585–1802
DEL 7	Bound volumes of printed appeal cases (these copy documents, produced by the court from which appeal was made, provide a summary of the proceedings in the lower court)	1796–1834

There is a parliamentary paper (Sessional Papers, House of Commons, 1867–8, 199) listing all the appeals taken to the High Court of Delegates between 1533 and 1832. This is available under the reference DEL 11/11 and can also be consulted in the reference library. It does not include document references, but is a useful point of departure—although many of the DEL series lists give the names of the parties and are searchable on the Catalogue.

A detailed analysis of the court's role and records is contained in G. I. O. Duncan's *High Court of Delegates* (Cambridge University Press, 1971).

8.6.4 *Court of High Commission*

In addition to the High Court of Delegates, until 1641 there was another ecclesiastical tribunal, called the Court of High Commission. This operated in the provinces of Canterbury and York and in the dioceses. In the province of York it was established in 1561. As with the High Court of Delegates, there was no right of appeal from the decision of the court, but a Commission of Review could be applied for.

At the National Archives, among State Papers, Domestic, Charles I (SP 16) there is a short run of minute books of the High Commission for Ecclesiastical Causes for Canterbury (1634–6 and 1641). These calendars group together all the cases for a period, but none of them concern wills or administrations. Along with some other records among the State Papers, these are the only records pertaining to the High Commission for Ecclesiastical Causes for Canterbury to have survived the destruction ordered by Parliament during the English Civil War.

High Commission records for York are held by the Borthwick Institute. There are also a number of surviving records for the High Commission courts of the dioceses, held by the relevant local archives, some of which have been transcribed and published.

8.6.5 *Commissions of Review*

Although there was no appeal against a decision of the High Court of Delegates, very occasionally, if there was an error in law or fact, a petition could be made to the king or queen in council asking for the matter to be heard before judges under an instrument known as a Commission of

Review. The petition was usually heard by the Lord Chancellor. Some of these documents survive among the records of the High Court of Delegates. In addition, petitions can be found among the State Papers (SP) and Privy Council (PC) records at the National Archives.

8.6.6 *Records of the Judicial Committee of the Privy Council, 1834–70*

PCAP 1 contains processes (copies of proceedings) in the lower courts from 1834 to 1870, while PCAP 3 consists of printed appeal cases for the same period. PCAP 3 contains copies of many of the documents in PCAP 1 and, additionally, the case for both sides. References to PCAP 3 are provided in the series list and index for PCAP 1. Both series are searchable by the names of the parties and by testator or intestate. These are searchable by name on the Catalogue.

8.7 Disputes in Courts of Equity and Common Law

Church courts dealt mostly with the validity of wills. Consequently disputes over the interpretation of a will often went to the courts of equity—typically to the Court of Chancery (especially from the eighteenth century), but also to the equity side of the Court of Exchequer. Moreover, equity courts were attractive to litigants because the judges were obliged to reach their judgments on the basis of 'fairness', and church courts had no real powers to call in the assets of an estate.

The majority of actions in the courts of equity related to claims for payment of legacies and the fulfilment of other provisions of wills—including complicated cases involving trusts or charitable bequests and actions brought to secure the assets of the deceased. Detailed studies of the equity courts are in Henry Horwitz's books *Chancery Equity Records and Proceedings 1600–1800* (PRO, 1998) and *Exchequer Equity Records and Proceedings 1649–1841* (PRO, 2001). Research guides about these records are on the National Archives website.

All disputed cases regarding issues of law ('law' is often used as shorthand for the unwritten common law of England) that concerned freehold property or questions such as whether the testator was of sound mind were heard by the common-law courts—namely the King's Bench, the Court of Common Pleas and the common-law side of the Court of Exchequer (sometimes referred to as the Exchequer of Pleas). Such common-law cases were also heard outside London, in the assizes courts of the provincial towns of England and Wales. There were also the courts of the Palatinates of Chester, Durham and Lancaster and the Duchy of Lancaster, which may need searching for disputes over wills and administrations, too. The relevant records are mostly held by the National Archives.

Although an action over the validity of a will bequeathing personal property could be heard by a church court, it might be necessary to bring an action in Chancery to gain an order authorizing the hearing in a common-law court to decide whether, for example, the testator was of unsound mind. As a result, you may find the Prerogative Court of Canterbury, the Court of Chancery and the Court of King's Bench all hearing cases involving the same will or estate. Also, a frequent reason why more than one court would be involved was that only the common-law courts were able to hear disputes regarding freehold property (often referred to as cases of *ejectment*).

8.7.1 *Relevant records*

• COURT OF CHANCERY / CHANCERY DIVISION The records of the Court of Chancery are mostly in English. They are also well indexed and contain much family, local and social history detail, especially among the depositions (witness statements). Some of the series of pleadings can be searched by name of plaintiff or defendant on the Catalogue. The phrase 'the estate of' is always a clue to an inheritance dispute. The Equity Proceedings Database (*www.nationalarchives.gov.uk/equity/*) includes some of the pleadings in the Chancery series C 6, dating from 1606 to 1722. It is searchable by name (including that of the testator in cases involving a will), places, and subject of dispute. On British Origins there is an index to lawsuits in the Court of Chancery concerning inheritance of money or real estate from 1574 to 1714. See *www.britishorigins.com/*.

Indexes arranged by name of plaintiff are available on the open shelves in the reading rooms at the National Archives, including indexes to decrees and orders (C 33 and J 15). Also at the National Archives there are unpublished alphabetical indexes, mostly compiled by P. W. Coldham, to the pleadings in the personal-estate cases in C 5 to C 8 and in C 10 (part of the Six Clerks Series), covering the period 1613–1714. These indexes are particularly useful because they are arranged by name of the deceased.

The masters' reports and certificates in C 38 for 1544–1875 and J 57 for 1876–1962 are worth mentioning as they often provide a rich source of information, especially for administration of estates, which was the responsibility of the masters. Judges frequently referred matters to masters —legally qualified officers of the court, subordinate to the judges—for further investigation, and their reports were often very detailed.

Many wills were deposited in Chancery as exhibits and are in the series C 103 to C 114. The names are searchable on the Catalogue.

Exchequer depositions by commission in E 134 are searchable by names of parties and name of the deceased on the Catalogue. The Bernau index held by the Society of Genealogists is an additional source for names of deponents in some of the Chancery and Exchequer depositions series.

• TREASURY SOLICITOR PAPERS A number of cases relating to wills, especially Chancery cases, were referred to the Treasury Solicitor (the government lawyer). Often the documents are merely court copies, but sometimes they include law officers' opinions. However, there is a straightforward route to these records, as they can be searched by names of parties and name of testator on the Catalogue. Series searchable in this way are TS 11 (1584–1858), which is an especially good source, TS 18 (1517–1953) and TS 27 (1706–1996).

• COMMON-LAW RECORDS Compared with the records of the courts of equity, the common-law records are formulaic. Also, a lot of the records were destroyed and up to 1733, apart from the Interregnum (1651–60), they are all written in Latin. For the detail of cases to 1875, consult the relevant plea rolls (King's Bench in KB 122, Common Pleas in CP 40, and Exchequer in E 13).

MAIN RECORD SERIES FOR WILL AND INTESTATE DISPUTES IN EQUITY AND COMMON-LAW COURTS

Name(s) of court	Decrees and orders (decisions)	Pleas/ pleadings	Affidavits	Depositions	Exhibits
Court of Chancery Chancery Division	C 33 (1544–1875) J 15 (1876–1954)	C 1–C 16 (c.1386–1875) J 54 (1876–1945)	C 31 (1611–1875) J 4 (1876–1945)	C 21 (Country) (1558–1649) C 22 (Country) (1649–1714) C 24 (Town) (1534–1867) J 17 (1880–1925, 1960–91)	C 103–C 114 (1180–1859) C 171 (1350–c.1850) J 90 (1700–1953)
Court of Exchequer, equity side (King's Remembrancer)	E 123–E 131 (1559–1841)	E 112 (1558–1841)	E 207 (to 1774)	E 133 Barons (Town) (1558–1841) E 134 Commission (Country) (1558–1841)	E 140 (1319–1842) E 219 (1625–1841)
Court of King's/ Queen's Bench King's/Queen's Bench Division	KB 122 (1702/3–1875) KB 168 (1699–1875) J 168 (1879–1937)	KB 122 (1702/3–1875) J 55 (1875–80) J 54 (1880–1945, 1979–1980)	KB 101 (1734–1874) J 4 (1881–95)	KB 144 (1792–1875) J 16 (1876–80)	
Court of Common Pleas/Common Pleas Division	CP 40 (1273–1875)	CP 40 (1273–1875) J 55 (1875–80)	CP 3 (1704–1876)	CP 22 (1831–79)	
Court of Exchequer, common-law side (Exchequer of Pleas)/ Exchequer Division	E 13 (1236–1875)	E 13 (1236–1875) J 55 (1875–80)	E 1 (1830–81)	E 20 (1853–67) J 16 (1871–80)	

8.8 Additional Sources for Research

Disputes over wills may also appear in a variety of other sources. Some key areas are outlined below.

8.8.1 *Newspapers*

Newspaper reports of trials usually provide a useful account of the proceedings, certainly from the eighteenth century onwards. You can search *The Times* online, plus the yearly indexes to *The Times* known as Palmer's (1790–1905) at the National Archives and many reference libraries. The online version of the newspaper has the advantage of enabling you to conduct a search easily when you are not sure of the date of a trial.

Newspaper reports are especially important for the period since 1858, when the Court of Probate was formed, as so few of the records are preserved at the National Archives (see 2.1).

8.8.2 *Law reports*

Some cases generated law reports, especially where they gave rise to legal precedents or new points of law. Before 1866 a high percentage of cases were reported; but from 1866, when law reporting became more structured, the percentage declined. Because law reports tend to be more concerned with legal points than with the facts surrounding a case, you need to treat details contained in them with caution, as they were often reported inaccurately and the spelling of names can be inconsistent. Where possible, you should therefore compare the information given in the reports with surviving original records. All the courts that heard will or intestate disputes generated law reports—including the church courts, though mainly those for London.

Examples of law reports that covered Prerogative Court of Canterbury cases are *Phillimore Ecclesiastical*, *Robertson Ecclesiastical* and *Haggard Ecclesiastical*. Known collectively as the *English Reports*, they are usually available in law libraries in that form. One significant series is the *Lee Reports* for 1752–8, which are especially valuable—not only because they were written by the presiding judge, but also because they are concerned with the facts of the cases, report witness depositions in much detail, and provide the judge's full reasons for his judgments. They are included in *English Law Reports 1220–1865* (see below) in electronic form; and in *British Trials 1660–1900* (Chadwyck-Healy) on microfiche, a copy of which can be viewed at the National Archives. The latter mainly consists of contemporary pamphlet accounts of criminal cases but, as well as the *Lee Reports*, it includes a small collection of reports on equity and common-law disputes over wills, which record in detail what was said in court by counsel and witnesses—something that is rarely found in other sources.

You can search for these and other publications on Google Books (*http://books.google.co.uk/*) which provides a full text search of publications. If the book is out of copyright, or the publisher has given permission, you can see a preview and in some cases the entire text.

• LAW REPORTS HELD AT THE NATIONAL ARCHIVES The National Archives holds *English Reports 1220–1865* (Juta Hart), which can be viewed on any of the computers in the National Archives reading rooms, and *Electronic Law Reports 1866–2004* (Justis) which are searchable on CD-ROM. *English Reports 1220–1865* is especially useful as it not only enables searches by names of parties but also provides a keyword-search facility covering the whole text of each report, so you can search for other people involved in a case, including the testator or intestate. *Electronic Law Reports 1866–2004* searches by names of parties and the subject matter of the dispute. Both sources enable you to conduct searches for very specific types of cases—for example, if you are interested in disputes that focused on the type of ink used by the testator in writing his or her will, you can use the keywords 'will' and 'ink' and enter a date range.

8.8.3 *Family papers*

Although most researchers seem to come across disputed cases almost by chance, sometimes family papers that they or a relative hold will contain legal documents and/or documents relating to a case. Such documents generally contain the names of the parties, a date and the name of the court—making it possible for you to locate other documents in the relevant archive. In addition, you may find that family papers have been deposited in local archives or libraries. The National Register of Archives database (*www.nationalarchives.gov.uk/nra*) is the best place to search for the location of private papers, some of which are also catalogued on the Access to Archives (A2A) database.

8.9 Records of the Courts of York

The records relating to the various courts of York are held by the Borthwick Institute. They fall into two categories:

- Court books (the equivalent of the Prerogative Court of Canterbury acts of court books), containing the formal proceedings and cause papers, which bring together the pleadings of both parties.
- Similar individual documents (at present only partly indexed).

Unlike the records of the PCC, those of the Prerogative Court of York encompass all types of church–court disputes. Details of their arrangement and references can be found on the Borthwick Institute's website. A brief summary of the records is given below:

• CAUSE PAPERS (EARLY FOURTEENTH TO TWENTIETH CENTURY) These include a separate collection of cause papers for the Court of High Commission dating from the late sixteenth to the early seventeenth century. A project to catalogue the files of cause papers has begun. Two volumes have been indexed: *Ecclesiastical Cause Papers at York 1301–1399* by D. M. Smith (Borthwick Text and Calendar 14, 1988) and *Ecclesiastical Cause Papers at York: Files Transmitted on Appeal 1500–1883* by W. J. Sheils (Borthwick Text and Calendar 9, 1983).

• COURT BOOKS
Court of High Commission 1562–1641.
Consistory Court 1417–1911.
Chancery Court and Court of Audience 1525–1956.
Exchequer Court and Prerogative Court 1548–1857.

• DEPOSITION BOOK 1676–8 This is the only PCY deposition book known to have survived.

• ABSTRACT BOOKS 1634–1948 These books, which cover all courts, are similar to court books.

• CAVEAT BOOKS 1521–1859 These include notes of caveats, including those relating to probate matters.

• CITATIONS Citation books 1611–92 (these generally cover all courts).
Citations 1595–1857 (these bundles derive from the Consistory, Chancery, Exchequer and Prerogative courts).
Citation notes (seventeenth to nineteenth centuries).

• COMMISSION BOOKS 1611–83 These record commissions issued to clergy out of all PCY courts (though mainly the Exchequer and Prerogative courts). They include commissions issued for granting probate and administration, as well as those issued for swearing executors, administrators and witnesses.

8.10 Litigation after 1858

From 1858 actions were brought before the new Court of Probate, which in 1873 became part of the Probate, Divorce, and Admiralty Division of the High Court. In 1970 this division was renamed the Family Division. Appeals were made to the House of Lords, whose records are held by the House of Lords Record Office.

From 1858 onwards, very few records relating to contentious probate cases are preserved at the National Archives—which is why newspaper reports and law reports are so valuable post 1858. Only 7 per cent of the case files were kept, in J 121, for the years 1858–1960. There is also a small sample of exhibits in J 165, which covers the years 1854–1934. Both of these series are searchable on the Catalogue by names of parties and name of testator. There is also a small run of minute books, covering the years 1858–66, in the series J 169. These include registrars' notes that provide details such as dates of the filing of documents, the reading of affidavits and wills, grants of administrations and the stopping of proceedings.

In the cause books in J 168, there are some entries regarding Probate

Division cases. These commence in 1876 and end in 1937, and are arranged by initial letter of name of plaintiff. However, the few entries for the Probate Division tend to give the names of parties and representatives and date of appearance only, with no judgment details.

The Court of Chancery and, from 1876, the Chancery Division of the newly created Supreme Court continued to hear cases concerning the interpretation of wills. You will find the decrees and orders for the Chancery Division (1876–1955) in J 15 and pleadings (1876–1942) in J 54. The reports and certificates of the Supreme Court masters (see 8.7.1) from 1876 to 1962 are in J 57. For other series, see 8.7.1. There is also a small sample of case files, mainly from 1968, in J 83 and J 84. Many of these files are still closed, but they are searchable on the Catalogue. For requests to see files that have not yet been transferred to the National Archives, contact the Head of Records Management Services and Departmental Records Officer at the Ministry of Justice.

8.11 Criminal Trials for Fraud over Wills and Administrations

Sometimes there was sufficient evidence to bring a criminal prosecution for fraud over wills and administrations. Such cases can be found among the records of the assize courts, the Old Bailey (Central Criminal Court) and the criminal side of the Court of King's Bench. Many examples of such trials, especially those concerning wills and administrations of Royal Navy seamen, can be found among the published Old Bailey session papers, which run from 1674 to 1913. These often give a verbatim account of what was said in court.

The records of the assize courts are mainly held by the National Archives—except for the Old Bailey records up to 1834, which are held by the Corporation of London Records Office and the London Metropolitan Archives.

Published accounts of the proceedings of the Old Bailey are available online for the period from 1674 to 1913 on *www.oldbaileyonline.org*. The text of the entries is fully searchable.

8.12 Non-Contentious Business

Non-contentious (non-contested) business was where there was no dispute but there was some complication or variation in the process of probate or administration. If you find there was a long interval between the dates of death and probate, then that may have been because of one of the circumstances described below.

• Special or limited grants of probate A grant of probate normally gives the testator powers to deal with the whole estate. But sometimes, for various reasons, a grant of probate or administration is limited to a particular part of the deceased's estate or to a specified period of time (see also 4.7).

- Lost or mislaid will When an original will was lost or mislaid but a true copy had been made, the executor might receive a limited grant of probate, conditional on either the original or an authentic copy being brought into the registry. Under certain circumstances, from the nineteenth century, the executor had to advertise for recovery of the lost will, usually in two newspapers. If the will was lost outside London, its loss was advertised in a local newspaper; if it was lost in London, then the advertisement had to be placed in *The Times* and one other London paper.
- Limited probate of an authentic copy of a will Similar to the above. When the executor could not obtain the original will but an authentic copy was available, probate was limited until the appearance of the original will.
- Probate of a married woman's will Until 1882 a married woman —in legal terminology referred to as a 'feme covert'—could only bequeath part of her goods. A grant of probate might therefore be made to her husband, limited to what she could legally dispose of.
- Probate limited to 'assign a term' This happened when a testator held all his goods in one diocese except for the lease of a property in another diocese for a term of years. In these circumstances probate was normally granted in the court of the diocese, and the Prerogative Court would assign a person to take over the lease.
- Probate limited to goods in Great Britain When someone left goods both at home and abroad, the Prerogative Courts would deal only with the goods in Great Britain. Any part of the estate abroad would be dealt with in the foreign country.
- Double probates These are separate grants made to two or more executors who were unable to apply for probate together—for example, because one of them was abroad.

8.12.1 *The National Archives' records relating to non-contentious business*

You will find that many of the entries in PROB 29 (acts of court books) and PROB 30 (acts of court) are concerned with non-contentious business, providing an account of the formal proceedings leading to the final order of the court.

Renunciations of rights of executors and next of kin can be found among the proxy records (see 8.13).

8.13 Children and the Appointment of Guardians

The church courts had the power to appoint guardians for orphaned minors. Sometimes the term used was 'curator' or 'tutor', instead of 'guardian'. A *tutor* was a guardian of a minor—under the age of 15 for a boy and 13 for a girl. A *curator* was a guardian for boys over the age of 14 and under 21, or for girls over 12 and under 21. Additionally, the term *tuition* is used in the Prerogative Court of York—but not in the Prerogative Court of Canterbury—to describe the testamentary guardianship of minors.

In the Prerogative Court of Canterbury a minor could choose his or her guardian from the age of seven. Regarding legacies left to children, many 'subtraction of legacy' cases were brought by minors. At the National Archives, there are many records of appointment of guardians. These are among the records of proxies—documents appointing proctors to act on behalf of parties (see 8.5.1)—in PROB 19 for the years 1674–1714, PROB 36/17–21 for 1654–1713, and PROB 31 (see 8.5.1) for 1722–1858.

The Court of Chancery also dealt with guardianship matters. To find documents relating to guardianship, you may therefore also need to search the Court of Chancery records (see 8.7.1).

8.14 Dormant Funds or Money in Chancery

There is a popular story handed down within many families that a large unclaimed pot of money has been gathering interest for generations because one or more legatees entitled to inherit it could not be found.

Such monies are variously referred to as dormant funds, funds in court, estates in chancery, or money in chancery. Where necessary, the central courts of law would take responsibility for money and property on behalf of people who could not be traced, or could not look after it themselves due to a disability or for other reasons. The traditional court for this role was the Court of Chancery, though the Court of Exchequer and the King's/Queen's Bench were also sometimes involved.

The normal practice was to sell the property and for the Crown to administer the residue, which was lodged with the appropriate court. Provided you have the necessary documentary evidence to prove your descent from the individual concerned, it is possible to claim this money back. After a fixed period of inactivity (set by the legislation under which the residue is lodged), accounts are classed as dormant funds and no longer attract interest. Most often, their value is less than £150.

8.14.1 Finding a dormant fund

The Offices of Court Funds, Official Solicitor and Public Trustee (*www.officialsolicitor.gov.uk*)—which receives, deals with and disposes of funds as directed by the civil courts of England and Wales—has an index to dormant funds in England and Wales. This can be consulted in person or by writing to the Offices of Court Funds, Official Solicitor and Public Trustee. If you write, you should provide as much detail about the case as possible. They request that no original documents, such as birth, marriage or death certificates, are sent. At this stage, photocopies are acceptable.

You will be notified of the result of the search, but should be aware that:

Records concerning dormant funds are confidential and they will not be disclosed to anyone who cannot produce evidence of beneficial interest

Fees are payable—consequently you are strongly advised to obtain details of these before initiating an investigation, as it is always possible that the value of the funds may turn out to be less than the fees charged

The Offices of Court Funds, Official Solicitor and Public Trustee does not hold any original court documents

The Offices of Court Funds, Official Solicitor and Public Trustee cannot answer any questions regarding entitlement by descent or relationship, or about legal procedures or selection of legal advisors.

8.14.2 *Proving a line of descent*

If you find a relevant entry in the dormant funds index, before any money is paid out you will have to prove to the satisfaction of the originating court that you are related to the individual whose money is lodged with it. The main sources for proving descent are the same as those used when tracing a family tree, namely:

Birth, marriage and death registers
Wills, grants of probate and letters of administration
Census returns
Orders of the High Court.

8.15 Case Studies

8.15.1 *A forged will disputed in the Prerogative Court of Canterbury*

The dispute surrounding the will of the Hon. Lieutenant General Charles Frampton was typical of many that occupied the sittings of the church courts, even if the will itself was not. The will that was produced after the general's death in September 1749 had only one beneficiary: Mary Grace, Frampton's housekeeper, who had supposedly found it pinned inside a book in a bureau at his home in Berkeley Square. Grace's claim was opposed by Frampton's cousin and next of kin, Henrietta Calemberg, who applied for administration of the estate. The case was brought before the Prerogative Court of Canterbury from whose records the following story emerges. Grace had first met and befriended the general in 1743 while he was staying at his country house in Newbury, Berkshire. She had then followed him back to London, moving into lodgings found by him and taking a position in his household. The supposedly close bond of friendship that existed between the pair was evidenced by her assertion that they regularly dined together.

Both sides produced numerous witnesses who gave depositions (sworn statements) in answer to prepared numbered questions called interrogatories.

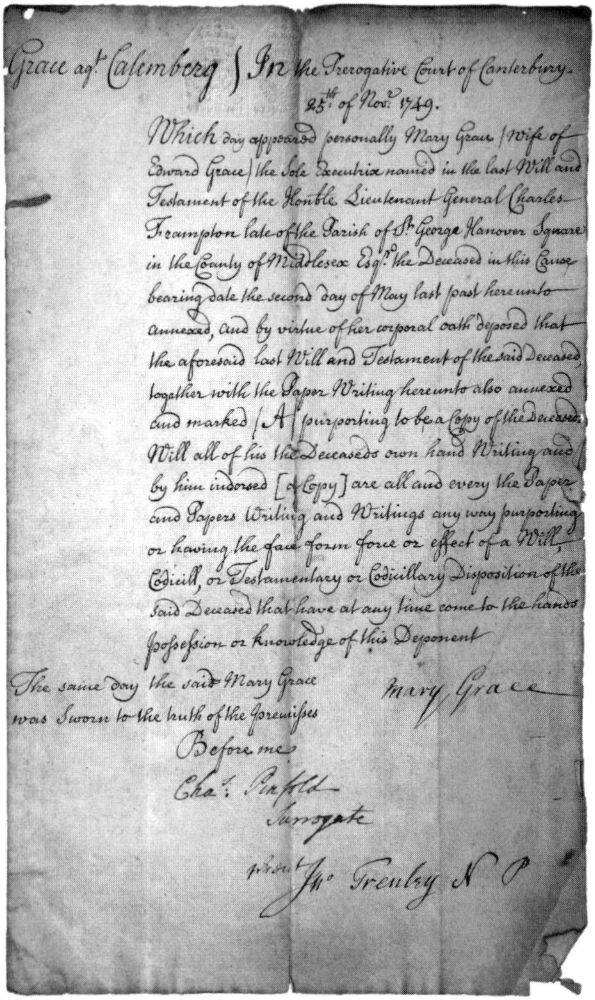
Grace agt. Calemberg } In the Prerogative Court of Canterbury.
25th of Novr. 1749.
Which day appeared personally Mary Grace (Wife of Edward Grace) the Sole Executrix named in the last Will and Testament of the Honble Lieutenant General Charles Frampton late of the Parish of St. George Hanover Square in the County of Middlesex Esqr. the Deceased in this Cause bearing date the second day of May last past hereunto annexed, and by virtue of her corporal oath deposed that the aforesaid last Will and Testament of the said Deceased together with the Paper Writing hereunto also annexed and marked (A) purporting to be a Copy of the Deceased's Will all of his the Deceaseds own hand Writing and by him indorsed [a Copy] are all and every the Paper and Papers Writing and Writings any way purporting or having the face form force or effect of a Will, Codicill, or Testamentary or Codicillary Disposition of the said Deceased that have at any time come to the hands possession or knowledge of this Deponent

The same day the said Mary Grace was Sworn to the truth of the Premisses
Before me
Chas. Pinfold
Surrogate

Mary Grace

present Jno. Trenley N P

Fig. 26 *An accompanying statement from 1749 to a will that purported to be Frampton's.* PROB 31/315

Some of the statements from those supporting Calemberg were clearly designed to give a bad impression of Grace's character. One witness, for example, described her as a 'woman of ill repute' well known to the army officers stationed at Newbury. Similarly, a servant at Frampton's country house recalled an occasion on which he and the other servants had been instructed not to take in any of Grace's letters or parcels or to let her in. A letter from her was refused and she was denied admittance but forced her way in. In the struggle in getting past the door she was hurt.

In contrast, witnesses for Grace described her in a far more favourable light: 'esteemed at Newberry', she apparently 'bore a good character, and was not extravagant but behaved with prudence … [paying] many debts after her husband left her'. One witness for Grace, Martha Reeves, who had previously been employed by Frampton, stated that Grace used to be 'much with' the general. According to her testimony Grace had breakfasted with him shortly before he died. Grace had apparently broken down in tears at the end of the meal as Frampton prepared to leave for Newbury. Asked the reason for her distress she had apparently replied 'To think you are going so far.' To this Reeves claimed the general had replied 'You have no need to cry. I have taken care of you. I have settled my affairs and provided for you to your satisfaction.' By this Reeves stated that she understood him to mean his will (PROB 24/76, f. 261).

The judge, Sir George Lee, gave his judgment on 9 May 1752. He stated that the will appeared not to be in the same handwriting as other exhibits. Consequently he gave a sentence against the will and declared administration to Mrs Calemberg. The orders of the judge are found in the Acts of Court Books in the series PROB 29. In the volume for 1752 (PROB 29/160) there are 14 separate orders for the case which are all indexed at the front of the volume. On f. 393 there is the judgment order or sentence. In the margin is written the word 'Interlocutory', which means it is an interlocutory decree that could be overturned if new evidence was produced. In common with the rest of the content of these books, it is written in a formulaic legal style. Documents relating to the case are shown above and in Figs. 24 and 25.

This was not quite the end of the matter, as in 1754 the case was taken to the High Court of Delegates on appeal but Grace failed to overturn the judgment. An unusually full account of this case and transcripts of the witness statements appear among the Law Reports (1 LEE 76, 161 ER 29). These are available at the National Archives in the electronic resource English Reports 1220–1865 (Juta Hart) and on microfiche among British Trials 1660–1900 (Chadwyk Healey) and can also be found on the internet by keyword searching Google Books.

8.15.2 *A forged will and a criminal trial*

The will of the theatrical costumier and wig maker William (Willie) Berry Clarkson, who died in 1934, was contested in the Probate, Divorce and Admiralty Division of the High Court of Justice in the following year. William Cooper Hobbs, former managing clerk at a firm of solicitors, sometime accountant and convicted fraudster, maintained that he was the executor of a will of 1929 that named him as the residuary legatee. This will was in the charge of solicitor Edmund O'Connor. Hobbs's claim was, however, disputed by Clarkson's friend Max Fred Brezinski, who maintained that there was a later will of 1931. Brezinski claimed to be the executor of this will, which left the entire Clarkson estate to him and his daughter.

What made this case particularly unusual was the fact that Brezinski, a conjurer, was unable to produce it. Brezinski was, however, able to produce a witness prepared to testify that he had acted as a signatory to the will and had noted its content. Asked by the barrister in court why he had looked at the will he answered, 'I wanted to see if I was there.' Another witness stated that he had been shown the will by Clarkson himself. The judge decided the 1931 will was the valid one, even though it had never been found.

Three years later, the story of the two wills took a criminal turn. Edmond O'Connor and William Cooper Hobbs appeared at Bow Street Police Station charged with conspiring together to 'utter a forged will' of the late William Berry Clarkson. There were even sensational reports in the press that Clarkson's body had been exhumed.

Both men were committed to the Central Criminal Court for trial. A handwriting specialist who was brought in expressed the opinion that Clarkson's signature on the 1929 will had been forged. He also believed the signature of the deceased in a letter produced by Hobbs in support of his claim was not genuine. In another the handwriting had been bleached out and typewritten matter superimposed. Yellow outlines of the original letter were still visible.

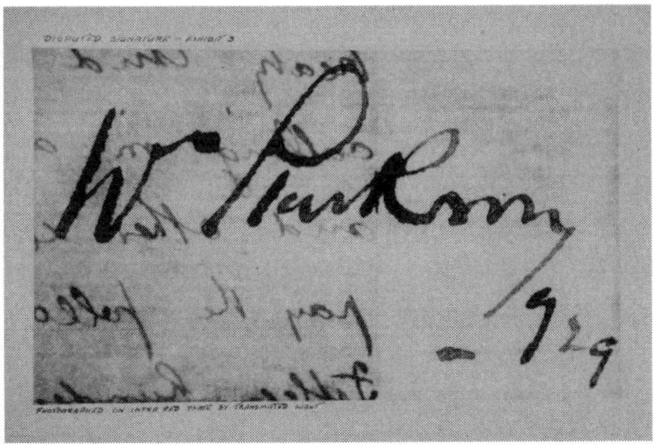

Fig. 27 *The forged signature of William Clarkson.* MEPO 3/1088

Hobbs and O'Connor were both found guilty of colluding together in forging the will of William Clarkson and sentenced to five and seven years' penal servitude respectively. The National Archives holds a very thick Metropolitan Police file (MEPO 3/1088) with witness statements and a

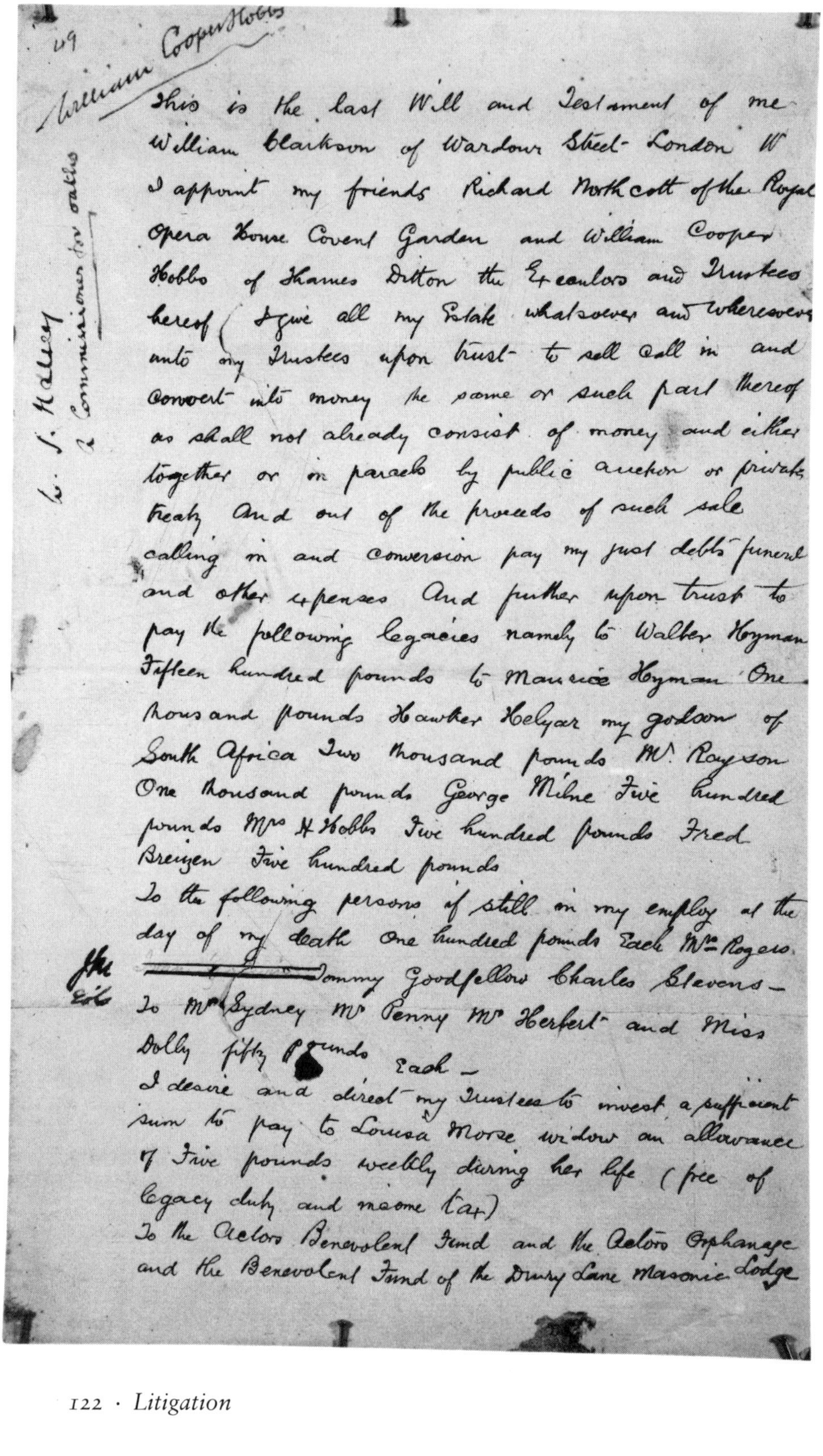

49

William Cooper Hobbs

L. S. Holley
a Commissioner for oaths

This is the last Will and Testament of me William Clarkson of Wardour Street London W I appoint my friends Richard Northcott of the Royal Opera House Covent Garden and William Cooper Hobbs of Thames Ditton the Executors and Trustees hereof I give all my Estate whatsoever and wheresoever unto my Trustees upon trust to sell call in and convert into money the same or such part thereof as shall not already consist of money and either together or in parcels by public auction or private treaty And out of the proceeds of such sale calling in and conversion pay my just debts funeral and other expenses And further upon trust to pay the following legacies namely to Walter Hyman Fifteen hundred pounds to Maurice Hyman One thousand pounds Hawker Helyar my godson of South Africa Two thousand pounds Mr. Rayson One thousand pounds George Milne Five hundred pounds Mrs H Hobbs Five hundred pounds Fred Breizen Five hundred pounds

To the following persons if still in my employ at the day of my death One hundred pounds Each Mr Rogers ~~[illegible]~~ Tommy Goodfellow Charles Stevens – To Mr Sydney Mr Penny Mr Herbert and Miss Dolly fifty pounds Each –

I desire and direct my Trustees to invest a sufficient sum to pay to Louisa Morse widow an allowance of Five pounds weekly during her life (free of legacy duty and income tax)

To the Actors Benevolent Fund and the Actors Orphanage and the Benevolent Fund of the Drury Lane Masonic Lodge folder of close-up photographs of signatures, including the signature on the fraudulent 1929 will. In addition, the National Archives also holds Central Criminal Court case files, again containing many witness statements (CRIM 1/1004).

8.15.3 *An intestate Probate case at the High Court of Justice*

Alice Hirst died in 1931 without leaving a will. Therefore she died intestate. In 1934 her two sisters Edith Hobson and Mary Emily Watson went to the High Court of Justice, Probate, Divorce and Admiralty Division to obtain an order granting an administration of the estate. There is a surviving file in the series J 121 (J 121/8001) and the case is typical of many litigation cases that were not party against party disputes – in other words a case brought by someone seeking a decision rather than the resolution of a dispute.

Contained in the file are four affidavits, including one each from the sisters. From these affidavits, part of the story of the family can be told. Alice's husband John had left his wife in 1893, after which no news about him had been received. Her son, Joseph, left home in 1909 to emigrate to America. In the last year of the Great War he enlisted in the Canadian Expeditionary Force, arriving in England on 28 August 1918. This is confirmed by the service record of Joseph Hirst, which is available on the Library and Archives Canada website (*www.collectionscanada.gc.ca*). This states that he was an expert mechanic, born in Sheffield, Yorkshire, who now lived in Los Angeles, California, with his wife. After his return overseas in 1919, nothing more had been heard of him.

As it was likely that Alice's estranged husband and son were potential beneficiaries it was important that some attempt to contact them was made. However, the lack of communication raised the possibility that the pair were no longer alive. As was expected in such cases, advertisements were placed in Sheffield, London and American newspapers, but no responses were received. It was therefore believed that both had been dead for a number of years. The file also includes the order granting letters of administration to the two sisters.

The National Probate Calendar includes the entry for the administration of Alice Hirst and gives a valuation of the estate of £550.

Fig. 28 *The forged will of William Clarkson, dated 1934.* MEPO 3/1088

9 OTHER PROBATE RECORDS

9.1 Military Wills and Powers of Attorney

9.1.1 *Royal Navy wills (1786–1882)*

The Royal Navy actively encouraged ratings to leave wills, so their families were taken care of in the event of death. From 1796, the office of Inspector of Wills was established in order to prevent alleged next of kin making fraudulent claims for prize money and unpaid wages. Naval wills were usually written on preprinted forms. These records are in the National Archives series ADM 48/1–105 and are available on DocumentsOnline. There are 19,927 wills searchable by name, rank or rating, name of ship and other keyword, for example the pay book number.

The documents provide name, date of will, name of ship, man's number in the ship's muster, current residence, name, address and occupation of executor, and name(s) of the beneficiary or beneficiaries.

• OTHER ROYAL NAVY WILLS AT THE NATIONAL ARCHIVES Applications by next of kin for unpaid wages or pensions due to deceased Royal Navy and Royal Marines officers, or their widows, and to civilian employees of the navy are in ADM 45 (1830–60). Some applications are supported by birth or marriage certificates or wills. This series is searchable by name on the Catalogue.

Applications from the next of kin of deceased Royal Navy ratings and Royal Marines other ranks for unpaid wages (1800–60) are in ADM 44. Some are supported by birth or marriage certificates or wills. The letter included in the piece number is the initial letter of the surname of the seaman or marine, and there is a range of certificate numbers for each letter of the alphabet. Indexes to ADM 44 are in ADM 141.

Registers of wills made at the Naval Hospital, Gibraltar (1809–15) are in ADM 105/40 and are searchable by name on the Catalogue. The wills in this register (which occupy only 12 pages) provide: name of ship, name of testator, date of will, in whose favour drawn (a brief abstract of the will), when sent to the Inspector of Wills, witnesses' names, by whom filled in and the name of physician or surgeon who certified the sanity of the patient.

Fig. 29 (opposite) *The will of able seaman Charles Stannard, proved at sea in 1808.* ADM 48/90

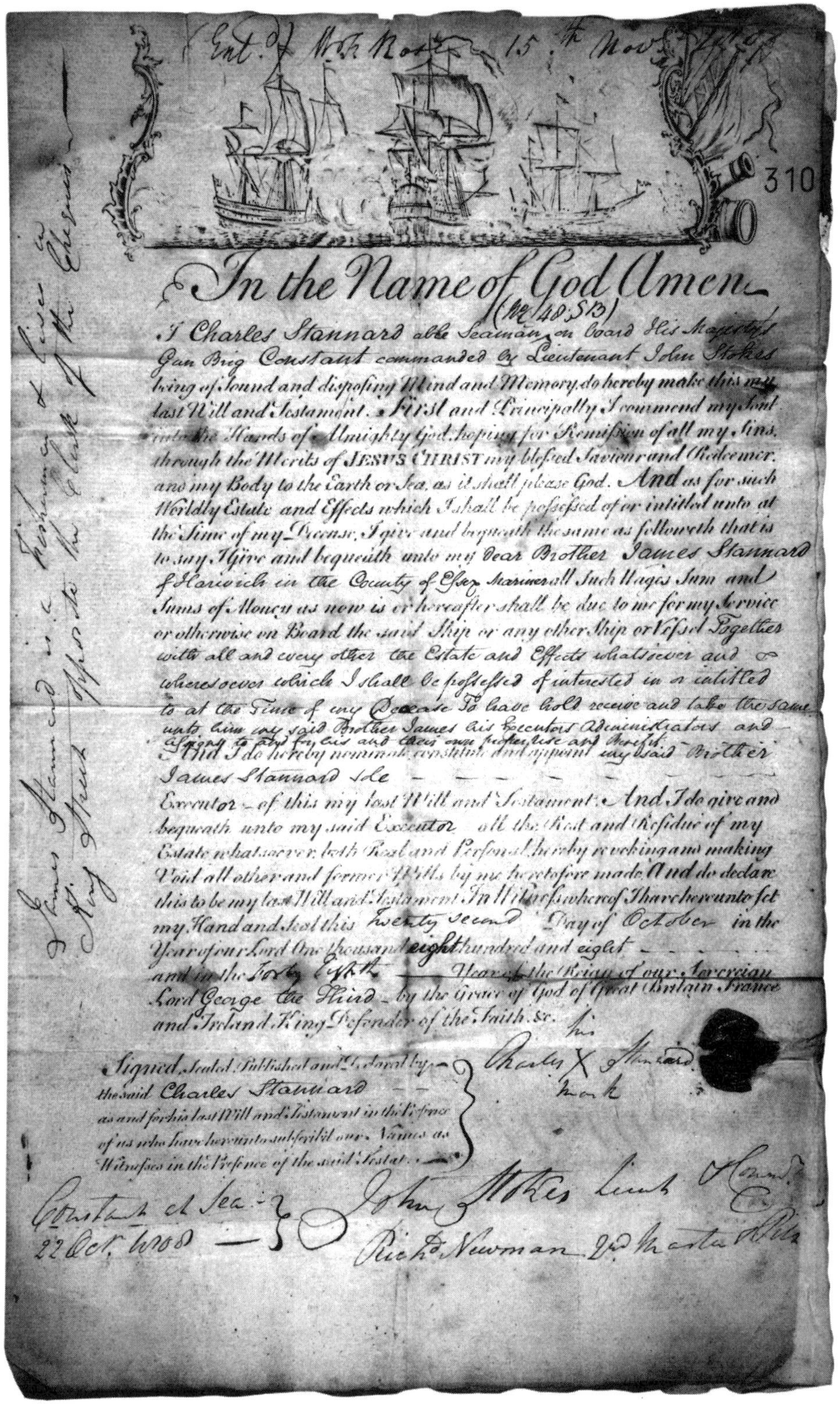
Ent. of W. R. Ross 15th Nov.

310

In the Name of God Amen

(M. 48.513)

I Charles Stannard able Seaman on board His Majesty's Gun Brig Constant commanded by Lieutenant John Stokes being of sound and disposing Mind and Memory do hereby make this my last Will and Testament. First and Principally I commend my Soul into the Hands of Almighty God hoping for Remission of all my Sins through the Merits of JESUS CHRIST my blessed Saviour and Redeemer, and my Body to the Earth or Sea, as it shall please God. And as for such Worldly Estate and Effects which I shall be possessed of or intitled unto at the Time of my Decease, I give and bequeath the same as followeth that is to say I give and bequeath unto my dear Brother James Stannard of Harwich in the County of Essex Mariner all such Wages Sum and Sums of Money as now is or hereafter shall be due to me for my Service or otherwise on Board the said Ship or any other Ship or Vessel Together with all and every other the Estate and Effects whatsoever and wheresoever which I shall be possessed of interested in or entitled to at the Time of my Decease To have hold receive and take the same unto him my said Brother James his Executors Administrators and assigns to and for his and their own proper use and benefit. And I do hereby nominate constitute and appoint my said Brother James Stannard sole Executor of this my last Will and Testament. And I do give and bequeath unto my said Executor all the Rest and Residue of my Estate whatsoever both Real and Personal hereby revoking and making Void all other and former Wills by me heretofore made And do declare this to be my last Will and Testament In Witness whereof I have hereunto set my Hand and Seal this twenty second Day of October in the Year of our Lord One thousand eight hundred and eight and in the Forty Eighth Year of the Reign of our Sovereign Lord George the Third by the Grace of God of Great Britain France and Ireland King Defender of the Faith &c.

Charles his X mark Stannard

Signed, Sealed, Published and Declared by the said Charles Stannard as and for his last Will and Testament in the Presence of us who have hereunto subscribed our Names as Witnesses in the Presence of the said Testat.

Constant at Sea 22 Oct. 1808

John Stokes Lieut. Command.

Richd. Newman 2d Master [illegible]

James Stannard in a [illegible] & [illegible] in [illegible] [illegible] [illegible] to the Clerk of the Cheque

In 1862 the Royal Navy began a new system of recording wills, which were registered after the death of the testator. These records are in ADM 142/15–19 (1862–1901). This series is part of the Digital Microfilm Project, which aims to put entire series of microfilm on the National Archives website unindexed. There is no charge to access these documents online. A partial name index to this series is available on Your Archives and a name index is included in *A List of Wills, Administrations etc. in the Public Record Office, 12th–19th Century* (Baltimore, 1968), which is available at the National Archives. The series contains original wills which the Admiralty accepted as valid; those not declared valid appear to have been returned to the executors. The registers provide: name, ship, date of registering the will and date of death. The survival rate for these wills is quite poor, but entries for those proved in or after 1858 should be in the National Probate Calendar. Information in ADM 154 (Registers of Men Discharged Dead, 1859–78) may also be useful.

There are registers of probates and administrations affecting the payment of pensions between 1836–1915 in the series PMG 50. Miscellaneous powers of attorney for the Royal Navy are in PMG 50 between 1836–1915 and PMG 51 between 1800–99.

The National Archives series PROB 20 contains a number of precautionary wills made between 1623 and 1838 by sailors and others embarking on hazardous voyages. These are usually little more than letters of attorney authorizing a named person to dispose of the estate if the traveller failed to return.

For more detailed information about naval wills, administrations, effects papers and associated records, see section 5.3 of *Tracing Your Naval Ancestors* by Bruno Pappalardo (PRO, 2003).

• ROYAL MARINES WILLS There is a collection of copies of Royal Marines wills and administrations (1740–64), extracted from probate registries, in ADM 96/524, which is searchable by name using the Catalogue. These were presumably obtained to settle questions relating to arrears of pay of officers and other ranks in the Marines. Later, after the establishment of the Inspector of Wills in 1796, Royal Marines other ranks were encouraged to deposit wills in the Navy Pay Office and are indexed in ADM 142 (1786–1909) and are available on DocumentsOnline in the series ADM (1786–1882).

9.1.2 *Army wills*

Before 1858, for soldiers who died abroad leaving assets over a certain amount, grants of probate or administration were issued by the Prerogative Court of Canterbury. Also useful are the casualty returns in WO 25/1359–2407 (1809–55). These sometimes include wills, or copies of wills, of deceased soldiers and inventories of their effects. They are arranged by regiment. Application papers for widows' pensions and dependants' allowances for army officers (1755–1908), which include wills, are in WO 42.

• Soldier's Effects Ledgers The National Archives holds the Soldier's Effects Ledgers for 1862–1881 in WO 25/3475–3501. The National Army Museum holds a set of ledgers for April 1901–March 1960. These ledgers were created as a list of the monies owed to a soldier who died in service. They do not list any of his personal items that were returned to the next of kin. The information they typically contain is:

Full name
Regimental number
The date of death and sometimes the place
Next of kin
Monies paid to the next of kin.

The records from 1901–1914 also include the date of enlistment and trade at the time of enlistment. There is a fee payable to provide a transcript of an individual's entry. Contact The National Army Museum at *www.national-army-museum.ac.uk/*.

• Army letters and powers of attorney Registers or entry books of letters and powers of attorney for army officers are in several series:

TNA reference	Content	Date range
WO 30/1	Registers of letters of attorney	1755–83
PMG 14/142–164	Registers of letters of attorney	1756–1827
PMG 14/104–125	Entry books of powers of attorney	1759–1816
PMG 14/165–167	Registers of letters of attorney granted by officers' widows	1802–21
PMG 14/126–137	Alphabetical entry books	1811–14
PMG 51	Registers of letters of attorney (includes Ordnance Officers from 1858)	1836–99
WO 54/494–510	Indexed registers of attorney Royal Artillery and Royal Engineers (officers, civilians and creditors)	1699–1857

See also WO 54/494–510, which are indexed registers of letters of attorney for Ordnance (Royal Artillery and Royal Engineers) officers, civilian staff and creditors, 1699–1857.

9.2 Deeds

These series relate mainly to records of conveyances and other deeds of title, but they also contain references to wills and grants of probate and administration. Most of the deeds in these series were probably lodged with the particular court either for enrolment or as evidence in legal proceedings. Some of these series are searchable, either wholly or in part, on the Catalogue.

TNA reference	Name of series	Date range
C 146	Ancient Deeds Series C	1100–1695
E 40	Ancient Deeds Series A	c.1100–1603
E 41	Ancient Deeds Series AA	c.1100–1642
E 42	Ancient Deeds Series AS	c.1100–1590
E 44	Modern Deeds Series A	1504–1764
E 210	(King's Remembrancer) Ancient Deeds Series D	c.1120–1609
E 211	Ancient Deeds Series DD (bundle 10)	c.1101–1645
E 214	Modern Deeds	c.1603–1851
E 326	Ancient Deeds Series B	c.1200–1592
E 327	Ancient Deeds Series Maddox	c.1100–1543
E 329	Ancient Deeds Series BS	1148–1560
LR 14	Ancient Deeds Series E	1223–1730
WALE 29	Ancient Deeds Series F	1265–1602

9.3 Overseas Probate Courts

The probate records of the British Consular Court at Smyrna, Turkey (1820–1929) and of the Shanghai Supreme Court (1857–1941) are to be found in FO 626 and FO 917 respectively. Other wills of Britons in China (1837–1951) are in FO 678/2729–931. Wills from the British Consulate in Russia are in FO 184/14 (1817–66), while wills and private papers from Tunis are in FO 335/164 (1866–85). A name index is available in *A List of Wills, Administrations etc. in the Public Record Office, 12th–19th Century.*

9.4 Royal Wills

The National Archives has a good collection of royal wills and other probate records. Others are held by the Royal Archives, Lambeth Palace Library and the British Library. See Jane Cox's *Wills, Inventories and Death Duties: A Provisional Guide* (Public Record Office, 1988) for a complete list of royal wills both before and after 1858. For transcripts of early royal wills see John Nichols' *A collection of all the wills, now known to be extant, of the kings and queens of England, princes and princesses of Wales, and every branch of the blood royal, from the reign of William the Conqueror to that of Henry the Seventh exclusive.* See 2.8 for the sealing of royal wills.

Date	Member of royal family	TNA reference
13th cent.	Henry II	E 164/12, f. 1 (illuminated); T 48/23 (copy)
*c.*1282–*c.*1292	Edward I	E 36/274
1399	Richard II	E 23/1/1; T 48/23 (copy)
1422	Henry V	C 65/87, m. 3; E 23/2
1509	Henry VII	E 23/3; T 48/23 (copy)
1547	Henry VIII	PROB 11/31; E 315/469 (contemporary transcript); E 23/4/1, E 23/4/2 and SP 1/227, f. 217–229 (drafts); T 48/23 (copy)

Date	Member of royal family	TNA reference
1557	Anne of Cleves (wife of Henry VIII)	PROB 11/39, f. 261
1661–2	Queen Elizabeth of Bohemia	PROB 1/41
1669	Henrietta Maria (wife of Charles I)	PROB 6/44, f. 114 (19 October 1669); T 27/2, p. 116
1682	Rupert, Prince Palatine of the Rhine	PROB 1/46
1706	Catherine of Braganza (wife of Charles II)	PROB 1/56; PROB 11/487
1708	George of Denmark (consort of Queen Anne)	PROB 6/85, f. 89–90; PROB 16/6, f. 133–148
1714	Anne, Queen of England	PC 1/2/260 (incomplete draft); T 48/23 SP 44/116
1720–36	Princess Amelia Landgravine of Hesse	PROB 1/94
1818	Queen Charlotte (wife of George III)	PROB 1/97; PROB 11/1612
1821	Queen Caroline (wife of George IV)	PROB 1/98; PROB 11/1653
1850	Queen Adelaide (wife of William IV)	PROB 1/99; PROB 31/1526/1482–1485

In the table above: f. = folio m. = membrane p. = page

Fig. 30 *The illuminated will of Henry II.* E 164/12

9.5 Miscellaneous Series at the National Archives

Wills, probates and other associated testamentary records occur in a variety of 'miscellaneous' series at the National Archives. Many of them can be found by trying a name search on the Catalogue along with an appropriate search term such as 'will', 'estate', 'administration' or 'probate'. However, catalogues of some series are not available online, in which case it is necessary to search the original documents, with the help of supplementary finding aids. Many of the series listed below are indexed by name in the publication *A List of Wills, Administrations etc. in the Public Record Office, 12th–19th Century.*

9.5.1 *Chancery*

• C 47 (1324–1577) Among the various items in this series are a number of ecclesiastical documents that relate to testamentary matters, including transcripts of wills, probates and administrations.

9.5.2 *Exchequer*

• E 135/7 (1325–1628) This series contains the transcripts of proceedings in various courts relating to ecclesiastical and monastic matters concerning the possession of church lands and tithes, rights of presentation, taxation and indulgences. Wills also feature among the collection, which does not have a name index. The origin of these wills is unknown, but it is assumed that they were sent to the Exchequer for financial or judicial reasons.

• E 315/31–54 (*c.* 1100 TO *c.* 1800) The main contents of this series are private grants to monastic houses and grants relating to property acquired by the monastic houses.

• E 315/483 (1648–59) This series contains copies of wills, grants of probate and letters of administration extracted from the Registers of the Prerogative Court of Canterbury during the Commonwealth. They relate mostly to individuals who served during the Commonwealth, either in the army or otherwise. Copies were presumably taken for the purposes of settling arrears of pay.

• E 403/2372–2378 (1681–1718) Documents contained in these volumes include copies of wills, grants of probate and letters of administration taken from the various courts of probate, though they mainly relate to the Prerogative Court of Canterbury. The entered documents were those which affected annuities and other payments from the Exchequer. There is a name index in each volume.

• E 406/27–44 (1677–1704) These books include brief entries concerning wills, copies of probates and letters of administration that affected assignments made as a result of the settlement between Charles II and the London goldsmiths in 1677.

• E 406/45–80 (1622–1834) Among the items in this series are deeds of assignment whereby pensions, annuities and other payments from the Exchequer were sold in whole or in part. It also contains letters of attorney, letters of administration and probates of wills, along with other documents recorded in the Auditors' Assignment Books. There is a name index in each volume.

9.5.3 *Lord Chamberlain's Department*

• LC 5/104–106 (1748–84) These are entry books of wills, letters and assignments of household servants that affected payment of salaries or pensions due to officials of the royal household.

9.5.4 *Lord Steward's Department*

• LS 13/195 (1712–26) Similarly, these are entry books of assignments of board wages in the Office of the Clerk of the Kitchen, together with letters of administration and probates of wills.

9.5.5 *Office of Land Revenue Records and Enrolments*

• LRRO 13/91 (1900–3) Includes probates of wills.

9.5.6 *National Debt Office*

• NDO 1/4 (1746–67) Consists of entry books of assignments and wills relating to life annuities granted in 1745, 1746 and 1757.

9.5.7 *Treasury*

• T 16/1–13 (1857–87) Contains letters relating to intestates' estates.

• T 64/292–293 (1792–4) These registers of wills proved in the Consistory Court of London were presumably compiled for Legacy Duty purposes, as they list the value under which the will was proved. They provide the following information:

The total amount (or proportion) of the whole estate bequeathed
The widow's name
The relationship of legatees to the testator.

9.6 Other Major Probate Collections

9.6.1 *East India Company and India Office: British Library*

The Oriental and India Office Collections (OIOC) at the British Library include records of estates and wills of 'home and overseas servants' of the East India Company and India Office. It also includes their dependants who died in the UK and Europe while in receipt of salary, leave pay or pension, and of members of the Indian civil and military services who died in India. The records, which give the name and address of the deceased, names of beneficiaries and sometimes of relatives, details of bequests and names of executors, cover the following:

1704–80	Court proceedings
1727–74	Bengal Mayor's Court proceedings
1774–79	Supreme Court proceedings
Up to 1783	Bombay Mayor's Court proceedings

Other records at the British Library include grants of administration (1774–1948), grants of probate (1865–1938) and inventories of deceased estates and copies of estate accounts (1780–1938).

For further information about probate records at the British Library see their website: *www.bl.uk/collections/oiocfamilyhistory/familywills.html*.

9.6.2 *Bank of England Probate records (1717–1845)*

These records consist of extracts of wills of people who died with monies in public funds, as well as abstracts of orders made for stockholders who went bankrupt or were declared lunatic. They extend from 1717 to 1845, when the process of recording bequests of stock ceased. In 1812 the Bank ruled that, from then on, it would accept grants of probate from the Prerogative Court of Canterbury only.

Since the Bank of England holds extracts only, for the full text of a will you need to consult the records of the court that proved it. However, although the extracts do not include all the information contained in the original wills, they often identify members of the deceased's family as beneficiaries.

Indexes to Bank of England extracts are available (for a fee) on the British Origins website. Hard copies of extracts can be ordered via British Origins. Access to the Bank of England's archives is restricted, but applications can be made, in writing only, to the Bank of England.

9.7 Case Studies

9.7.1 *A navy will*

The seaman's will of Charles Stannard, Able Seaman, is dated 22 October 1808 (see Fig. 29). The Navy Office form used for writing the will is one of several designs that were used and lodged in the Navy Office so that they could easily be found at time of death. Although formulaic in nature, these wills can contain a surprising amount of information, often of a very specific nature. From Stannard's, for example, we learn that he had served on board His Majesty's gun brig *Constant* under the command of Lieutenant John Stokes. He also names his brother, James, of Harwich, as executor, writing in the margin that he was a fisherman and lived in King Street opposite the Clerk of the Cheques.

The will also provides the ship's pay book number. The ship's pay book for the *Constant* for the years 1807–11 can be found under reference ADM 35/2696. This provides additional information, such as Stannard's birthplace (Walton in Suffolk) and his age when he came on board the ship (22).

9.7.2 *A death abroad*

Sometimes the very absence of a will can be responsible for a fascinating series of records, particularly if the death occurred abroad. When Thomas Vincent Lee died in Rome, Italy, on 25 May 1871, responsibility for dealing with his death fell to the British Consul in the capital as Lee was a British subject. A record of his death can be found in the General Register Office Consular Deaths for 1871, and letters relating to it among the British Consul at Rome's correspondence for 1871 (FO 45/191). These establish that Lee died in his apartment on the second floor of 9A Via della Croce. A letter from the Vice Consul describes how seals were used to protect his goods and then removed in the presence of three witnesses so that an inventory could be taken. This lists a variety of items, from coats and trousers to a travelling carpet, a thermometer and a medal of Pope Pius IX. Among his papers was a certificate from the Italian Ministry of Agriculture and Commerce granting a patent of invention for a means of making artificial coal. However, neither a will nor any money was found.

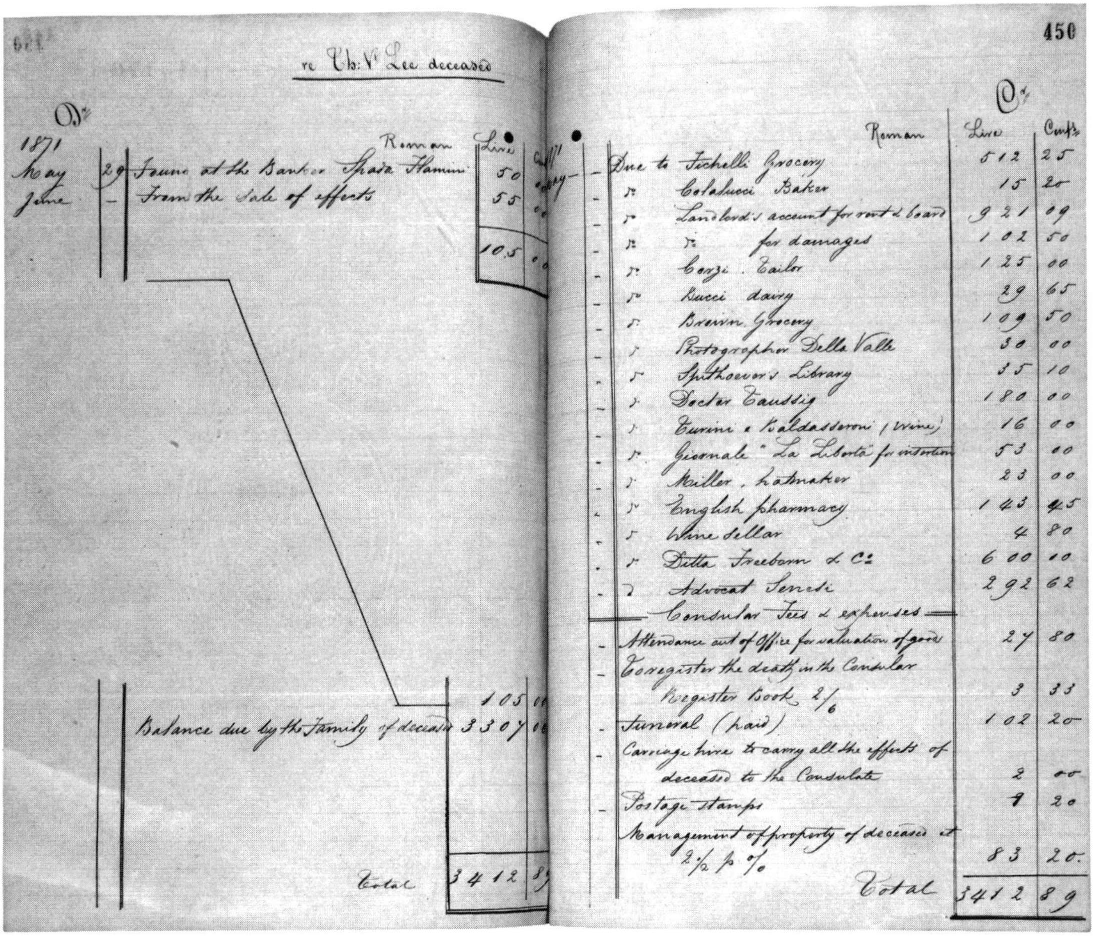

re Th: Vt Lee deceased

450

Dr

1871			Roman Lire	Cents
May	29	Found at the Banker Spada Flamini	50	
June	–	From the sale of effects	55	
			105	
			105	
		Balance due by the Family of deceased	3307	
		Total	3412	89

Cr

	Roman Lire	Cents
Due to Fichelli Grocery	512	25
" Coladucci Baker	15	20
" Landlord's account for rent & board	921	09
" " for damages	102	50
" Cenzi Tailor	125	00
" Bucci dairy	29	65
" Brown Grocery	109	50
" Photographer Della Valle	30	00
" Spithoever's Library	35	10
" Doctor Taussig	180	00
" Turini e Baldassaroni (wine)	16	00
" Giornale "La Libertà" for insertion	53	00
" Miller, hatmaker	23	00
" English pharmacy	143	45
" Wine cellar	4	80
" Ditta Freeborn & Co	600	10
" Advocat Senesi	292	62
Consular Fees & expenses		
Attendance out of Office for valuation of goods	27	80
To register the death in the Consular Register Book 2/6	3	33
Funeral (paid)	102	20
Carriage hire to carry all the effects of deceased to the Consulate	2	00
Postage stamps	7	20
Management of property of deceased at 2½ p %	83	20
Total	3412	89

Fig. 31 *A record of the debts of Thomas Vincent Lee, who died in Rome in 1871.* FO 45/191

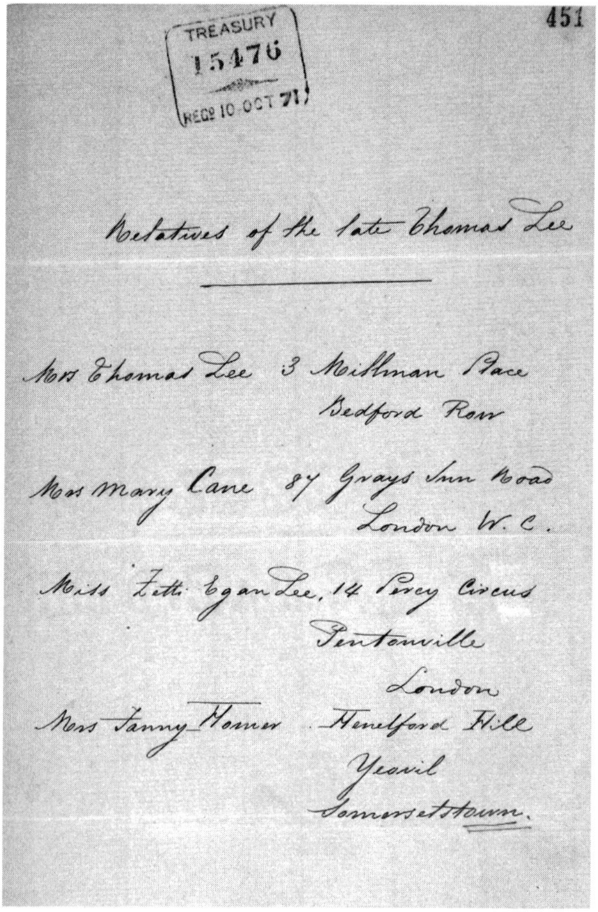

TREASURY
15476
REGD 10 OCT 71

451

Relatives of the late Thomas Lee

Mrs Thomas Lee 3 Millman Place
Bedford Row

Mrs Mary Cane 87 Grays Inn Road
London W.C.

Miss Letti Egan Lee, 14 Percy Circus
Pentonville
London

Mrs Fanny Homer Henelford Hill
Yeovil
Somersetshire.

Fig. 32 *A list of four of the relatives of Thomas Vincent Lee from 1871.* FO 45/191

All the effects were then packed up in order to remove them to the consulate building, apart from a gold watch that was returned to the watchmaker as he had not been paid. An account of the credits and debts was also included with the outstanding debts in lire to, among others, the grocer Tichelli and the baker Colalucci.

As Lee had potentially died intestate a list of four of his relatives in England, including Mrs Thomas Lee, was drawn up. Notification of death was to be passed via a firm of London solicitors, but as no reply was received the Consul was forced to write to the Foreign Office in London. From this letter, which was addressed to the then Foreign Secretary, Lord Granville, we learn that Lee was an engineer by profession and had been residing at the same address for nearly two years. There were also no relatives present. As he was now being pressed by the creditors for their money, the Consul asked if it was possible to avoid any responsibility for the claims under the General Consular Instructions.

From *The Times* newspaper we can learn more about Thomas Vincent Lee and possibly what induced his demise. While living at Macclesfield in 1865 Lee had been involved in a train accident on the line between Manchester and York. He asked for damages of £3,000 from Lancashire and Yorkshire Railway. The company offered a much smaller sum, which they stated Lee had accepted. The matter came to the Court of Chancery in December 1870 and then, in April 1871, to the Lord Justices of Appeal, where the case was dismissed. It seems Lee had been incapacitated with some form of spinal injury. The reports of the trials mention that Lee was the owner of seven patents. A check of the Index to Patents for the year 1868 confirms that he took out a patent in that year for producing charcoal fuel and firelights from peat, and machinery for making coal dust into coke.

A search of the National Probate Calendars for wills and administrations for 1871, 1872, 1873 and 1874 yields no entry for Thomas Vincent Lee. If a will was to be found it was likely to have been within this period. Without it there may have been insufficient estate to justify a grant of administration. Alternatively, if all of the estate was in Rome, the administration may have been granted in the Italian capital under the Italian laws.

10 SCOTLAND, IRELAND, THE ISLE OF MAN AND THE CHANNEL ISLANDS

10.1 Scottish Probate Records

England, Wales and Scotland still maintain separate legal systems and have historically different legal structures for wills. In Scotland, from 1804 property was divided into 'heritable', and 'moveable'. *Heritable property* is what is known in England as freehold property or real estate. *Moveable property* is what is called personal estate in England. Before 1804, in Scotland, testaments dealt with moveable property only. After this date heritable property was transferred via other types of legal documents, such as settlements, but it was not until the Heritable Jurisdictions Act of 1868 that heritable property figured on a regular basis in wills and inventories.

It is interesting to compare the practices concerning wills, intestates and inheritance in Scotland with those in England and Wales. In Scotland anyone over the age of 16 can make a will, whereas in England and Wales the age is 18. An old will is not invalidated when someone north of the border gets married, legally separated or divorced. Widowed spouses, children and other descendants in Scotland are entitled to a fixed share of moveable or personal property, regardless of what is expressed in a will. And when someone dies without leaving a will, the rules of intestate succession are different.

10.1.1 Terminology

The Scottish system of probate differs slightly from the practice in England and Wales. In Scotland *testament* is a collective term used to describe documents relating to the estate of a deceased person. These may include an inventory (of varying length) of the testator's property and (occasionally) a will detailing how the testator wished his or her goods to be divided. The latter is called a *testament testamentar*, and the equivalent of letters of administration is a *testament dative*.

While the form and process of probate differs from the system in England and Wales, the type of information that can be obtained from Scottish wills is, however, similar to that described in 5.3. It is also just as difficult to estimate what proportion of Scottish people left wills as it is to estimate the proportion that left them in England and Wales (see 1.3.2).

10.1.2 *Scottish court structure*

From 1515 to 1823 the secular commissary courts were responsible for the proving of wills. These were based on the same administrative areas as the medieval dioceses (the authority of the bishops being abolished in 1560). Between 1824 and 1875 all but one of the commissary courts were abolished and replaced with sheriff's courts (the sheriff being the chief judge of a county or district). The one exception was the Edinburgh commissary court, which continued until 1830. The courts also held jurisdiction for non-residents dying in Scotland; and residents dying outside Scotland could have their wills registered there. The records of all these courts are held by the National Archives of Scotland.

10.1.3 *Where to find the records*

• 1513–1901. Scottish wills from 1513 to 1901 have been digitally imaged by the Scottish Archive Network and are on the website (*www.scotlandspeople.gov.uk/*). All of these wills can now be searched on this site, although the digital images of some wills are not yet available. The index (which covers testaments and inventories, too) is free to search, but there is a fee to download the image of a will. This excellent website also has information on reading old handwriting, weights and measures, and occupations.

• 1876–91. From 1876 there are annual indexes of testaments, known as the Calendar of Confirmations, which can be found at the National Archives of Scotland, large Scottish libraries and local archives. From 1876 to 1959 they are in the form of printed or typed volumes; from 1960 to 1984 they take the form of microfiche cards.

These indexes give:

The name of the deceased
The place of death
The date of death
The date when the testament was recorded.

• 1992 ONWARDS. Records from 1992 to the present day are held by the Commissary Department.

10.1.4 *Inheritance rules*

Before 1868, Scottish wills could transfer moveable property only. Heritable property (real estate) could be inherited by two methods. One was by *retour* (also known as *services of heirs*), which was part of the Scottish feudal land system. Local landowners would decide whether an individual was the rightful heir. Their decision was communicated by a retour (return) to the Scottish Chancery, who would then give full title to the lands. These

Chancery records are held at the National Archives of Scotland. The other method was by trust deposition and settlement (*testamentary deed*), which would be recorded in the relevant registry of deeds. These records are also held at the National Archives of Scotland.

From 1868 Scottish wills could transfer both moveable and heritable property, and from 1964 the formal abolition of the retour procedure began. However, for a few properties, this method is still used even today.

10.1.5 *Estates without next of kin* (bona vacantia)

For enquiries concerning Scottish estates that have fallen to the Crown in default of heirs, contact the Queen's and Lord Treasurer's Remembrancer.

Funds lodged in the Court of Session and other unclaimed sums resulting from situations such as company liquidations, bankruptcies and judicial factories (the placing of the affairs of a person under the control of someone appointed by the court) are held for seven years from the date of consignation (lodgement) by:

Office of the Accountant of Court
1st Floor
Hayweight House
23 Lauriston Street
Edinburgh
EH3 9DG

After seven years, they are transferred to the Queen's and Lord Treasurer's Remembrancer.

10.1.6 *Death duties*

The National Archives of Scotland holds Estate Duty records commencing in 1804, among the records of the Inland Revenue in Scotland. However, these records may not contain more genealogical information than can be found in the commissary and sheriff court records.

Death duty records held at the National Archives of Scotland comprise:

- Personal legacy registers, 1804–29
- Return ledgers for Inventory Duty, 1831–92
- Residue Duty account books and legacy receipt books, 1819–38
- Register of inventories received from commissary offices, 1824–76; indexes, 1863–84
- Testate register and indexes, 1828–79
- Intestate register and indexes, 1829–79
- Succession Duty register and indexes, 1853–68
- General registers and separate indexes to the last three series in the list above, 1829–79.

At the National Archives in series IR 7, there is a small amount of correspondence concerning contentious cases relating to Scotland for the years 1839–41.

10.2 Irish Probate Records

Before 1858 wills were proved and administrations granted by the courts of the Church of Ireland, which consisted of the Prerogative Court of Ireland and 28 diocesan consistory courts (note that the boundaries of the dioceses do not coincide with county boundaries). There are separate indexes for each of these courts.

After 1858, grants of probate and administration were made in the Principal Registry and district registries of the Probate Court up to 1877; and from 1877 in those of the High Court.

Wills proved up to 1903 held in the Four Courts building in Dublin were destroyed by a fire during the troubles of 1922. No original wills survive from the Principal Registry in Dublin, nor for the counties of Dublin, Kildare, Meath and Wicklow.

However, the National Archives of Ireland holds the following records:

Original wills and administration papers for the Principal Registry from 1904; and for most district registries since 1900.

Will books, containing copies of most wills proved in district registries since 1858; and, for a few years, some of the wills proved in the Principal Registry.

Grant books containing copies of grants of wills and administrations made in the Principal Registry from 1922 and also for a few earlier years; and most grants made in the district registries since 1858.

The Calendars of the Grants of Probate and Letters of Administration made in the Principal Registry and the district registries from 1858. These were produced annually and give basic details, including occupation and address of deceased, date of death, name and address of executor, and value of estate. Sets also survive in the Public Record Office of Northern Ireland and at the district registries. There are indexes for some years.

Betham's abstracts of wills before 1827; Inland Revenue registers of wills and administrations 1829–39 (indexes cover 1829–79); and Charitable Donations and Bequests will extract books 1800–1961 (there is a separate card index for 1800–58). And there are other copies of wills and administrations, too.

The Society of Genealogists, in London, holds abstracts of Irish wills from 1569 to 1909.

There is now an *Index of Irish Wills, 1484–1858* on British Origins (*www.Britishorigins.com*), which covers the wills held at the National Archives of Ireland, including miscellaneous collections of wills or will abstracts. There are also a number of published indexes in book form. These include *Index to Prerogative Wills, 1536–1810*, edited by Arthur Vicars (Dublin, 1897), which is available at the National Archives of Ireland and in the library of the National Archives.

Republic of Ireland grants of probate and administration for the last 20 years, as well as the original wills, schedules of assets and associated documents, are available for public inspection at the Probate Office, High Court.

For Northern Ireland, for wills and administrations up to the last five years, contact the Public Record Office Northern Ireland. For wills and administrations for the last five years (only the last two years are held on site), contact the Probate and Matrimonial Office, Royal Courts of Justice.

Before 1858, because wills were proved and administrations granted by the diocesan bishops of the Established Church, the probate records are arranged by diocese, namely Armagh, Clogher, Connor, Derry and Raphoe, Down and Dromore.

• BEFORE 1900. All original wills prior to 1900 were destroyed in the fire in Dublin mentioned above. But before sending an original will to Dublin the local registry copied it into a register, and these copies have now been put onto microfilm.
• 1900 ONWARDS. From 1900 all proved wills and grants of administrations and associated documents are available, filed in a separate envelope for each testator. There are bound indexes to wills from 1858 to 1984, arranged by date of probate.

Also, printed and manuscript indexes to pre-1858 wills, administrations and administration bonds exist. These records are of value to the genealogist because, although the wills themselves have not survived, the indexes make it possible to determine whether there was a will.

10.2.1 *Estates without next of kin* (bona vacantia)

• NORTHERN IRELAND For funds lodged in court in Northern Ireland since 1921, write to the Court Funds Office. For records prior to the institution of the Supreme Court in Northern Ireland in 1921, contact the Accountant of the Courts of Justice in Dublin.
• REPUBLIC OF IRELAND For funds under the control of the Supreme Court and High Court of Justice in Ireland, write to the Accountant of the Courts of Justice, the Courts Service.

10.2.2 *Death Duties*

The only identified sources relating to death duties are the Inland Revenue registers of wills and administrations for 1828–39, with indexes for 1828–79. These are held at the National Archives of Ireland. No other records appear to have survived.

10.3 Isle of Man Wills

The Isle of Man was in the diocese of Sodor and Man—which included the Consistory Court of Sodor and Man and the Archdeaconry of the Isle of Man—and came within the jurisdiction of the province of York. Some Isle of Man probate records may be held at the Borthwick Institute of Historical

Research. From 1874 the consistory court had sole jurisdiction on the island, then in 1885 the civil High Court of Justice took over jurisdiction for the probate of wills and grants of administrations.

The Manx National Heritage Library holds wills proved by the two consistory courts from around 1600 to 1910; and on microfilm up to 1916. The majority of the wills have been indexed. These records are held at Manx National Heritage. Wills and administrations for 1912–39 are held at the Isle of Man Public Record Office. Those for 1940 to the present day are held at the Deeds and Probate Registry.

10.4 Channel Island Wills

10.4.1 *Jersey*

The church court, that of the Dean of Jersey, had responsibility for the probate of wills and granting of administrations up to 1949. Jersey Archive has a searchable online catalogue (*www.jerseyheritagetrust.org*).

From 1851, as well as the wills of personalty, there are also wills of realty. These are in French and are held by the Jersey land registry at The Judicial Greffe.

10.4.2 *Guernsey*

Wills and administrations were, and still are, proved or granted in the Ecclesiastical Court of the Bailiwick of Guernsey, including those for Alderney, Sark, Herm and Jethou. Wills in Guernsey are split between wills of personalty and wills of realty, and there are separate indexes for these two types of wills. Make enquiries to the States of Guernsey, Island Archive Service.

11 RESEARCH TECHNIQUES

Researching probate records can be particularly frustrating for researchers before 1858 as there is no comprehensive index of names. Wills are legal documents governed by strict rules, and changing government legislation affected both their contents and process. Understanding this will help you determine the best sources for your research and help you interpret what you find.

11.1 Wills before 1858

• WHICH DATE IS MORE IMPORTANT — THE DATE THE WILL WAS WRITTEN OR PROVED? Wills are arranged by the date the will was proved. If the will was written when the testator was close to death then these dates should be fairly close to each other and probably within several months. Remember that some testators wrote their wills earlier in life — for example, when they got married, before setting out on a long journey, or to make provision for their children. If you know the date of death, search for two to three years from this point. If you get numerous results on Documents Online relating to the same name, click on the 'date' heading on the results screen to sort your results into date order.

• I'VE SEARCHED 3 YEARS FROM THE DATE OF DEATH, BUT I CAN'T FIND THE WILL. If there was any kind of deviation from the standard probate process or a dispute, it could take several years, and occasionally decades, to prove the will. The probate clause often provides useful information about any former grants made by the court before it granted probate. There are sometimes formal annotations on registered copy wills that are worth spending the time trying to decipher as these can sometimes lead to further information about the case.

• I HAVE A NAME THAT IS SPELT IN MANY DIFFERENT WAYS. HOW CAN I FIND IT? Early wills in particular can be difficult to find as the spelling of surnames was inconsistent. On DocumentsOnline you can use an asterisk (*) as a wildcard to replace a letter or letters. Thus, a search for Car* brings up results for Card, Carr and Cary. You can use this research technique for both first names and surnames.

It is possible that online search engines contain transcription errors, so if you are really stuck, it might be worth looking at wills that partially match your search criteria. Tell a member of staff if you identify transcription errors so the indexes can be amended.

Some courts indexed testators in unusual ways, particularly if they were titled. So, for example, the will of the Right Reverend Herbert Marsh, Lord Bishop of Landaff, formerly Lord Bishop of Peterborough, could be indexed under M for Marsh, B for Bishop, L for Landaff or P for Peterborough. Online indexes makes this type of searching much quicker, but where this is not the case you should be prepared to search all possible permutations.

• I CAN'T FIND A REGISTERED COPY WILL BUT I'VE FOUND AN ORIGINAL WILL. WHY IS THAT? The Prerogative Court of Canterbury required the executor to pay a fee to have a copy of will recorded permanently in the registered wills. Although the executor could claim this cost back from the testator's estate, some executors chose not to follow this part of the process.

• WHY IS THE WILL NOT WRITTEN OR SIGNED BY THE TESTATOR? Registered wills are copies of original wills made by clerks as a permanent record for the benefit of the ecclesiastical court. If you want to see the testator's signature or seal (or sometimes their mark) you need to look at the original will, if it survives. However, original wills proved by the Prerogative Court of Canterbury before 1600 were often copies. We believe the clerk would 'forge' the testator's signature to give the document an air of authenticity. Sometimes the testator would write the entire will or codicil in his or her own hand. These 'holograph' wills are unusual as clerks were often employed to undertake this task.

• I CAN'T FIND A WILL EVEN THOUGH I KNOW THERE WAS ONE.

It is possible that the will was proved by a local church court or by a Scottish or Irish court or a court even further afield.

Check the various act books, as these record every grant of probate and administration issued by the court.

The will was never proved. This could occur if the will was disputed or if the court decided the will was invalid for any reason. When a court declared a will invalid they usually granted letters of administration instead.

It is possible that your information is incorrect and there is no will. This could be because the person died suddenly or at a young age; the person did not own the capital he or she was living off but merely a life interest; or the property was disposed of before death, making the need for a will redundant.

11.2 Wills after 1858

• Do all wills go to probate? No. The current threshold for wills in England and Wales is £5,000 for money held in accounts. However, executors go to probate with smaller amounts as it is the easiest way to fulfil the conditions contained in the will.

• Why is Llandudno the place of probate and administration in the indexes of 1940–6 instead of London? During the Second World War, the government evacuated key records from central London. The records of the Principal Registry were moved from London to Llandudno for safety.

11.3 Death Duties

• My ancestor was quite wealthy. Why can't I find an entry in the death duty registers? When death duties were introduced in 1796, duties were payable on legacies and residues of the personal estate only and the children, spouse, parents and grandparents were exempt. The number of people excluded from paying tax was gradually reduced until, by 1815, only the spouse was exempt from the tax. Real estate did not become subject to death duties until 1853. Between 1796 and 1903 death duties were not levied on the estates of people who lived abroad or who died in service of their country.

• I've found the reference *NE* in the index to death duties. What does this mean? *NE* is an abbreviation for 'no entry'. This means that although the Inland Revenue anticipated that duty was payable on the estate, in the end, it did not apply. There are no other death duty sources available.

• I've found a death duty entry, but I don't understand it. Death duties can be difficult documents to interpret. However, as they provide important genealogical information, it is worth the effort. Individual entries were kept 'open' by Inland Revenue clerks for numerous years after the person's death in order to record important updates to the family's history—for example, when a child reached the age of 21 or when a beneficiary died. These additions are usually abbreviated and scrawled across the entry, often in different coloured inks.

To start, take copies of both halves of the register and stick them together so you can read the entry across the page. If there is a will, read it carefully so you are familiar with its contents. The death duty entry may contain references to old Inland Revenue files that no longer exist, for example OF 1345/98, so eliminate any of these. A reference such as RR/41/J/12 is to reversionary registers, which are available in IR 26/4856–67. In this instance, the year is [18]41, J is the initial letter of the surname and 12 is the folio. A reference such as RA 767/46 1 LD relates to residual accounts. Most of these have been destroyed, but a few still survive in IR 19 and IR 59.

11.4 Intestacy

• WHAT HAPPENS TO ESTATES WHERE THERE WAS NO NEXT OF KIN? Where someone dies intestate and there is no obvious next of kin, the estate reverts to the Crown. This is known as *bona vacantia* or 'ownerless goods'. Such estates are administered by the Bona Vacantia Division of the Treasury Solicitor's Department (*www.bonavacantia.gov.uk*) and you can search their website to see if you are entitled to the estate of a deceased relative. If you do think you are entitled to the estate, you need to prove a line of descent from the deceased using documentary evidence (such as birth, marriage and death certificates).

• I HAVE FOUND THE ADMINISTRATION, BUT IT GIVES ME LITTLE GENEALOGICAL INFORMATION. WHAT ELSE IS THERE? When you finally track down your ancestor you might be disappointed to find that they died intestate. Although there is no will, there may be other sources that you can use to find further information. Estates of intestates were subject to death duties depending on the date and the value of the estate. This information is particularly rewarding as it may include all the family members with a share in the estate.

Administration bonds provide a rough estimation of the value of the estate, which is useful if there is no death duty. The bond provides some basic genealogical information about the administrator (not the intestate), which is useful if the next of kin is a member of the family.

Where inventories survive they can be particularly rewarding. They can provide a detailed breakdown of the deceased's personal estate, but they are unlikely to reveal any genealogical information.

APPENDIX 1

The National Archives' Prerogative Court of Canterbury (PROB) Series

PROB 1 **Wills of selected famous people** (1552–1854) *The original wills of famous people removed from* PROB 10, *including the wills of Shakespeare, Drake and Nelson.*

PROB 2 **Inventories compiled before 1661** (1417–1660) *These are the small number of pre-1661 inventories that have survived. A few of the inventories are accompanied by executors' or administrators' accounts.*

PROB 3 **Filed engrossed 18th-century inventories and associated documents** (1701–82) *Engrossed copies of inventories preserved in their original filing arrangement. A few of the inventories are accompanied by executors' or administrators' accounts.*

PROB 4 **Engrossed inventories exhibited from 1660** (1660–*c*.1720) *Engrossed copies of inventories. Some of them are copies of those in* PROB 5 *and* PROB 32. *A few of the inventories are accompanied by executors' or administrators' accounts.*

PROB 5 **Miscellaneous inventories, accounts and associated documents** (1643–1836) *Inventories, executors' and administrators' accounts and associated documents, including commissions to appraisers to make or receive inventories and accounts.*

PROB 6 **Administration act books** (1559–1858) *These books record letters of administration. They include limited grants to 1809.*

PROB 7 **Limited administration act books** (1810–58) *These books record limited grants of administration.*

PROB 8 **Probate act books** (1526–1858) *These books record both probate acts and letters of administration with will annexed. They also record limited grants of probate for 1780, 1782–99, 1801 and 1805.*

PROB 9 **Limited probate act books** (1781–1858) *These books record limited grants of probates for 1781, 1800, 1802–4 and 1806–58.*

PROB 10 **Original wills and sentences** (1484–1858) *The majority of the documents are original wills signed and sealed by testators and attested by witnesses. However, many of the pre-1600 wills are merely copies.*

PROB 11 **Will registers** (1383–1858) *These are the will registers into which the court clerks copied the text of the wills. Most of the PCC wills were registered and can therefore be found in* PROB 11.

PROB 12 **Indexes of wills and administrations grants** (1383–1858) *This is the main series of original indexes to* PROB 6–PROB 11.

PROB 13 **Original calendars and indexes of wills and administrations** (1384–1800) *These are original indexes to* PROB 6 *and* PROB 8–PROB 11. *Many of them were transcribed to produce the indexes in* PROB 12 *and* PROB 15.

PROB 14 **Warrants** (1657–1858) *These warrants were used to authorize the issue of a grant of administration or probate.*

PROB 15 **Original calendars and indexes of wills and administrations** (1655–1858) *These consist of several series of original indexes to* PROB 6–PROB 11.

PROB 16 **Muniment books** (1611–1858) *These volumes contain registration of exhibits, orders and decrees, and appointments of officers of the court.*

PROB 17 **Commission books** (1678–1857) *These books document the issue of commissions and requisitions to swear executors and administrators.*

PROB 18 **Allegations** (1661–1858) *The allegations (plaintiffs' pleas) are arranged in bundles.*

PROB 19 **Bundles of proxies** (1674–1718) *Documents appointing proctors to act on behalf of persons involved in litigation or in non-contested business. The most common are those relating to the renunciation of executors or of next of kin in the case of administrations.*

PROB 20 **Supplementary wills, Series I** (1623–1838) *Mostly wills rejected by the court on the grounds that they were not the latest will of the deceased.*

PROB 21 **Supplementary wills, Series II** (1623–1857) *Court copies of wills made when the original was to be removed from the registry for exhibition in another court of law. There are also affidavits setting out reasons why the original document was required.*

PROB 22 **Supplementary wills, Series III** (1782–1851) *Wills lodged for safekeeping.*

PROB 23 **Supplementary wills, Series IV** (1629–1827) *Mostly court copies of wills originally proved in lower church courts.*

PROB 24 **Depositions** (1657–1809) *Statements of witnesses given in court during litigation cases. Also referred to as town depositions.*

PROB 25 **Answers** (1664–1854) *These bound volumes contain the response (known as the answer) made by the opposing party to the plaintiff's plea (the allegation).*

PROB 26 **Bound volumes of depositions** (1826–58) *These volumes contain statements of witnesses produced in evidence during litigation cases.*

PROB 28 **Cause papers taken by commission** (1641–1722) *Answers sworn by commission and depositions taken by commission. Sometimes known as country depositions, to distinguish them from those taken at the court in London.*

PROB 29 **Acts of court books** (1536–1819) *These volumes contain the minutes of the proceedings of the court. They summarize each stage of the proceedings and the judgment reached. They record information concerning disputed wills and administrations, along with non-contested business such as renunciations by executors and the appointment of guardians.*

PROB 30 **Acts of court** (1740–1858) *These contain the same information as* PROB 29, *but take the form of individual documents bound into bundles.*

PROB 31 **Exhibits, main series** (1722–1858) *This is the main series of exhibits brought into the registry of the court – including affidavits, depositions, inventories, accounts, draft wills, and personal items such as account books and diaries.*

PROB 32 **Files of exhibits** (1661–1723) *These files contain exhibits from the period preceding the establishment of* PROB 31.

PROB 33 **Indexes to exhibits** (1722–*c.*1900) *These yearly indexes were compiled at the same time as the registration of the exhibits. They mainly index* PROB 31, *but also provide an index to* PROB 37, PROB 26 *and* PROB 49.

PROB 34 **Special jurisdiction miscellanea** (1536–1698) *These consist of volumes and loose documents that were found among the Prerogative Court of Canterbury records but did not originate from that court.*

PROB 35 **Original files, 16th century: exhibits** (1529–86) *This small collection contains at least one example of almost every type of exhibit.*

PROB 36 **Miscellaneous exhibits, pre-1722** (1653–1721) *Exhibits for the period preceding the establishment of* PROB 31.

PROB 37 **Cause papers, later series** (1783–1858) *These papers include allegations, answers, depositions, draft wills, inventories and personal items such as account books and diaries.*

PROB 38 **Orders of court books** (1817–57) *These are volumes containing entries of various orders made by the court subsequent to grants of probate or administration. The orders are duplicated in* PROB 30.

PROB 39 **Correspondence and papers of officials** (1659–1857) *Miscellaneous correspondence and papers of officers of the Prerogative Court of Canterbury (mainly registrars, record keepers, clerks and proctors).*

PROB 40 **Caveat books** (1666–1858) *Entry books of caveats (notices or warnings) preventing the issue of grants of probate and administration.*

PROB 41 **Court caveat books** (1678–1857) *Court caveat books record the next stage in litigation after the issue of a caveat.*

PROB 43 **Assignations** (1665–1858) *These include assignation books and draft acts recording appointments for court hearings concerning disputes over wills or administrations.*

PROB 44 **Instruments from other courts** (**Commonwealth to George III**) *Various documents directed to the Prerogative Court of Canterbury, by the King's Bench or other common-law courts or by the High Court of Delegates, to suspend an action in the PCC while a related case was taking place in one of these courts.*

PROB 46 **Files and bundles of administration bonds** (1713–1858) *These are bonds entered into by administrators and by administrators with will annexed. They include name and place of residence of sureties and give the approximate value of the estate.*

PROB 48 **Files and bundles of citatory mandates** (1666–1857) *This is the main series of citatory mandates summoning parties and witnesses to appear in court for disputed will or administration cases.*

PROB 49 **Exhibits (volumes)** *Now searchable on the Catalogue, by name of deceased and names of parties.*

PROB 51 **Administration bonds before 1601** (1542–65) *These are bonds entered into by administrators and by administrators with will annexed. They include name and place of residence of sureties and give the approximate value of the estate. This series has only been partially sorted and catalogued. The majority of the bonds are therefore unavailable.*

PROB 52 **Files of commissions and requisitions for wills** (1796–1857) *These files contain commissions authorizing local officials to administer an oath to executors unable to visit the court in London.*

PROB 57 **Accounts and papers of record keepers and other officials** (1676–1857) *This series of records gives details of the Prerogative Court of Canterbury staff and the administrative mechanisms of the court.*

These items are classified as 'Not available. Unsorted and uncatalogued': PROB 27 **Sentences**; PROB 42 **Supplementary exhibits (sixteenth–nineteenth centuries)**; PROB 45 **Miscellaneous registers, lists and indexes**; PROB 47 **Unpublished evidence and miscellaneous depositions**; PROB 50 **Bills of court**; PROB 53 **Early proceedings**; PROB 54 **Administration bonds (1601–1713)**; PROB 55 **Proxies (sixteenth century)**; PROB 56 **Files of commissions and requisitions for wills before 1796.**

APPENDIX 2

Glossary

Term [Abbreviation] ***Definition***

Account [Acc] *Details of the executor's or administrator's expenditure in settling the deceased's personal estate (see* Charge and Discharge).

Ad litem *For the purpose of the suit—for example, a guardian appointed pending the settlement of a lawsuit.*

Administration [A, admon, ad] *A grant made by the court to an administrator in order to settle the deceased's estate in accordance with the rules of intestacy.*

Administration bond *Bond entered into by the administrator, with one or more sureties, to guarantee the proper administration of the deceased's estate.*

Administratio cum testamento annexo [Ad cum testo] *See* Administration with will annexed.

Administratio cum testamento annexo de bonis non administratis [Admon dbn, de bo non] *See* Administration with will annexed of goods not administered.

Administratio de bonis non administratis *See* Administration of goods not administered.

Administration of goods not administered [AW] *Grant made following the death or renunciation of the initial administrator, in order to complete the administration of the estate.*

Administration with will annexed *Grant authorizing the implementation of a will when the testator has failed to name an executor or when the named executor renounces his or her right to execute the will or is incapacitated in some way, or fails to respond to the summons asking him or her to prove the will.*

Administration with will annexed of goods not administered *Grant made when the named executor dies after probate has been granted but the estate has not been completely administered.*

Administrator (m. or f.), administratrix (f.) *Person appointed by the court to administer an estate following the death of an intestate, or to administer the estate of a testator where an executor has not been appointed or an appointed executor fails to act.*

Advocate *In church courts, the equivalent of a barrister.*

Affidavit [Aff] *A written statement supported by the swearing of an oath or by affirmation.*

Affirmation *Declaration by a witness who has no religious belief that the evidence he or she is giving is the truth.*

Allegation *The pleading of the plaintiff in a lawsuit.*

Amita *Father's sister.*

Amita uxoris *Wife's father's sister.*

Annuity *A sum paid annually.*

Answer *The defendant's response to the plaintiff's case, or to interrogatories.*

Appeal *Application to a higher court for review of a court's decision.*

Archdeaconry court *The lowest ecclesiastical court.*

Arches, Court of *The court of the Archbishop of Canterbury, which also acted as a court of appeal within the province of Canterbury.*

Archidiaconus *Archdeacon.*

Archiepiscopus *Archbishop.*

Assizes *Regional civil and criminal common-law courts—see Common Pleas, Exchequer (common-law side) and King's Bench for types of cases heard.*

Attestatio *See* Affidavit.

Avia *Grandmother.*

Avunculus *Mother's brother (or, sometimes, father's brother).*

Avus *Grandfather.*

Avus relicta *Grandfather's widow.*

Beneficiary *Someone entitled to benefit under a will or trust.*

Bequeath *To leave personal property by will.*

Bequest *A gift of personal property by will.*

Bona *Goods.*

Bona notabilia *'Noteworthy goods'. Refers to the requirement of the Prerogative Courts that only estates valued at £5 or more in more than one diocese should come within their jurisdiction.*

Bona paraphernalia *Personal items belonging to a widow, such as her clothes, jewels and ornaments.*

Bona vacantia *An unclaimed estate, where no person entitled to inherit the estate is known.*

Breve *Writ.*

Canon law *The law of the Church of England. Unless canons (ecclesiastical decrees) received parliamentary endorsement, they were binding only on those holding ecclesiastical office.*

Catalla *Chattels.*

Cause Case or lawsuit.

Caveat *A notice that effectively prevents action by another party without first notifying the party entering the caveat.*

Cessate *A grant of limited duration that has come to an end. Usually applied to a child coming of age.*

Chancery, Court of *Equity court hearing cases such as those concerning wills, lands, inheritance, trusts or debt.*

Charge *The assets of the deceased's personal estate. Usually takes the form of a citation of the valuation given in the inventory.*

Chattels [Cat] *A person's moveable goods and belongings.*

Citation *A mandate (summons), obtained by a proctor at the request of a party to a lawsuit, ordering the attendance of another party so the case could be heard.*

Codicil *A properly executed (signed and witnessed) addendum to a will, amending, revising or revoking something in the will or making additional provisions.*

Comitatus [Com] *County.*

Commissary *An official deputizing for a bishop.*

Commissary court *Bishop's court. Large dioceses might be divided into smaller areas, each covered by a commissary court. See also* Consistory court.

Commission [Com] *A document appointing a person to a specific task. Such a document was used when executors and administrators were unable to attend court personally and were 'sworn by commission', usually by a local clergyman. Inventories and the examination of witnesses could also be undertaken by commission. See also* Requisition.

Common form *The straightforward proving of a will by oath of executor.*

Common law *Law established by precedent, based on custom and judicial decisions.*

Common Pleas, Court of *Common-law court that heard cases such as those concerning chattels, freehold, debt or damages.*

Compos mentis *'Of sound mind'—used to describe a person judged fit to leave a will or act as an executor or administrator, or to participate in other legal matters.*

Compulsory *A strongly worded decree requiring a witness to attend court after repeated failure to comply with an order to do so.*

Consanguinity *Blood relationship.*

Consistory court *Bishop's court, covering the whole of the diocese. See also* Commissary court.

Contra *Can mean before, against or contrary to.*

Coparcener *A person who has jointly inherited a property.*

Court for the Probate of Wills and the Granting of Administrations *Court that exercised probate jurisdiction throughout England and Wales from 1653 to 1659.*

Coverture *The status of a wife during marriage.*

Curation *A form of guardianship. See* Curator.

Curator *Guardian appointed by the court for boys over the age of 14 and under 21, or girls over 12 and under 21.*

Custantia *Costs.*

Death duties *Collective name for Estate Duty, Legacy Duty and Succession Duty, payable by beneficiaries from 1796.*

De bonis non administratis [Admon dbn, de bo non] *See Administration of goods not administered.*

Declaration in lieu of inventory *Declaration submitted by some executors or administrators in place of an inventory, usually after the elapse of a considerable period of time since the death of the deceased.*

Decree [Dec] *Sentence (final judgment). Can also mean an interlocutory decree. See* Sentence and Interlocutory decree.

De facto *As a matter of fact.*

Defendant *Person defending a legal action.*

Denarius [d] *Penny.*

Deposition *A statement of evidence supported by the swearing of an oath or by affirmation.*

Desperate debt *A debt unlikely to be recovered.*

Devise *To leave real estate by will.*

Diocesan courts *See* Consistory court and Commissary court.

Discharge *The disbursements made by the executor or administrator, which may include medical and funeral expenses, legal fees for probate or administration, payment of legacies, settling the deceased's debts, and expenses incurred in the maintenance of dependants.*

Doctors' Commons *The building where the London ecclesiastical courts and the High Court of Admiralty were formerly situated.*

Dominus [Dnus, dns] *Sir or lord.*

Domus [Dom] *House.*

Double probate *Separate grants made by the court to two or more executors who could not be sworn at the same time (e.g. because one was a child or abroad).*

Episcopus *Bishop.*

Equity *Law based on principles of fairness and natural justice.*

Estate *A deceased person's estate encompasses all his or her assets, including both personal estate and real estate.*

Examination *The putting of questions to someone giving evidence.*

Exchequer, Court of *The equity side of the Court of Exchequer heard cases concerning matters such as wills, land, inheritance, trusts and debt. The common-law side (Exchequer of Pleas) heard cases concerning matters such as chattels, freehold, debt or damages.*

Executor (m. or f.), executrix (f.) [Exec] *A person appointed to carry out the provisions of a will—whose duties include burying the deceased, proving the will, paying debts and legacies, and distributing the residue.*

Exhibit *Item or document referred to in an affidavit or used as evidence during a court hearing.*

Feme covert *A married woman.*

Feme sole *An unmarried woman.*

Filius *Son.*

Folio [F, f] *A leaf of a document or book, numbered only on its front (recto). A page is one side of a folio.*

Frater [Frat] *Brother.*

Freehold *See* Real estate.

Generosus [Gen] *Gentleman.*

Grant of administration *See* Administration.

Guardian *A person appointed to safeguard, protect or manage the interests of a child or of a person legally incapacitated due to mental disability. See also* Curator *and* Tutor.

Heres *Heir.*

Heresy *The ecclesiastical offence of holding opinions contrary to the tenets of the church.*

High Court of Delegates *The court of appeal from the Prerogative Court of Canterbury (1534–1834).*

Holograph *Will written entirely in the hand of the testator.*

Imperpetuum *For ever, in perpetuity.*

In partibus transmarinis [Partibus, ptibus, parts, pts] *Died abroad.*

In servitio regis/reginae *In the service of the Crown (King/Queen).*

Instance cases *Cases heard by ecclesiastical courts concerning disputes over matters such as probate, defamation, breach of promise, adultery or fornication, separation and divorce.*

Inter alia *'Among other things'—often used to indicate that the details given are only an extract from the whole.*

Interlocutory decree *A judgment that can be revoked (often used in administration cases where someone might subsequently appear and prove they were the true next of kin).*

Interrogatory *A formal question prepared by a litigant and put to a witness.*

Intestate *A person who has died without leaving a will, or leaving a will declared invalid by a court.*

Intimation *A decree including a clause warning a party who had failed to respond to an earlier summons that he would be liable to censure or excommunication, or that the case would be heard in his absence if he persisted in his contumacy.*

Intra vires *'Within the power of'—indicates that an act falls within the jurisdiction of the court.*

Inventory *List of the deceased's personal estate and its appraised value.*

Judex *Judge.*

Judgment *Final decision of a court.*

Judicial Committee of the Privy Council *The court of appeal for the Prerogative Court of Canterbury (1834–58).*

Jurat *A statement at the end of an affidavit that gives the name of the person making the affidavit and states before whom and where the oath or affirmation was taken.*

Jurisdiction *The area and matters over which a court has authority.*

King's Bench, Court of *Common-law court hearing cases concerning matters such as chattels, freehold, debt or damages. Criminal court (Crown side) hearing cases concerning matters such as breach of the peace, forgery, deceit or high treason.*

King's warrant *Royal warrant for a grant of administration to revert the deceased's estate to the Crown.*

Leasehold property *Land or tenement conveyed by the owner to a tenant for a term (specified period of time).*

Legacy *Gift of personal property by will.*

Legantia, Legantio *Legacy.*

Legatee *Person to whom personal estate is given by will.*

Legatorius *Legatee.*

Lego *'I bequeath'.*

Letters of administration *Legal document, issued by a relevant court, authorizing an appropriate person to administer the estate when no valid will has been left by the deceased. The letters allow the administrator to carry out duties similar to those of an executor.*

Liberi *Children.*

Libra [L, li] *Pound.*

Limited administration [Ad limit] *A grant of administration limited to a specified period of time or to a particular part of the estate.*

Limited probate *A grant of probate limited to a specified period of time or to a particular part of the estate.*

Maritus *Husband.*
Mater, matris *Mother.*
Matertera *Aunt, mother's sister.*
Medietas *Half or moiety.*
Messuagium *Messuage.*
Ministrant *Another word for defendant.*
Moiety *A half share.*
Monition *A form of decree normally used only when the court required both a person and some evidence to be brought before it—for example, when a party was required to bring in testamentary scripts, or when the registrar of a lower court was ordered to bring in all relevant papers in a case that had been transferred to a superior court.*

Nepos *Grandson, nephew, descendant.*
Neptis *Niece.*
Non compos mentis *'Not of sound mind'—used to describe a person judged unfit to leave a will or act as an executor or administrator, or to participate in other legal matters.*
Nuncupative will [Nunc] *Spoken will—often from the deathbed.*
Nuncupativus [Nunc] *Nuncupative. See* Nuncupative will.
Nuper *Can mean either the late or lately or recently deceased.*
Nurus *Daughter-in-law.*

Oath *A promise to tell the truth sworn, usually on the Bible, by a person with religious beliefs.*
Obsequia *Funeral, funeral rites.*

Paraphernalia *See* Bona paraphernalia.
Para rationabilis *A reasonable portion.*
Parochia [Par] *Parish.*
Party *Any of the participants in a lawsuit or in other legal proceedings.*
Pater *Father.*
Patruelis *Cousin on father's side.*
Patruus *Paternal uncle, father's brother.*
Peculiar court *An ecclesiastical court exempt from the authority of the local archdeacon, and sometimes from the authority of the bishop.*
Personal estate, personal property, personalty *Possessions such as chattels (moveable goods), cash, credits and leasehold property.*
Plaintiff *Person bringing a legal action.*
Pratum *Meadow.*
Prerogative courts *The courts of the archbishops of Canterbury and York.*
Primogenitus *First-born.*
Privigna *Stepdaughter.*
Privignus *Stepson.*
Proavus *Forefather, great-grandfather.*
Probate *The legal recognition of the validity of a will.*
Probatio *See* Probate.
Probo *'I prove'.*
Proctor *In ecclesiastical courts, the duties of a proctor were similar to those of solicitors in other courts.*
Promoter *In ecclesiastical courts, another word for plaintiff.*
Province *The jurisdiction of an archbishop.*
Proxy *Document appointing a proctor to act on behalf of a person involved in litigation or in non-contested business.*
Pur autre vie *For/during the lifetime of another person.*

Quire *In the Prerogative Court of Canterbury, a section of 16 pages in the series of registered wills* (PROB 11).

Real estate, real property, realty *Immoveable property, such as land and buildings held on a freehold basis.*
Relict [Rel] *The person remaining after the death of a spouse. Widow.*
Requisition *In the Prerogative Court of Canterbury, a commission outside the jurisdiction of the court was known as a requisition. See* Commission.
Residuary devisee *A person who takes the residue of the real property after the payment of all debts and legacies charged on the deceased's real estate.*
Residuary legatee *A person who takes the residue of the deceased's personal property after the payment of all debts and legacies.*
Residuum *Residue, remainder.*
Reversion *See* Reversionary interest.
Reversionary interest *An interest in property that reverts to its grantor or the grantor's heirs at the end of a specified period of time (e.g. the life of the grantee).*

Seat *From 1719 the Prerogative Court of Canterbury's probate and administration business was divided into five administrative divisions based on geographical areas. Each of these divisions was called a seat (also known as 'walk').*
Sentence, definitive sentence [Sent, S] *The final judgment in a cause.*

Solemn form *Procedure for proving a will by witnesses before a judge.*
Solidus [Sol, S] *Shilling.*
Sororius *Sister's husband or son or wife's brother.*
Special administration. See Limited administration.
Special probate *See* Limited probate.
Sperate debt *Debt thought likely to be recovered.*
Sponsa *Wife.*
Sponsus *Husband.*
Spurius *Illegitimate.*
Surrogate *In church courts, a deputy judge—an official deputizing for the archbishop, bishop or archdeacon.*
Susceptores *Godparents.*

Terra *Land.*
Testament *Originally the term 'testament' referred to personal estate only; but from the sixteenth century it has been used interchangeably with 'will', referring to both personal and real estate.*
Testamentum *See* Testament.
Testator (m. or f.), testatrix (f.) *A person who makes a will.*
Trust *The conveying of property (e.g. by will or by drawing up a trust) to a trustee or trustees with instructions to hold or administer it for the benefit of a beneficiary or beneficiaries.*
Trustee *A person who holds or administers property in trust for another or others.*
Tuition *Guardianship of a minor. See* Tutor.
Tutor *Guardian of a minor (a boy under the age of 15 or a girl under 13).*

Ultra vires *'Beyond the power of'—indicates that an act falls outside the jurisdiction of the court.*
Uxor *Wife.*
Uxoratus *Married, married man.*

Vacatur [Vacat, vac] Void

Walk *See* Seat.
Warrant *Document issued by a church court authorizing a commission or requisition to swear an executor or administrator unable to come to court.*
Will *From the sixteenth century 'will' has been used to refer to both personal and real estate (originally 'testament' was used for personal estate).*
Writ *A document, issued under seal, conveying either a royal command or an order from a court of law.*

USEFUL ADDRESSES AND WEBSITES

England

BANK OF ENGLAND (archive information and appointments)
The Archivist, Archive Section HO-SV
The Bank of England
Threadneedle Street
London EC2R 8AH
TEL *020 7601 4889/5096*
bankofengland.co.uk/about/history/archive

BORTHWICK INSTITUTE OF HISTORICAL RESEARCH
University of York
Heslington
York YO10 5DD
appointments and archive enquiries:
TEL *01904 321166*
www.york.ac.uk/inst/bihr

BRITISH LIBRARY
96 Euston Road
London NW1 2DB
reader enquiries: TEL *020 7412 7676*
switchboard: TEL *0870 444 1500*
www.bl.uk

BRITISH LIBRARY, Newspapers
Colindale Avenue
London NW9 5HE
TEL *020 7412 7353*
www.bl.uk/collections/newspapers.html

BRITISH LIBRARY, Oriental and India Office Collections
96 Euston Road
London NW1 2DB
TEL *020 7412 7873*
www.bl.uk/collections/asiapacificafrica.html

CATHOLIC NATIONAL LIBRARY
St. Michael's Abbey
Farnborough Road
Farnborough
Hants GU14 7NQ
www.catholic-library.org.uk

CORPORATION OF LONDON RECORDS OFFICE
PO Box 270, Guildhall
London EC2P 2EJ
TEL *020 7332 1251*
www.corpoflondon.gov.uk

FEDERATION OF FAMILY HISTORY SOCIETIES
The FFHS Administrator,
PO Box 2425
Coventry CV5 6YX
www.ffhs.org.uk

GUILD OF ONE-NAME STUDIES
Box G, 14 Charterhouse Buildings
Goswell Road
London EC1M 7BA
www.one-name.org

GUILDHALL LIBRARY
Aldermanbury
London EC2P 2EJ
TEL *020 7332 1862/3*
www.history.ac.uk/gh

LAMBETH PALACE LIBRARY
Lambeth Palace Road
London SE1 7JU
TEL *020 7898 1400*
www.lambethpalacelibrary.org

LONDON METROPOLITAN ARCHIVES
40 Northampton Road,
London EC1R 0HB
TEL *020 7332 3820*
www.corpoflondon.gov.uk/lma

LONDON PROBATE DEPARTMENT
Principal Registry of the Family Division
First Avenue House
42–49 High Holborn
London WC1V 6NP
TEL *020 7947 7191*
www.hmcourts-service.gov.uk

MINISTRY OF JUSTICE
Departmental Record Officer
Record Management Services
5th Floor, 30 Millbank
London SW1P 4XB

THE NATIONAL ARCHIVES
Kew, Richmond
Surrey TW9 4DU
TEL *020 8876 3444*
www.nationalarchives.gov.uk

OFFICES OF COURT FUNDS
Official Solicitor and Public Trustee
22 Kingsway
London WC2B 6LE
www.officialsolicitor.gov.uk

PARLIAMENTARY ARCHIVES
Houses of Parliament
London SW1A 0PW
TEL *020 7219 3074*
www.parliament.uk

POSTAL SEARCHES & COPIES DEPARTMENT
York Probate Sub-Registry
1st Floor, Castle Chambers
Clifford Street
York YO1 9RG
TEL *01904 666777*
www.hmcourts-service.gov.uk

Royal Archives
Windsor Castle
Windsor
Berkshire SL4 1NJ
TEL *01753 868286*
www.royal.gov.uk/output/page4978.asp

Society of Genealogists
14 Charterhouse Buildings,
Goswell Road
London EC1M 7BA
TEL *020 7251 8799*
www.sog.org.uk

Channel Islands

Channel Islands Family History Society
PO Box 507
St Helier
Jersey JE4 5TN
http://channelislandshistory.com

Jersey Archive
Clarence Road
St Helier
Jersey JE2 4JY
TEL *01534 833333*
www.jerseyheritagetrust.org

Judicial Greffe (Jersey)
Royal Court House
Royal Square
St Helier
Jersey JE1 1JG
TEL *01534 441300*
www.gov.je/JudicialGreffe

Société Guernesiase
Candie Gardens
St Peter Port
Guernsey GY1 1UG
TEL *01481 725093*
www.societe.org.gg

Société Jersiase
Lord Countanche Library
7 Pier Road
St Helier
Jersey JE2 4XW
TEL *01534 730538*
www.societe-jersiaise.org

States of Guernsey
Island Archive Service
29 Victoria Road
St Peter Port
Guernsey GY1 1HU
TEL *01481 724512*
http://user.itl.net/~glen/archgsy.html

Ireland

Accountant of the Courts of Justice
The Courts Service
15–24 Phoenix Street North
Smithfield, Dublin 7
TEL *00 353 1 888 6214*
www.courts.ie

Court Funds Office
18th Floor, Windsor House
Bedford Street
Belfast BT2 7LT
TEL *028 9072 8888/8895/8891*
www.courtsni.gov.uk

Irish Genealogical Research Society
Stratford Avenue
Rainham
Kent ME8 0EP
www.igrsoc.org

National Archives of Ireland
Bishop Street
Dublin 8
Republic of Ireland
TEL *00 353 1 407 2300*
www.nationalarchives.ie

Probate and Matrimonial Office
Royal Courts of Justice
PO Box 410
Chichester Street
Belfast BT1 3JF
TEL *028 9072 4678*
www.courtsni.gov.uk

Probate Office
High Court
First Floor, 15/24 Phoenix Street North
Smithfield, Dublin 7
Republic of Ireland
TEL *00 353 1 888 6174*
www.courts.ie

Public Record Office of Northern Ireland
66 Balmoral Avenue
Belfast BT9 6NY
TEL *028 9025 5905*
www.proni.gov.uk

Isle of Man

Deeds and Probate Registry
Registries Building
Deemster's Walk
Bucks Road
Douglas
Isle of Man IM1 3AR
TEL *01624 685250*
www.gov.im/registries/general/deedsandpro.xml

Isle of Man Public Record Office
Unit 40a, Spring Valley Industrial Estate
Douglas
Isle of Man IM2 2QR
TEL *01624 693569*
www.gov.im/registries/publicrecords

Manx National Heritage,
Douglas,
Isle of Man IM1 3LY
TEL 01624 648000
www.gov.im/mnh

Scotland

Association of Scottish Genealogists and Researchers in Archives
259 Broad Street
Cowdenbeath
Fife KY4 8LG
TEL *01383 515465*
www.asgra.co.uk

The Commissary Department
Edinburgh Sheriff Court
27 Chambers Street
Edinburgh EH1 1LB

National Archives of Scotland
HM General Register House
Edinburgh EH1 3YY
TEL *0131 535 1334*
www.nas.gov.uk

National Library of Scotland
George IV Bridge
Edinburgh EH1 1EW
TEL *0131 623 3700/4531*
www.nls.uk

The Queen's and Lord Treasurer's Remembrancer
Crown Office, 25 Chambers Street
Edinburgh, EH1 1LA
TEL *0844 5613805* or *0844 5613804*
www.copfs.gov.uk/About/roles/qltr/Bona-Vacantia

Scots Ancestry Research Society
8 York Road
Edinburgh EH5 3EH
TEL *0131 552 2028*
www.scotsancestry.co.uk

Wales

National Library of Wales
Aberystwyth
Credigion SY23 3BU
TEL *01970 632800*
www.llgc.org.uk

Useful Websites

Access to Archives (A2A)
www.nationalarchives/a2a
Catalogue
www.nationalarchives/catalogue
DocumentsOnline
www.nationalarchives/documentsonline
Independent Researchers
www.nationalarchives.gov.uk/irlist
Manorial Documents Register
www.nationalarchives/mdr
National Register of Archives
www.nationalarchives.nra
Palaeography tutorial
www.nationalarchives.gov.uk/palaeography
Your Archives
http://yourarchives.nationalarchives.gov.uk
British Origins
www.britishorigins.com
Her Majesty's Court Service
www.courtservice.gov.uk
Findmypast
www.findmypast.com
Offices of Court Funds,
Official Solicitor and Public Trustee
www.officialsolicitor.gov.uk
ScotlandsPeople
www.scotlandspeople.gov.uk

FURTHER READING

FFHS = Federation of Family History Societies;
PRO = Public Record Office; **TNA** = The National Archives

Addy, John *Death, Money and the Vultures: Inheritance and Avarice, 1660–1750* (Leopard's Head Press, 1992)

Arkell, Tom; Evans, Nesta and Goose, Nigel (eds) *When Death Do Us Part: Understanding and Interpreting the Probate Records of Early Modern England* (Leopard's Head Press, 2000)

Baker, J.H. *An Introduction to English Legal History* (OUP, 4th ed., 2002)

Barrett, John and Iredale, David *Discovering Old Handwriting* (Shire Publications, 2001)

Bevan, Amanda *Tracing Your Ancestors in the National Archives* (PRO, 7th ed., 2006)

Bristow, Joy *Local Historian's Glossary of Words and Terms* (Countryside Books, 2001)

Buck, W.S.B. *Examples of Handwriting 1550–1650* (Society of Genealogists, 1985)

Burn, Richard *The Ecclesiastical Law* (S. Sweet, 4 vols, 1842)

Camp, Anthony *Wills and their Whereabouts* (Anthony J. Camp, 1974)

Chapman, Colin R. *Ecclesiastical Courts, Officials and Records: Sin, Sex and Probate* (Lochin, 2nd ed., 1998)

Chapman, Colin R. *Ecclesiastical Courts, their Officials and their Records* (Lochin, 1992)

Christian, Peter *The Genealogist's Internet* (TNA, 4th ed., 2009)

Coldham, P.W. *American Wills and Administrations in the Prerogative Court of Canterbury, 1610–1857* (Baltimore, 1989)

Collinge, Michael 'Probate Valuations and the Death Duty Registers: Some Comments' (*Bulletin of the Institute of Historical Research*, vol. LX, 1987, pp. 240–5)

Collins, Audrey *Wills After 1858* (FFHS, 1998)

Colwell, Stella *Family Roots* (Weidenfeld & Nicolson, 1991)

Colwell, Stella *The Family Records Centre: A User's Guide* (PRO, 2002)

Coote, Henry Charles *The Common Form Practice of The High Court of Justice in Granting Probates and Administrations* (Butterworths, 7th ed., 1878)

Coote, Henry Charles *The Practice of the Ecclesiastical Courts With Forms and Tables of Costs* (H. Butterworth, 1847)

Cox, Jane *Affection Defying the Power of Death: Wills, Probate and Death Duty Records* (FFHS, 1993)

Cox, Jane *Hatred Pursued Beyond the Grave* (HMSO, 2nd ed., 1995)

Cox, Jane *Wills, Inventories and Death Duties: A Provisional Guide* (PRO, 1988)

De L'Hoste, D.F.; Ranking and others *Executorship Law and Accounts* (Isaac Pitman, 1933)

Duncan, G.I.O. *The High Court of Delegates* (Cambridge University Press, 1971)

Ellis, Mary *Using Manorial Records* (PRO, 1997)

English, Barbara 'Probate Valuations and the Death Duty Registers' (*Bulletin of the Institute of Historical Research*, vol. LVII, 1984, pp. 80–91)

English, Barbara 'Wealth at Death in the nineteenth century: The Death Duty Registers' (*Bulletin of the Institute of Historical Research*, vol. LX, 1987, pp. 246–9)

Franklin, Peter *Some Medieval Records for Family Historians* (FFHS, 1994)

Gibson, Jeremy and Churchill, Else *Probate Jurisdictions: Where to Look for Wills* (FFHS, 5th ed., 2002)

Grannum, Karen *Using Wills* (PRO, 2001)

Grenham, John *Tracing Your Irish Ancestors: The complete guide* (Genealogical Publishing Company, 2nd ed., 2006)

Hair, P.E.H. and Alsop, J.D. *English Seamen and Traders in Guinea, 1553–1565: The New Evidence of Their Wills* (Edwin Mellen Press, 1992)

Heal, Felicity *Of Prelates and Princes: A Study of the Economic and Social Position of the Tudor Episcopate* (Cambridge University Press, 2008)

Helmholz, R.H. *Canon Law and English Common Law* (Selden Society, 1983)

Helmholz, R.H. *Canon Law and the Law of England* (Hambledon Press, 1987)

Hindle, Paul *Latin for Family Historians* (Phillimore, 2000)

Holdsworth, Sir William *A History of English Law* (Methuen, 17 vols, 1903–72)

Horwitz, Henry *Chancery Equity Proceedings 1600–1800* (PRO, 1998)

Horwitz, Henry *Exchequer Equity Records and Proceedings* (PRO, 2001)

Houston, Jane (ed.) *Index of Cases in the Records of the Court of Arches at Lambeth Palace Library 1660–1913* (British Record Society, Index Library, vol. 85, 1972)

Howell, P.A. *Judicial Committee of the Privy Council, 1833–1876, its origins, structure and development* (Cambridge University Press, 1979)

Ingram, Martin *Church Courts, Sex and Marriage in England 1570–1640* (Cambridge University Press, 1987)

ISON, Alf *A Secretary Hand ABC Book* (Berkshire FHS, 3rd ed., 2000)
JAMES, Alwyn *Scottish Roots: The Step by Step Guide to Tracing Your Scottish Ancestors* (Luath Press, reprinted 2003)
KITCHING, Christopher 'Probate during the Civil War and Interregnum. Part 1: The survival of the Prerogative Court in the 1640s' (*Journal of the Society of Archivists*, vol. 5, no. 5, April 1976, pp. 283–93)
KITCHING, Christopher 'Probate during the Civil War and Interregnum. Part 2: The Court of Probate, 1653–1660' (*Journal of the Society of Archivists*, vol. 5, no. 6, October 1976, pp. 346–56)
KITCHING, Christopher 'The Prerogative Court of Canterbury from Warham to Whitgift' (chapter 8 of *Continuity and Change: Personnel and Administration of the Church of England, 1500–1642*, edited by Rosemary O'Day and Felicity Heal, Leicester University Press, 1976)
LAWTON, George *A Brief Treatise of Bona Notabilia: Together with an Account of the Archiepiscopal Courts of Probate, Within the Province of York* (J. Butterworth & Son and others, 1825)
MCLAUGHLIN, Eve *Reading Old Handwriting* (FFHS, 2nd ed., 1996)
MCLAUGHLIN, Eve *Simple Latin for Family Historians* (FFHS, 1999)
MCLAUGHLIN, Eve *Wills from 1858* (FFHS, 1995)
MARCHANT, Ronald A. *The Church Under Law: Justice, Administration and Discipline in the Diocese of York 1560–1640* (Cambridge University Press, 1969)
MARCHANT, Ronald A. *The Puritans and the Church Courts in the Diocese of York 1560–1642* (Longman, 1960)
MARSHALL, G.W. *A Handbook to the Ancient Courts of Probate and Depositories of Wills* (Horace Cox, 1895)
MARSHALL, Hilary *Palaeography for Family and Local Historians* (Phillimore and Co., 2004)
MARTIN, G.H. and Spufford, Peter *The Records of the Nation* (Boydell & Brewer, 1990)
MILWARD, R. *A Glossary of Household, Farming and Trade Terms From Probate Inventories* (Derbyshire Record Society, Occasional Paper no. 1, 3rd ed., 1993)
MOORE, Susan T. *Family Feuds* (FFHS, 2003)
MORRIS, Janet *A Latin Glossary for Family and Local Historians* (FFHS, 1989)
MUNBY, Lionel; Hobbs, Steve and Crosby, Alan *Reading Tudor and Stuart Handwriting* (British Association for Local History, 2002)
NICHOLS, John *A collection of all the wills, now known to be extant, of the kings and queens of England, princes and princesses of Wales, and every branch of the blood royal, from the reign of William the Conqueror to that of Henry the Seventh exclusive* (London, 1780)
PAPPALARDO, Bruno *Tracing Your Naval Ancestors* (TNA, 2003)
PHILLIMORE, Sir Robert Joseph *The Ecclesiastical Law of the Church of England* (Henry Sweet, 1873)
PURVIS, J.S. *An Introduction to Ecclesiastical Records* (St Anthony's Press, 1953)
RAYMOND, Stuart A. *Words from Wills and Other Probate Records 1500–1800, A Glossary* (Federation of Family History Societies, 2004)
RYCRAFT, Ann *Sixteenth and Seventeenth Century Wills, Inventories and Other Probate Documents* (Borthwick Institute of Historical Research, 1973)
SCOTT, Miriam *Prerogative Court of Canterbury Wills and Other Probate Records* (PRO, 1997)
SENIOR, William *Doctors' Commons and the Old Court of Admiralty: A Short History of the ...* (BiblioBazaar, 2008)
SHEEHAN, Michael M. *The Will in Medieval England* (Pontifical Institute of Mediaeval Studies, Toronto, Studies and Texts no. 6, 1963)
SINCLAIR, Cecil *Tracing your Scottish Ancestors: A Guide to Ancestry Research in the Scottish Record Office* (The Stationery Office, revised ed., 1997)
SLATTER, M. Doreen 'The Records of the Court of Arches' (*Journal of Ecclesiastical History*, vol. IV, 1953, pp. 139–53)
SPUFFORD, Peter (ed.) *Index to the Probate Accounts of England and Wales*, Part I: A–J, Part II: K–Z (British Record Society, 1999)
SQUIBB, G.D. *Doctors' Commons* (Clarendon Press, 1977)
SWINBURNE, Henry *A Brief Treatise of Testaments and Last Willes* (Companie of Stationers, 1611)
TARVER, Anne *Church Court Records: An Introduction for Family and Local Historians* (Phillimore, 1995)
TATE, W.E. *The Parish Chest* (Phillimore, 1983)
THOMAS, David *Shakespeare in the Public Records* (HMSO, 1985)
WARNER, Gerald *Being of Sound Mind: A Book of Eccentric Wills* (Elm Tree Books, 1980)
WATERS, Colin *A Dictionary of Old Trades, Titles and Occupations* (Countryside Books, 2002)
WEBB, C.C. *A Guide to Genealogical Sources in the Borthwick Institute of Historical Research* (University of York, 1983)
WHITELOCK, Dorothy *Anglo-Saxon Wills* (Cambridge University Press, 1930)
WILSON, H.A.R.J. *Executorship Law and Accounts* (Sir Isaac Pitman & Sons, 11th ed., 1933)

INDEX

A

B

C

D

E

F

G

H

I

J

K

L

R

S

T

V

W

Y